Olin, Oskeegum & Gizmo

GROWING UP IN A
SMALL SOUTHERN COLLEGE TOWN

1950-1970

JAMES B. PUCKETT

Published in the United States of America
by Blackwell Ink, Inc. (Publishers)

ISBN 0-9702713-1-X
Library of Congress Control Number: 2003104286

Printed by Walsworth Publishing Company
Marceline, MO

Jacket Art: David Teague

Address inquiries to:
Blackwell Ink, Inc.
PO Box 434
Davidson, NC

DEDICATION

For Jim

AUTHOR'S NOTE

AND

ACKNOWLEDGMENTS

This book deals with a number of unique individuals who over a period of twenty years, in one way or another, influenced my life. It is not feasible to mention them all here, but the reader will meet them as the story progresses. I am grateful to each of them. Because of a lapse of so many years and the atrophy of memory, however, other worthy individuals who deserve mention may not appear here. For that I apologize.

My father, William Olin Puckett, passed on to me much of the lore of northern Mecklenburg County and Davidson College. In recalling all of that in recent years, I realized that there was so very much more that was special to this community. I was afraid that it would be lost forever were it not recorded. I wanted to preserve that brief history of my time in Davidson as a source of gratitude to the community that reared me. Hence follow stories and lore I learned along the way and descriptions of Davidson and Davidson College from 1950 to 1970, the years of my memory of the town.

I have tried to give voice to my years in Davidson. The colloquialisms and quaint expressions used in the book are faithful to that particular time and place. The maps included in this work are drawn entirely from memory. It is not my intent to be professional or precise; the maps hopefully will serve to orient the reader and help him or her to navigate the storyline.

I wish to be clear at the outset about the limitations of this book. The town I describe in the 1950's and early 1960's is by no means the whole of the town as it then existed. It is the eastern part of Davidson, the world I inhabited and knew well when I was coming of age. The Southern Railway tracks divided the town east and west along racial and social class lines, and Jim Crow customs still prevailed. Other than my occasional bike forays across the tracks into western Davidson and some wonderful people I came to know from that side of town, I was a stranger to its life and daily rhythms. A complete social history of Davidson has yet to be written—a work that would include a broader perspective of town life that my memoir lacks.

The chemistry of memory is complex. Individuals often view events from entirely different perspectives. What one considers important, another may consider banal. What one considers humorous or enlightening, another may find offensive. Such are the unavoidable foibles of a memoir of this nature.

My publisher and long time friend, Taylor Blackwell, saw enough merit in this memoir in its most rudimentary form to encourage me to enlarge the work and publish it. Taylor and his wife, Irene, provided hospitality for my wife, Margaret, and me during our visits to Davidson. Irene assisted with editing and proofing the manuscript.

Mary Beaty, daughter of beloved professor Ernest Beaty, wrote histories of both Davidson and Davidson College. Her extensive works, *A History of Davidson College* (1988) and *Davidson: A History of the Town from 1835 until 1937* (1979) gave me precise dates rather than my own approximations and the correct spelling of some of the faculty names.

The Washam family genealogy is complex owing to the fact that its patriarch, Henry Jackson Washam, married three times, and one of his many children had twelve children of his own. My cousins Margaret Washam Kelly and Martha Barnhardt Usilton helped me to ascend the family tree and guided me in the right direction when I lost the trail.

My sister, Ginger Puckett Grizzard, read the original manuscript and made suggestions on grammar and syntax. Ginger shared with me memories of people and events that I might have otherwise omitted.

The late Dr. Chalmers Davidson embodied just about everything good about Davidson College. I knew him as I grew up, and he was my mentor in college. He provided me a wealth of information on Peter Stuart Ney and the Marshal Ney controversy as well as other aspects of the college's history. Dr. Leland Park and the Davidson College library staff assisted me with the Ney story on details I had long forgotten from my conversations with Dr. Davidson. The library also graciously gave me access to old annuals and books.

I am grateful to Dr. and Mrs. Samuel R. Spencer and Dr. and Mrs. Samuel W. Newell for allowing me to visit with them in the Spencer's Montreat home in June 2001. Where memory failed, they helped clarify people and events.

When I began this book, I envisioned including the graduation painting commissioned for Davidson College's sesquicentennial in 1987. What the artist created, I believe, captures the spirit of both Davidson College and the town of Davidson. Wendy Roberts put me in touch with David Teague, the painter, and he has graciously allowed me to use his work for the dust cover of the book. The Davidson College communications office created the digital file of the painting for the cover.

My friend and erstwhile object of my youthful affections, Kristi Scott Boykin, uncovered a cornucopia of photographs from which I selected some for publication here. She was particularly helpful with information on her father, Dr. Tom Scott, coach and athletic director at Davidson College in the 1950's and 1960's.

Our town doctor was the late Dr. James Baker Woods, who tended to the medical needs of both town and gown for almost fifty years. His daughter, Lacy Woods Dick, helped to clarify details of his extraordinary life. She and her brother, John Woods, contributed the photograph of Dr. Woods that appears in this book.

Nancy Withers Dishman has lived in Davidson all of her life and as town librarian knows just about everybody. She was a great help on details from our high school years. She rummaged through old annuals to make certain I had recorded name spellings and details correctly. Nancy has contributed a picture for inclusion in the photographic part of this book.

The late Dr. Frontis Johnston was an influential history professor and dean of faculty at the college. I am grateful to his daughter Tish Johnston Kimbrough, who helped me with the material on both her father and family.

Along the way I had lost memories of my family's time on Pawley's Island on the South Carolina coast. Van Lear Logan was on Pawley's Island during those summers and was of great assistance in filling in the gaps.

Scholar extraordinaire Dr. Malcolm Lester was my faculty advisor during my freshman year at Davidson College. He is the leading authority on the old college burial ground on North Main Street. Dr. Lester came to my rescue and gave me direction when I had difficulty locating specific graves of people mentioned in the book.

Diane Neil Maye was my "girl next door" during our years together at North Mecklenburg High School. She recently retired from teaching at North after over thirty years. She helped me with details from our high school years and pointed me to Margaret Smith's *Golden Reflections: A History of North Mecklenburg High School 1951-2001*, which helped me to correct mistakes in my final revision.

Tom McEver's parents, Gene and Joy McEver, play an important role in my life's story. Tom, his brother Jim, and I grew up together. Tom assisted me in providing specifics on his father's life and the contributions the McEvers made to the community.

Two of the memorable characters presented here are Scotty and Peter Nicholls. Their son, Sandy, who continues to live in Davidson, filled in gaping holes in my memory and updated me on the family history.

My next-door Davidson neighbor Mrs. Nancy Smith survived my years at her house and graciously contributed the delightful photograph of the Smith family that appears in the book. Her son Shaw Smith, Jr., helped me with details of the North Mecklenburg-Myers Park football game in 1965—perhaps the most memorable game any of us have ever attended.

I am also indebted to James Raeford, who began barbering at Johnson's Barbershop in Davidson in 1957 and today maintains his own shops in Davidson and Cornelius. James allowed me to interview him about the barbering scene in Davidson in the 1950's and 60's. One of the memorable characters I profile in this book is Oskeegum. James gave me considerable background information on this man, who was a fixture on Main Street during those years.

Mary Fetter Stough reviewed and critiqued an early draft of the manuscript. She was particularly helpful in pointing out substantive mistakes and enlightening me on some of the historical content of the work.

One of my father's best friends was his first cousin George Tugend. George and his wife, Emilie, who today live in Delaware, helped me to clarify their ties to the Washam family and their own relationship with my parents.

They say you never forget your first kiss, and I certainly won't forget mine. Pattie Newell Williams was the college minister's daughter and one of my dearest friends during our years together in Davidson, 1953-1961. She spent time recently adding memories of her own to this book and allowed me to update her on the years she missed during my odyssey through junior and senior high school.

Tom Northcutt was one of my Sunday school teachers at the Davidson College Presbyterian Church. His wife, Neena, graciously gave me information on his life and contributions to both his country and community. I have included much of that in the book.

I owe an everlasting debt to my wife, Margaret, and son, Jim, who patiently endured my many hours at the computer compiling this work. They encouraged me to go on when I felt that the whole thing would never come together. Along the way Jim lent me considerable technical support. Margaret agreed not to read the book until publication lest the perspectives of her own moral upbringing in any way influence the work. This has given me free reign over the spicier parts.

My appreciation to Jan Blodgett, of the Davidson College Library staff, for her interest in my boyhood home and its history and for following in the footsteps of my mentor, Professor Chalmers Davidson, as a keeper of the Davidson story. Her review of the work was most helpful.

Finally, I had a fellow traveler. Our father called my identical twin and me "womb mates." John shared memories with me and encouraged me throughout the writing of this book. With the exception of a year John spent in Germany in 1968-69, he and I shared the journey described in this book from the moment of our birth in October 1947 until our graduation from Davidson College in June 1970. He was an amiable companion.

James B. Puckett
Asheville, North Carolina
December 2002

The Davidson College Motto

Alenda Lux Ubi Orta Libertas
(Let Learning Be Cherished Where Liberty Has Arisen)

—The motto of Davidson College, in reference to the
Mecklenburg Declaration of Independence, May 20, 1775

TABLE OF CONTENTS

Chapter		Page #

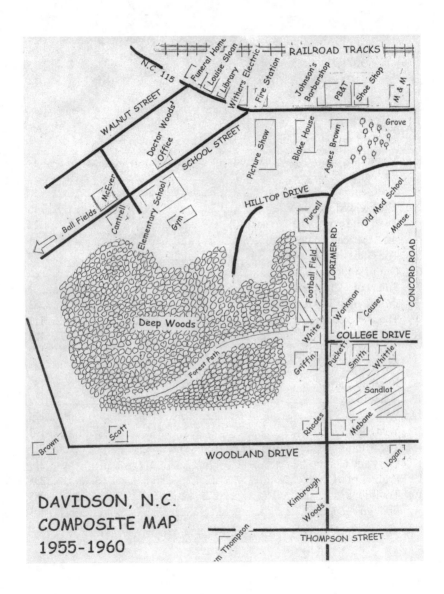

DAVIDSON, N.C.
COMPOSITE MAP
1955-1960

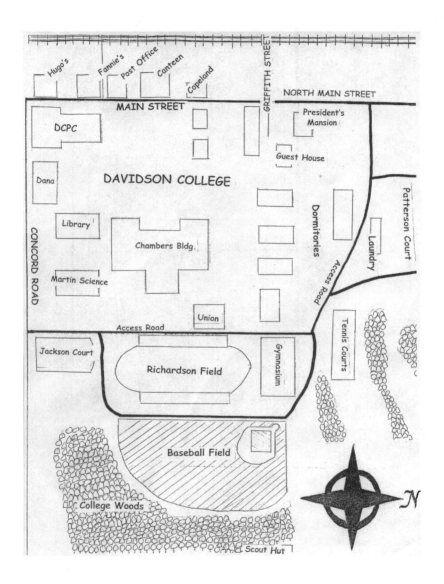

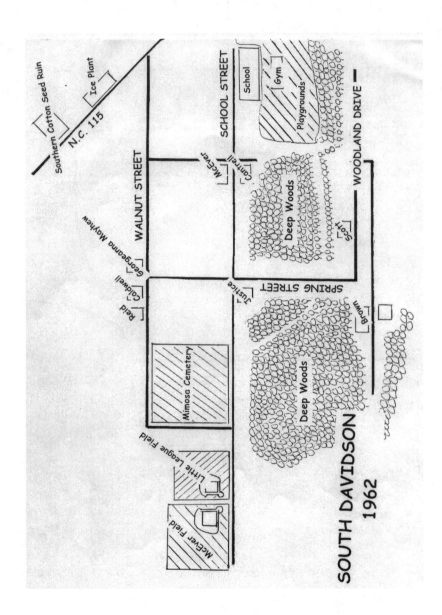

SOUTH DAVIDSON
1962

Southern Cotton Seed Ruin

Ice Plant

N.C. 115

SCHOOL STREET

School

Gym

Playgrounds

WOODLAND DRIVE

WALNUT STREET

McEver

Cantrell

Georgeanna Mayhew

Caldwell

Reid

Deep Woods

Scott

Justice

SPRING STREET

Brown

Mimosa Cemetery

Deep Woods

Little League Field

McEver Field

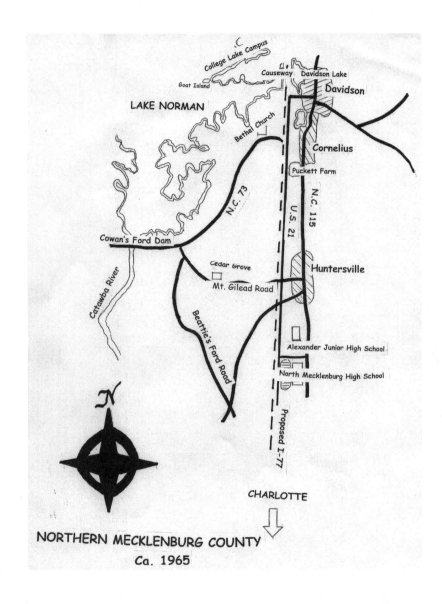

College Lake Campus

Goat Island

Causeway Davidson Lake

Davidson

LAKE NORMAN

Bethel Church

Cornelius

Puckett Farm

N.C. 73

N.C. 115

U.S. 21

Cowan's Ford Dam

Cedar Grove

Mt. Gilead Road

Huntersville

Catawba River

Beattie's Ford Road

Alexander Junior High School

North Mecklenburg High School

Proposed I-77

N

CHARLOTTE

NORTHERN MECKLENBURG COUNTY

Ca. 1965

PROLOGUE

Wonderful ghosts from my childhood haunt me into my middle age. They are the memories of the little place where I passed my youth—Davidson, a small college town, located in northern Mecklenburg County in the rolling Piedmont of North Carolina. My memories come, some in full and vivid colors, and others in fragmented, dimly recalled monochromes.

One of my ghosts is a Revolutionary War general who died in a battle with Lord Cornwallis at an obscure place that is a footnote to history. Another ghost is a famous field marshal who fought with Napoleon and led the shredded remnants of the Grand Army from Moscow in the terrible winter of 1812, and some say came to my town long after his supposed resurrection to design the seal of its small college. There is a young woman, daughter of the college's first president, who became the second wife of General Stonewall Jackson and was with him after Chancellorsville when he crossed that eternal river to rest in the shade of the trees. The old college cemetery holds a famous Confederate general who left his mark at Antietam, Gettysburg, and Malvern Hill. My father told me about a grave-robbing operation that centered in the medical school that once stood opposite the main college campus. There is in my recollection the tale of a skeleton found in a massive column that stood with three others as the only remains of a burned-out antebellum college administration building. My aging next-door neighbor told me about another ghost—an eccentric religion professor whose biblical trivial pursuits became legendary. I came to know President John Tyler's granddaughter in her old age, whose stories of Captain Kidd enthralled me as a small child. There is in my memory the story of a Persian youth who came to Davidson as a student and gave his life for a classmate. The great Louis Armstrong is still there trumpeting through the conflagration that took our last picture show. I fondly recall the former high school basketball coach who in five seasons raised college basketball teams from a student body just short of one thousand to national prominence and even had a chance to win it all. There is a group of devoted friends who called themselves "townies" and immortalized one of their own for his infamous midnight ride along the Southern Railway line. I have in memory a family who devoted themselves to youth and their development and taught us how to play baseball and to dance. Shining brightly is a family doctor who was the finest physician I have ever known.

It was the occasion of my twenty-fifth college reunion that drew me back to Davidson in the spring of 1995. I left my home in Asheville in the North Carolina mountains late one warm Friday afternoon in April. The dogwoods and azaleas were in full bloom, and the hills were resplendent in spring color as the sun settled behind the Smoky Mountains to the west. Once across the Eastern Continental Divide at Old Fort, memories of my youth came flooding back. I resolved that I would walk the town that weekend and try to come to grips with what I had left there twenty-five years before.

I spent that Friday night with my aunt, Louise Puckett, at The Pines, an upscale retirement community on the eastern end of town. The next morning I was up early and on the street. I first went up Main Street. As is typical of many small college towns, the town is on one side and the gown on the other. Most of the town buildings date from the early part of the twentieth century, but some are older. The college buildings that front Main Street date from the original 1837 campus and are fine examples of the Georgian architecture of the period. Woodrow Wilson, who came to Davidson as a student in 1874 and returned as President of the United States in 1916, would probably recognize the place if he could see it today.

Up the street I visited the old Carolina Inn, which had become the Dean Rusk International Studies Center. (The former Secretary of State was a Davidson graduate.) This structure was built as an inn by Lewis Dinkens in the 1840's, sold to Hanson Pinckney Helper, and was called the Helper Inn by 1860. Hanson was the brother of Hinton Rowan Helper, whose book *The Impending Crisis* was one of the flashpoints that ignited the Civil War. In my time the building was largely abandoned until the McEver family and others remodeled it for the town Teen Canteen in the late 1950's. I peeked through a window. Computers, desks, and chairs cluttered the spaces where I once had tripped the light fantastic on the Canteen's dance floor.

My next stop was down the street at the old Chairman Blake House. As a child I spent seven years in this house, which my father rented from the college. It is a rambling, antebellum, wooden affair with a colonnaded front porch. Out back was an old brick building, which in my time was in ruins and had served in worse times as a slave kitchen and quarters. For us in the 1950's it was the playhouse for the entire neighborhood. The college has long since removed the structure, but behind that place stood a living memory, one of my favorites. It was an old oak tree under whose protective boughs, legend has it, Daniel Boone once rested. When I was a child, its largest branch supported our favorite swing.

My old house fronted Main Street, and in my day was directly across the street from the firehouse. We were always the first to know when there was a fire in town. The alarm siren for the volunteer fire department was in our front yard, and it tested loud and clear at 5:30 p.m. each weekday—an ear-spitting "Ahhhhhhhhhhh." Just south of the Blake House, School Street (our name for South Street) meets Main Street.

I chose School Street. I first paused next door to our old house— where Bub Cashion's Gulf, no longer in business, still stood. This filling station replaced the old movie house that had stood on that site for more than twenty-five years until February 14, 1955. I remember that the first thing we heard that night was the fire siren, but it took us a while to realize that the fire was next-door. Despite the fact that the firehouse was directly across the street, the fire department couldn't save the building. That's the subject of another chapter.

At the top of School Street stands the old Davidson School. The night my dad arrived in Davidson in 1946, after leaving Princeton University to become the chair of the biology department at the college, the school building burned down. The present structure was erected in 1947, and after more than fifty years of service, is little worn. It is a fine building, once housing grades one through twelve. In 1951 the high school merged with the newly opened North Mecklenburg High School eleven miles to the south near Huntersville, and thereafter the Davidson School was known as the Davidson Elementary School.

The building had changed little over the years. I walked around it to the gymnasium, which was part of the original school complex and predates the post-1947 school building. I peered through a dusty window, and the interior was the same as I had remembered. I brought my first date, Georgeanna Mayhew, here to a sock hop in the early 1960's. I was in the seventh grade and she in the eighth. Henry Jarman, the janitor, was the chaperone. That night Jane Withers tried to teach me the Cha Cha and the Shag, but it didn't work, and I never learned to dance well.

After the dance I remember walking Georgeanna home. It was a small town, and the streets were safe at night. I desperately wanted to hold her hand but couldn't muster the courage. I don't know what I did wrong, but she hardly gave me the time of day after that. The following year she went to Alexander Junior High School near North Mecklenburg High. By the time I got to high school we were at least on speaking terms again.

Leaving the school grounds, I headed further down School Street, where it ends at the Mimosa Cemetery. My parents are buried there, and I visited their graves. For some reason the experience was more emotionally draining than I had anticipated. As a physician I fully understand and accept that death is a natural process, and as a Christian I know that all of this is taken care of, but I still miss Virginia and Olin Puckett. I suppose we never quite stop missing our folks. Nearby I visited Dr. James Woods' grave—one of the townspeople I describe in this book. On the way out I saw the marker of a young man from Davidson who perished at the Battle of Midway in June 1942. He was one of several hundred Americans who died in that major turning point in history, and I suppose that like most of them, he died at sea. The stone serves to mark his life and heroism.

Just beyond the cemetery is the Little League ball field and beyond that the Pony League field. I sat in the bleachers above the Pony League field, named McEver Field after Gene McEver, who directed its construction. This place is about family and the fathers and sons who built the fields. My own father had to watch in despair as I almost single-handedly dropped the biggest game we ever played in this ballpark. That incident comes in a later chapter. I looked out at the fences, which after almost thirty-five years seemed so close now but so distant back then. I only hit one ball out of the park, and that was over the right field fence in practice. But this was a lot more than a game because what we learned here was sportsmanship, teamwork, and rules of fair play.

My next stop was back on Main Street at the north corner of Concord and Main. The Davidson College Presbyterian Church (DCPC) stands on this site. When I was a little boy, the old church was a decrepit structure that fronted Concord Road away from the college campus. In the late 1940's the president of the college, Dr. John R. Cunningham, raised the money (I recall the amount as $1.7 million) to demolish the old church and replace it with a fine new building facing the campus. This new church building was completed in the spring of 1952, and I will always remember hearing the chimes ring at 6 p.m. on that first afternoon. They really weren't chimes, but a recording that Oscar Thies had placed in the top of the steeple. Thereafter, recorded peals emanated from the steeple on the hour each afternoon. My relationship with the new church would last eighteen years. In later years I would return here for the funerals of several members of my family. The church has had numerous pastors, and the size of the congregation has increased through the years; yet it remains an enormously intellectual, vital, and compassionate church, which is still a center of campus life.

Across Concord Road from the church is a vacant lot that was planted with dogwood trees in memory of my father who died in 1972. On this lot stood the old North Carolina Medical College, which was established in 1886. Doctors here took the first radiographs ever made in the United States shortly after Roentgen discovered X-ray technology in Germany late in the nineteenth century. The films were of some medical instruments. By my time the medical school entity had long since moved to Charlotte and later merged with the University of Virginia, but the building was still extant during my younger years. This was the center of the grave-robbing operations that kept the medical school in the anatomy business, a subject I detail in Chapter 5.

I then walked east out Concord Road to the Manse, which housed the college's Presbyterian ministers and their families for over fifty years. Pattie Morris Newell, who lived here from 1953-1961, was the main attraction of that house in my childhood. Her father, Sam Newell, hailed from Charlotte, graduated from Davidson, and later returned to the town as pastor of the college church. I was in and out of puppy love with Pattie over the years; in fact, I was practically a permanent resident of the house. My mother told me that Mrs. Newell was taking out adoption papers on my twin brother, John, and me. Pattie left between the seventh and eighth grades when her father accepted the pastorate of a church in Richmond, Virginia. I describe the ministers in Chapter 9.

Heading out Concord Road, I came to the intersection of College Drive and Concord. I walked down the hill to my old neighborhood. This was a wonderful place to grow up. This whole area was once Johnsie Shelton's horse pasture, and Daisy Whittle would take all of her nursery school students here on a picnic in the spring. In the mid-fifties the college bought the land and sold lots to faculty members. I stopped in front of the corner house that my father and mother built in 1955-56. I can still remember when it was an empty lot with a giant oak out back and a maple tree on the side. The house is a large two-story structure with a small colonnaded porch and a brick walk leading to the street. In 1956 we planted the dogwood trees that still stand in the front yard and are living reminders of a childhood and a generation of elders come and gone.

We have no precise and defined present moment that we can latch onto for the journey into the future. Our lives become one long memory as every moment passes into retrospect. Before my old home that day I resolved to put my memories of Davidson into writing. I knew it would take years to think through all of this and put it down in some coherent form, but I wanted to do it for my son. I wanted him to know a small part of a world that was so vastly different from the one in which he has grown to maturity. Having said all of that, I will start at the beginning.

The General
and
the River

On May 20, 1775, a group of American patriots met under a giant oak tree in the woods of northern Mecklenburg County, North Carolina. Here they supposedly drew up a document proclaiming their independence from Great Britain. This was the first formal American declaration of independence, and it took place more than a year before the declaration in Philadelphia. The site of the signing came to be revered in the county as the Independence Oak, and even during my high school years, the old tree supposedly stood in a stand of woods just north of Huntersville.

No such document has ever been found. If there was a written declaration, then it probably didn't survive the Revolution. Interestingly, a number of years back my family visited Independence Hall in Philadelphia and purchased a packet of famous American historical documents among which was a document spuriously entitled "The Mecklenburg Declaration of Independence." I have seen copies of this same document adorning the walls of many a Mecklenburg home.

It seems that someone took the story to heart and wrote his or her version of how a declaration should have read even if it never existed in the first place. My father added a different twist to the story.

He said that on warm, spring Sunday afternoons during those years, fervent patriots would become intoxicated on beer and stand up on tables proclaiming their independence from Great Britain, their wives, and just about anybody else. One cannot deny the importance of what may or may not have happened because the date May 20, 1775, appears on the North Carolina state flag. That day is still celebrated each year as Mecklenburg Independence Day.

In the autumn of 1780 events in the American Revolution in the South would dramatically reverse the setbacks suffered at the hands of Lord Cornwallis at Charleston and Camden. Cornwallis advanced northward into North Carolina and encamped at Charlottetown (now Charlotte). On October 7, 1780, a force of approximately two thousand frontiersmen, later called the Over Mountain Men, crossed the Appalachians and routed a Loyalist force under British Major Patrick Ferguson at Kings Mountain along the Carolina borders. This defeat effectively destroyed Cornwallis' left wing. The battle was the turning point of the Revolution in the South.

Things began to heat up for Cornwallis in little Charlottetown, and he decided to withdraw his army, calling the place "a damned hornet's nest." He moved his men to Winnsboro, South Carolina. Shortly afterwards, General Nathanael Greene brought his American army into Charlotte. Greene divided his forces, sending General Daniel Morgan south to an area called the Cowpens, near what is today Spartanburg, South Carolina. In the meantime, Greene, ever short on supplies, established camp in Cheraw, South Carolina, arriving there on December 26, 1780.

Cornwallis sent Colonel Banastre Tarleton (infamous for his ruthless tactics) to destroy Morgan's contingent. Morgan baited the trap at Cowpens, and on the morning of January 17, 1781, the American force double-enveloped the British and thoroughly routed them. Cornwallis' plans for a decisive victory in the Carolinas were evaporating.

Morgan retreated to Charlotte after Cowpens. Cornwallis began to move in that direction, hoping to cross the rain-swollen Catawba River several miles north of Charlotte. American soldiers carefully watched the British movement up the west bank of the Catawba, where there were several fords in that vicinity.

On January 31, 1781, the Redcoats feigned a movement northward to a crossing point at Beatties' Ford, approximately eighteen miles upriver from Charlotte. General Greene, General Morgan, and General William Lee Davidson met at Beatties' Ford, anticipating a possible British move there. That same night General Davidson, the commander of the Mecklenburg Militia, joined the men under his command at Cowan's Ford, the next crossing down the river that separated Mecklenburg and Lincoln counties. Davidson and his militia encamped some distance from the river, leaving sentries at the water's edge to warn of any British activity. They didn't know that Cornwallis had decided to order his main force across at Cowan's Ford.

The morning of February 1, 1781, dawned in a wet, cold drizzle. The British crossing may have gone unobserved had the traitor Frederick Hager not changed allegiance back to the Patriot cause. Hager, who had switched allegiance several times already in this conflict, is reputed to have had a pang of conscience. The British had hired him as a guide. He had planned to take them across the Catawba through the shallower but longer foot ford, but at the last moment his newfound patriotic fervor apparently overrode his greed, and he switched to the shorter but more treacherous wagon ford. The swift current swept several British soldiers down the river, and it was their cries that alerted a sleeping sentry on the Mecklenburg side of the river and brought the American forces scurrying down to the water's edge.

It wasn't much of a battle; the Redcoats overpowered the outnumbered militia. In the melee General Davidson was fatally shot through the heart while trying to rally his hapless soldiers. British losses were comparatively small. After the battle, family and friends retrieved Davidson's naked body and buried him that night by torchlight at nearby Hopewell Presbyterian Church.

The next day British Colonel Banastre Tarleton and some of his cavalry arrived at a little country inn and demanded refreshment. The innkeeper, a corpulent little woman with a heart of steel, recognized that he was the butcher Tarleton and swatted him over the head with her broom. Mercifully she was spared the infamous "Tarleton's Quarter."

She was our Molly Pitcher, and we called her little tavern Tarleton's Tavern and her swat the Battle of Tarleton's Tavern. The structure stood near Centre Presbyterian Church in southern Iredell County, just a few miles north of the patch of woods that in due time good Presbyterians would transform into Davidson College.

Cornwallis marched on to Guilford Courthouse, near modern-day Greensboro, where he fought the American army led by Nathanael Greene. The British claimed victory there, but in reality they were greatly weakened. History has overlooked Cowan's Ford, but for every British soldier lost on the Catawba, there was one less in contention at Guilford Courthouse and Yorktown. Cornwallis continued northward to Yorktown, and there his world turned upside down.

A triumphal arch was later erected in memory of General William Lee Davidson at Guilford Courthouse. A number of years ago the National Park Service decided that it needed to enlarge the road leading through the arch, and in so doing, workers chose to remove the structure rather than to reroute the road. I will never understand that decision.

In the early 1960's Duke Power Company bought up thousands of acres of farmland in Mecklenburg, Lincoln, and Iredell counties of North Carolina and began clearing land for the Cowan's Ford Dam-Lake Norman project. The dam began to rise on the site of the ford and the 1781 battle. On Sunday afternoons we would ride our bikes down to the dam site and take in the slowly moving construction. In a few years the lake would fill in and become one of the largest man-made lakes in the United States.

The Army Corps of Engineers blew up the Beatties' Ford Bridge while we listened from a distance. The bridge itself wasn't the loss. The Catawba crossed the fall line at Beatties' Ford, and the large rock outcroppings and deep pools provided an ideal swimming area. This was our old swimming hole, and it had been used as such dating back to colonial times.

Another victim of the rising waters was the beautiful old pre-Revolutionary Graham plantation home. Preservationists carefully disassembled the old house, numbered each piece, and carted them to Winston Salem for later reconstruction. Sadly, the storehouse and all of its contents were lost in a fire.

This was our Aswan and our Nubia. Familiar farmlands and forests were cleared and homes either razed or moved. Entire cemeteries were relocated, and this had ghoulish repercussions. There were all kinds of complaints raised about mishandlings of caskets and corpses. Somebody would load up a truck on Saturday and place caskets out on a lawn for the remainder of the weekend before reburial on Monday morning. Occasionally a casket would drop out of a pickup and spill its wretched contents into the path of an oncoming vehicle.

By the mid-1960's the lake had virtually filled. Just as we had predicted, Charlotteans began coming out in droves to overuse this lake just as they had overused nearby lakes along the Catawba system. This time they were in for a surprise. Engineers had cleared the land that would be the lakebed, but as the lake filled, debris kept surfacing. There followed a rash of serious and sometimes fatal boating and water-skiing accidents. We discovered that the drinking water had its own special hazards when Davidson converted to Lake Norman as its primary reservoir. The chemicals used to make the water potable actually made it resemble effluent from the Skoda Steel Works, and it was dreadful for almost a month.

The dam stood right on top of Cowan's Ford. To the best of my knowledge, after the completion of the dam, there was nothing to commemorate the battle fought there in 1781. The local matrons came to the rescue. Women from all over northern Mecklenburg County organized the Cowan's Ford Chapter of the Daughters of the American Revolution (we called it "The Damn Committee"), and my mother was one of the charter members. She had been a member of the D.A.R. for years thanks to her grandmother Virginia Hale, who had documented that she had a Revolutionary ancestor named Richard Stuart, who fought with George Washington in the Continental Army. Before helping to organize the Cowan's Ford Chapter, Mom belonged to the Hornet's Nest Chapter of the D.A.R.

The chapter chose Rutledge Withers (who had Revolutionary ties), my brother, and me to be the honor guard for the dedication of the memorial plaque at Cowan's Ford on the morning of May 20, 1965. We garbed up in military regalia donated by the ROTC Department at Davidson College and carried the North Carolina and American flags. We stood at rigid attention in front of the memorial as

Mrs. Maddie Sadler read the dedicatory speech. At the time I felt silly in all that military regalia, but in retrospect I'm very proud to have been a part of that ceremony. General Davidson finally received long overdue recognition on the precise site where he had bravely fought and died for American independence.

Townies in Davidson—among whom I counted myself, my father's position at the college notwithstanding—considered William Lee Davidson the first and foremost member of the august Davidson Townie Society. We respected him as a great hero even though we actually knew very little about him. Our predecessors saw him that way, too. Davidson County, North Carolina, Davidson College, and the town of Davidson all bear his name.

The Field Marshal

Peter Stuart Ney, who designed the seal of Davidson College in 1840, lived near Statesville, North Carolina. He was an educated man who came from obscure origins in South Carolina. Some said that he spoke fluent French, was an expert horseman and swordsman, and had a remarkable knowledge of French military history. Some said that he was Grand Marshal Michel Ney of France, the famous field marshal who led the Grand Army on its agonizing retreat from Moscow in the winter of 1812.

Napoleon, author of all the misery, had left his suburban Moscow palace in a flurry and was taken by fast sled to Paris in only nine days. Despite this, Ney remained loyal to Napoleon; but after his commander was exiled to Elba, Ney grudgingly swore allegiance to the new Bourbon king of France. When Napoleon returned for the "Hundred Days," Ney betrayed the French crown and joined his old command in time for the Battle of Waterloo. The British and loyal French captured Ney after the battle, and the restored Bourbon king asked the victorious Duke of Wellington to execute him for high treason. History records that on December 7, 1815, Ney fell before a

British firing squad and was interred in his family's mausoleum outside Paris. After that the events become murky.

Approximately one month later a packet ship from Bordeaux, France, arrived in Charleston, South Carolina, carrying a man rumored to be none other than Marshal Michel Ney of France. He called himself Peter Stuart Ney, and he became an itinerant schoolteacher who eventually migrated into Mecklenburg and Iredell Counties in North Carolina. Wherever he went, people questioned him regarding his true identity. Witnesses said that in the delirium of fever or intoxication of alcohol, he would confess that he was Marshal Ney of France. He seemed to know trivia of Napoleonic military history that only one close to Napoleon could have known. He once divulged a name, later confirmed as factual, that Marshal Ney had used while traveling incognito in Switzerland. Only the field marshal or someone very close to him could have known that.

Peter Stuart Ney became interested in the development of a new college in the woods of northern Mecklenburg County. The founders of Davidson College, knowing of his myriad talents, asked him to design the seal of the fledgling institution. The result is startling and typically Napoleonic—a sword stabs downward through a serpent. The motto reads *Alenda Lux Ubi Orta Libertas* (*Let Learning Be Cherished Where Liberty Has Arisen*). Ney, sensitive to the pride the locals had in their supposed declaration of independence from Great Britain in 1775, included a reference to the Mecklenburg Declaration of Independence.

Peter Stuart Ney died in 1847. On his deathbed friends asked, "Who are you? Some say you are Marshal Ney." He replied just before he died, "I am Marshal Ney of France." He was buried in the cemetery of the Third Creek Presbyterian Church in Cleveland, North Carolina.

He did not rest long in peace. Supposedly Marshal Ney had suffered a battle injury and had a steel plate in his skull. Late one night shortly after his internment, a group of history-minded grave robbers pillaged his remains, but found no steel plate. Forensic experts later would report that the job was so hopelessly bungled that no one could draw any firm conclusions from such a post mortem.

My father told me about Peter Stuart Ney early in my childhood, and I grew up with the story. On occasion we would drive up to Third Creek and visit the gravesite. When I entered Davidson College in the autumn of 1966, my interest in the Ney story was rekindled when my English professor, Dr. Tony Abbott, assigned a term paper. I used this as an opportunity to research this subject. Dr. Chalmers Davidson, director of the Davidson College Library and resident historian, was an invaluable resource. As a humorous aside, one afternoon he showed me an oriental rug donated to the college late in the nineteenth century, which bore the seal of the college. Ney's *Libertas* has been adulterated to *Ubertas*, so the piece loosely reads *Let Learning Be Cherished Where Fertility Has Arisen.*

Dr. Davidson took me to the rare book collection and pulled a volume from one of the shelves. It was the *History of Napoleon* written in 1842. In it there is a lithograph of Marshal Ney when he fought with Napoleon. In the right margin of that page an aged Peter Stuart Ney has sketched a small self-portrait, and he declares in writing that he is the same man portrayed in the lithograph—only much older. This and numerous other books on the subject gave me a wealth of information for my paper.

Although I gained a clearer understanding of this man, I still was unable to completely solve the mystery of who he really was. I asked Dr. Davidson for his opinion on the matter and how Ney could have survived the firing squad. He certainly knew more about Peter Stuart Ney than anyone, and he offered a plausible explanation.

According to Dr. Davidson, both Wellington and Marshal Ney were Masons. In those days Masons took their fraternal vows quite seriously; so seriously that Wellington rigged the firing squad to spare the life of a man whom he greatly respected. As the musket balls whistled over his head, Ney, a more than eager participant in the plot, fell to the ground, rupturing small pouches of chicken blood concealed inside his shirt. Wellington's personal physician pronounced him dead, and stretcher-bearers carted the "corpse" away for transport to a packet ship leaving the port of Bordeaux.

Dr. Davidson was actually noncommittal regarding the validity of the story. He did point out to me a major historical problem—the Ney family had never permitted historians to open the field marshal's mausoleum near Paris. That probably would have resolved the issue once and for all. The Ney controversy and the Lost Colony remain the two great mysteries of North Carolina history. My own research convinced me that the story is true.

The

Professor

A number of years ago my Sunday school department asked me to talk on the meaning of Father's Day. This occasion gave me the opportunity to reflect on my father's life and my relationship with him.

We don't know much about the Puckett genealogy. My paternal grandfather, William Lawrence Puckett, was born in Mississippi in 1880. His parents died of typhoid fever, and he was orphaned at an early age. Lawrence picked up the nickname "Lonnie" and moved from Mississippi to the Long Creek area of Mecklenburg County, where relatives raised him. His grandchildren would call him "Papa." We do know a little more about my grandmother Molly's side of the family. I have been able to piece together some of that history from several of her relatives.

In the early morning hours of July 30, 1864, coal miners from Pennsylvania had just completed a long tunnel under a key Confederate stronghold that was strategic to the defense of Petersburg, Virginia—during that agonizing period of trench warfare that preceded the collapse of the Confederacy. The miners packed the distal end of the tunnel with high explosives, and at approximately 4:45 a.m. Union soldiers lit the fuses. There followed a tremendous explosion, which blew a deep rent in the Confederate line, leaving a crater thirty feet deep. The blast stunned the Union soldiers as much as it did their Southern counterparts. In the darkness and smoke, thousands of Union troops poured into the crater and stood around in utter confusion not knowing what to do next. This gave the Confederate forces time to organize a counterattack. Thus began the Battle of the Crater.

One of those Confederate soldiers was young Henry Jackson Washam from North Carolina. During the battle a Yankee soldier shot Henry in the leg. His comrades carried him from the field, and he survived the battle and the war. Had his wound been mortal, I would have never arrived here, at least not in my present form. Henry married three times, thus expanding the branches of the Washam family tree. Three of his close family members would touch my life. The most influential was one of his daughters, Molly.

Molly Washam was the offspring of Henry and his second wife Belzora (Belvy). Lonnie Puckett married "Miss Molly," and they settled on Catawba Street in Cornelius, just one mile from Davidson. They had two children, William Olin and Mary Louise, born in 1906 and 1908, respectively. Papa (our name for Lonnie) ran a general store two blocks down the street, and he purchased several buildings in town that were leased for other businesses. The Puckett family attended the Cornelius Presbyterian Church, just across the street from their house. At one time Papa served as the town mayor.

We have pictures of Papa and Miss Molly. Papa had a dog he named Piddler, who was white and fluffy, got along well with children, and became our pet also. I have a picture of Papa and Piddler, and the dog's coat complements Papa's snow-white hair. A favorite family photograph is one my sister has had restored, showing the Puckett family in Papa's brand new 1912 Model T Ford. My grandfather appears his usual jovial self; whereas, little Olin and Louise look a little bewildered by all the high technology. Miss Molly is seated in the rear staring sternly at the camera—a pose that, by all descriptions, belied her true gentle nature.

I never knew Miss Molly. She died in 1945 of a prolonged stroke condition well before my birth in 1947. I understand that she was a very religious, kind, and compassionate woman, and judging from her children, I believe that is an accurate description. Dad and Louise were cut from the same mold; both could get along with just about anybody under any circumstances.

My memories of Papa come from late in his life. I remember him as a kindly old gentleman who, unlike his son and grandsons, had a full head of hair. Papa developed what we probably would call Alzheimer's disease today. Louise was constantly attending to him. On Saturdays Dad and Louise would put Papa in his favorite rocking chair, bundle him in sheets, and cut his hair—a ritual in which he seemed to delight.

We were frequent visitors at the home Papa and Louise shared on Main Street in Cornelius. During those years Louise taught history at the Cornelius School. It was always a treat to sleep over. I was small enough to fit snuggly into one of Papa's large dresser drawers, and that's where I always wanted to sleep.

In the early 1950's television was still in its infancy. Papa bought one of those early Sylvania sets, and I remember watching Douglas Edwards and the CBS evening news program. It was during the Korean War, and although I was too small to fully grasp what was happening, I did learn that Communism was a bad thing.

In the early 1900's Papa purchased a small farm out on Bailey Road just south of the Cornelius town line. An old two-story frame farmhouse came with the property. Papa had a close relationship with an African American farmer named James Davis. Papa wanted the land kept in good order, so he allowed Mr. Davis and his family to live in the house and run the farm. I don't believe that Papa ever derived a cent of income from rent or from Mr. Davis' work. He just wanted him to keep up the land.

I remember the spring morning in 1953 when the town fire siren went off in our front yard. I was alone in the house when someone from the fire station came over to tell me that the farmhouse was ablaze. I was in a virtual panic. I finally got in touch with Dad, and we picked up Papa and drove down to the property. By that time all that was left standing were the chimneys.

Papa and Dad went straight to work on building another house. At one story it was smaller than its predecessor but much more comfortable for the Davis family. It was an attractive house, and the family took excellent care of it, as they did all of the property. I fondly remember picking blackberries, corn, and cotton on the farm. One of the Davis daughters, Mary Frances, remained very close to Mom and Louise through the years.

Papa built a small cabin on the property along a branch that cut through the wooded area a few hundred yards from the farmhouse. It was for summer use only. We went there frequently for cookouts or just for an excuse to get out of Davidson. In those years the town closed down at 5 p.m., and there wasn't much for us to do after dark. The one thing I remember most about the cabin was Aunt Louise's "cabin tea." I never have been able to get the exact recipe. It was a very tasty concoction of ice tea, lemon, and mint leaves brewed precisely to get the best flavor out of it, and Louise made it in abundance during those summers.

Dad decided that we needed a swimming hole on the property, and he built a small concrete dam on the creek, giving us a place to splash about. That was always the first place we went to during those summer outings. After supper at the cabin, we would swim well past dark. Dad hung a lantern on a nearby tree to give us light.

In March 1960, we experienced big snowfalls on three consecutive Wednesdays. Before one batch would melt, along came the next. One of the casualties of that period of snow was our cabin. The roof couldn't support the weight of the snow and collapsed. Dad didn't feel it was worth the money it would take to rebuild it.

Papa died in his sleep in the summer of 1954. Dad told us the news, and we all sat down and cried together. Dad told us, "I know how you feel." I suppose that he sensed that we knew Papa as more than a grandparent. Mom and Dad would not allow us to attend Papa's funeral saying that we were too young. That was my first encounter with personal family loss, and I feel that they should have allowed me to see the whole thing through.

The family buried Papa beside Miss Molly in the Bethel Church cemetery outside Cornelius. Today it overlooks an arm of Lake Norman. The cemetery has expanded greatly over the years. Louise visited her parents' graves regularly and put out flowers until her own death in 1997. Today she rests beside her mother and father.

Henry Washam had a son named Jesse, who with his wife, Mary Elizabeth Knox, settled on a farm on Concord Road several miles east of Davidson. Louise told me that they had twelve children, and most of them attended college. We all called Mary, "Aunt Mae." Jesse and Mae's daughter Margaret (one of Dad's first cousins) married Murray Kelly and had two children—Mike and Judy. I don't remember much about the Kelly children from my early years, probably because I was in a stupor from fisticuffs with Mike on most of the occasions that brought us together.

The Henry Washam clan gathered yearly for a family reunion out at Aunt Mae's place. Mike Kelly always came along, and what started as friendly banter usually wound up in a big free-for-all and my flight from reality with a fist or blunt instrument. Because of that I particularly dreaded the yearly Ramah Presbyterian Church barbecue.

Ramah Presbyterian Church is a beautiful old wooden structure located several miles east of Davidson near the Cabarrus County line. The road that passes it connects Concord Road to Huntersville. Every autumn Ramah sponsored a crafts sale and barbecue. I never wanted to go—fearing what would happen at the hands of Cousin Kelly. At the last barbecue that I can remember, Mike pummeled me with a telescope.

During our early teen years we played on opposing teams in Pony League baseball. Mike was the star player for the Cornelius team. By that time we were on speaking terms, and the competition was friendly. John and I became telephone-chat-pals with Mike for a while in the eighth grade.

We all attended North Mecklenburg High together. Mike was All-State in football and baseball. He was tall, and as an end led North to a third place finish in 4-A football in 1965, and as the catcher led the baseball team to the state championship in 1966. Mike was also the starting center on the high school's basketball team. *The Charlotte Observer* named him Mecklenburg County Athlete of the Year in 1966.

Mike attended Davidson College with John and me. He was an honorable mention All-America end on the college football team. After graduation he played professional football for the Cincinnati Bengals in the NFL. I learned that he grew tired of injuries and left the game. He received a master's degree in animal science from N.C. State and worked in Florida with an agricultural extension program. Today he is in real estate. I last saw him at our thirtieth college reunion. He didn't clobber me then.

Another of Henry and Belzora Washam's progeny who touched my life was their daughter Addie, who was one of our dearest relatives. She married George Tugend. Their son George (Dad's first cousin), his wife, Emilie, and daughter, Georgia Lea, lived in Delaware City, Delaware, where George was the postmaster. Aunt Addie went to live with them when her husband died. The Tugends came south on a regular basis and visited their ever-expanding relations. They always brought Aunt Addie along. They were very close to Dad and Louise. Addie was very thin and frail looking, and every time I saw her I thought that would be the last. She was always partial to John and me and sent us presents at Christmas. In the end she proved she wasn't so frail after all. She lived to be a ripe old ninety-eight years. Many of her Mecklenburg relatives, including Mom and Louise, attended her sendoff, which was more of a church social than a funeral. Aunt Addie lived a gracious long life and was loved by many.

Another of Dad's many cousins in the Henry Washam clan was Robert Barnhardt. Henry Washam's wife, Belzora, was the daughter of Eli Barnhardt. Her brother Jesse Barnhardt married Cora Stenhouse. They had seven children, including John Robert, whom we called Robert, or "Grundy." Robert married Gladys Swift, and they settled on Concord Road, three miles east of Davidson, not far from Aunt Mae's place. They had three children—Bobby and twin daughters Martha and Jane.

Mr. Barnhardt was a farmer. John and I were frequent visitors at their home several miles east of Davidson. We played with our cousins Martha and Jane, who were ahead of us in school by one year. We spent a lot of time chasing the girls around the barnyard. They were very attractive, but there were never any romantic inclinations from either side.

Gladys Barnhardt was my second grade teacher at Davidson Elementary. She and Mr. Barnhardt drove a green Studebaker, and we always knew when they came to town. It was the only car like it in the northern end of the county. It became a fixture and source of conversation at the school parking lot. They stopped making

Studebakers eons ago, but every time I've seen one of the few remaining, I'm reminded of the Barnhardts.

During my second grade year I was up to considerable mischief. I briefly cultivated the bad habit of stealing books and *objets d'art*. I would wait until after school when everyone had left but the janitor, then sneak in and remove the books from some of my classmates' desks. I don't understand why I did that; I suppose I just wanted attention. At all events, I chuckled with glee when the kids came in the following day and found books and other things missing—usually to be found in the bathroom at the back of the classroom or dropped out the window and lying behind the bushes that bordered the building. Jim McEver and Jack McGeachy were my primary targets. My classmates referred to the culprit as the "Phantom."

This went on for a week, and with practice I was really getting good at it. I think that Gladys knew all along. One afternoon in February 1956, she confronted me and told me she wanted to have a little chat after school. I remember that she sat me down on the front row and took her seat at her desk. She sternly asked me why I was doing all of this. She made me feel very ashamed, and I cried a lot over it. My only excuse was the proverbial "The Devil made me do it" explanation. The spanking I got at home completed my exorcism.

Bobby Barnhardt graduated with my sister from North Mecklenburg High School in 1963. The Barnhardt twins were immensely popular at the high school, where they were cheerleaders. They graduated in 1965, and both attended East Carolina University. I was out of touch with the girls for years, but I recently contacted Martha and also learned that Jane became an attorney and later a state senator in Minnesota.

Dad told me all about growing up with his many cousins and also gave me an idea what it was like growing up in the early twentieth century. He spent a lot of time during his younger years working in Lonnie's country store on Catawba Street in Cornelius. During the winter months he would get up early and fire up the store furnace before the start of the school day. I remember his conversations about the abundance of goods that Lonnie sold in the store. Dad particularly loved oysters, and they came in barrels on ice, shipped west from the coast on the Southern Railway. Lonnie let him eat all he wanted.

Dad attended the Cornelius School, which was a combined elementary and high school. In 1923, at the age of seventeen, he enrolled as a freshman at nearby Davidson College. He showed a particular talent and love for the biological sciences. He also had a passion for soldiering and was so good at it that the Reserved Officers Training Corps (ROTC) cadre made him commander of the Davidson College ROTC battalion. Dad remembered with pride how he led General John "Black Jack" Pershing around the campus and stood with him on the ROTC review stand in the spring of 1927.

After his graduation in 1927, Dad stayed on at Davidson as an instructor in biology. He moved on to the University of North Carolina at Chapel Hill, where he did his master's work under Dr. "Froggie" Wilson. Dad next received his Ph.D. in biology from Princeton University in 1934. He did his embryology work under Drs. Speymann and Conklin, the founders of that field of biology.

Although the details are a bit blurry, Dad joined the faculty at Princeton as an assistant professor and went on loan from the university to Memphis, where he taught at Southwestern University (now Rhodes University) for the academic year 1934-1935. The following year he was back at Princeton teaching in the biology department. He chose to remain on the faculty, and that was a pivotal decision of his academic life.

Dad acquired a fine reputation as a teacher at Princeton, where he founded and directed the premedical program. He had a unique teaching style that involved lots of blackboards and colored chalk. He rose rapidly to associate professor under the guidance of his mentor and dear friend, Dr. Elmer Butler, who gave me my middle name.

Both Dad and Aunt Louise remained unmarried through the 1930's. Louise drove up to Princeton each spring to drive him home to Cornelius. During some of those summers before Dad married, he spent time doing research at Camp Alice, high atop Mt. Mitchell. Louise and Dad attended Franklin D. Roosevelt's second inauguration in Washington in 1937. Interestingly, his future wife was also in the crowd that day. In 1939 Louise and Dad attended the New York World's Fair. Both of them told me how remarkable that was. Even today after learning more about it, I still marvel at the technology that first went on display there.

Dad came to know many academic luminaries at Princeton through the Institute for Advanced Study, which was developed there in the years before World War II. He and Albert Einstein became friends. Dad told me how he once inducted Einstein into a scientific society at Princeton. After the program Dad took Einstein over to his lab and showed him a chick embryo under a phase microscope. He said that the old theorist sat there mesmerized, exclaiming, "*Wunderbar! Wunderbar!*"

I once asked Dad who he believed was the smartest man he ever met. I expected him to say Einstein. Without hesitation he replied, "Johnny Von Neumann," the great Jewish mathematician who fled to America from Hungary before the Holocaust. Von Neumann did the mathematics and computer work for the implosion device with the Manhattan Project, and today he is widely considered the father of the computer.

Dad recalled a mathematics Ph.D. candidate at Princeton who was working on his dissertation. This individual had multiple blackboards filled with his background work. After six weeks he came up with the solution but had not yet written it down. As fate would have it, Von Neumann walked into the room, saw the problem, and immediately solved it in his head. The student, unaware of Von Neumann's presence, wrote the answer on the board. Von Neumann was astonished that the student had done the calculations as rapidly as he!

In the prewar days the Government allowed young men to fulfill ROTC obligations by doing summer duty in the Army. Dad began his service as a second lieutenant at Ft. Moultrie on Sullivan's Island (the setting for Edgar Allan Poe's *Gold Bug*) near Charleston, South Carolina. My father thoroughly enjoyed those summers in the South Carolina sun. He fondly reminisced about his "Colonel" and how the "Old Man" had his junior officers over on Sundays for cocktails and small talk on a veranda overlooking the ocean. Dad obviously thought a lot of his commander. It was not until after George Catlett Marshall (Army Chief of Staff in World War II, author of the Marshall Plan, Nobel laureate, and Secretary of State) died in 1959 that I learned that he was Dad's colonel at Ft. Moultrie.

In the early 1940's a clear plastic was developed. Dad had a number of prehistoric insects preserved in amber, and from those marvels of nature came his idea for mounting biological specimens in the new plastic. It worked so well that Dad published the first scientific paper on the subject in 1941, but he couldn't patent the process because Du Pont had developed the plastic. From that discovery grew a cottage industry that would in time include just about everything mountable in clear plastic. I still have some of those old specimens.

In 1941 Dad met a twenty-eight year old woman from Wilson, North Carolina, named Virginia Lewis House. They married in 1942. My sister still has the newspaper clippings and photographs of the wedding party in front of my grandmother's house. Apparently it was quite a social event, which one paper described as "an occasion that generated considerable interest among state social circles."

I have more information on my mother's genealogy than Dad's. My maternal great-grandmother, Virginia Northington Hale, spent the last years of her life tracking down her roots. Her search carried her to numerous graveyards and courthouses all over eastern North Carolina and tidewater Virginia, and she managed to trace seven family lines back to the seventeenth century.

After my parents died, as I was cleaning out our attic, I came across her material in an old worn-out trunk. What I discovered was fascinating. She had preserved a mini-history of plantation life in Virginia and eastern North Carolina. I was astonished to see wills, which mentioned, among other details, where and to whom the decedents' slaves were sent. I learned that I am a direct line descendent of Betty Washington, George Washington's sister, and Fielding Lewis, a planter in Fredericksburg, Virginia. The Lewis' home, Kenmore, still stands on the heights above the town. The Daughters of the American Revolution restored the house in 1923, and it remains open to the public. It must have been right in the middle of the Battle of Fredericksburg in 1862. There is no original furniture in the house—all are period pieces. My sister, Ginger, has a pair of candlesticks reputed to have come from the Lewis household. From my study of the Lewis family I learned that Meriwether Lewis (of Lewis and Clark fame) and I share a common Lewis ancestor.

William and Virginia Northington Hale had an only daughter, whom they named Virginia. She was born in 1889 in Halifax, North Carolina, and she grew up in the former home of William R. Davie, the founder of the University of North Carolina. Nearby stood the ruins of the Wiley Jones home. A man named John Paul lived with old Wiley for a short time in the eighteenth century and took Jones' name to become John Paul Jones, the father of the American navy. When I visited the Jones place, all that remained of the house was a chimney covered in brush.

Young Virginia Hale met and married John House and settled in Roanoke Rapids, North Carolina, in 1911. John had a brother, Joe, who lived in Beaufort, on Pamlico Sound. Uncle Joe's home has survived and is on the National Registry of Historical Places. In time the Houses moved to Wilson, where John opened up a thriving wholesale grocery business. They had an only daughter, Virginia Lewis House, born in 1913. "Gin Lewis," as little Virginia was called, graduated from high school in Wilson in 1931. She attended Mary Baldwin College in Staunton, Virginia, and graduated in 1935. She did her masters work in English at the University of North Carolina and taught in public schools in Oxford and Burlington, North Carolina.

Dad and Mom spent the war years in Princeton, where Dad taught and also worked for the Office of Research and Development for the U.S. Government. He and Dr. Elmer Butler studied the ballistics of wounding—what happens when a ballistic enters human flesh. They had the fastest X-ray equipment in the world at Princeton. Mom told me how Dad once took her to New York City for an afternoon show. After dinner he took a taxi over to Bellevue Hospital to do some "business." When he later emerged with a wrapped package, Mom thought he had purchased some roses for her. On the train back to Princeton she finally asked Dad what was in the box to which he casually replied, "An arm."

Dad's work would culminate in the book *Wound Ballistics*, which was part of the large collection entitled *The United States Army Medical Corps in World War II*. His work demonstrated graphically for the first time why exit wounds are larger than entrance wounds, and the Warren Commission used the material in investigating the Kennedy assassination. Dad was always proud of the letter of gratitude Franklin Roosevelt wrote to him before the President's death in 1945. Presidents actually signed their correspondence in those years.

In December 1944, my parents had their first child, a daughter named Virginia Northington Puckett. One year later Dad accepted a position as professor of biology at his alma mater, Davidson College. I think he was tired of the publish-or-perish mentality coming into academics after the war. He just wanted to teach. He and Mom moved to Davidson in 1946, arriving the night the old school house burned down.

The small family settled into a faculty home on Concord Road. My identical twin, John, and I arrived in late 1947. Our first Christmas was the only White Christmas we would know as children. We lived in that house (which still stands) for our first two years. Some pictures of John and me romping in the yard have survived, but I have no memory of my years there.

In 1949 Dad moved us into a large, rambling antebellum house on Main Street—the old Chairman Blake House. We would live there until the fall of 1956, when we moved to our new home on College Drive. That old house, which had been built in the 1850's, was a remarkable place. Out back was the ruin of an old slave quarters and kitchen. The former slave kitchen, replete with a crumbling cooking chimney, served as a garage, which was seldom used. The quarters consisted of a single room with a rotting wooden floor. We spent many hours playing there.

Our backyard neighbors, Tom and Blanche Johnson, kept a chicken coop on the hillside beside their white frame house—a structure that was used as the college infirmary from the 1910's to the mid-1930's—in what is now the bend in Lorimer Road, just below that street's intersection with Concord Road and the Davidson College Presbyterian Church. Tom was a stern and humorless man when it came to his chickens. Once after John and I had stirred up the hen house, shaking on the chicken wire, whooping and yelling, Tom scared us to tears and probably worse—I vividly recall Tom standing in our kitchen, pointing his finger, vowing that he would throw both of us into the chicken coop with his ill-tempered rooster if we ever came near his chickens again. Of course, it was Tom and not the rooster that scared us straight.

In the early 1950's Mom hired Alberta Harvell, an African American woman, to do domestic work for her. Alberta was just two generations removed from her slavery ancestry. The Harvells lived in Smithville, a small community just outside Cornelius on N.C. 73. Alberta would remain with us for almost a decade. As small children, she bathed us, dressed us, cooked for us, and most of all loved us. She was a powerful Christian woman whose values carried over to her charges. I believe that on one occasion she may have saved my life.

As a small child I had temper tantrums. John had the same problem. He took it all out on his right hand—biting it hard on the dorsal surface, venting anger in that manner and developing a large callous in the process. I did it with a little more flair. I recall one afternoon when my sister hid one of my favorite toys, a plastic red fire engine. I was furious. I remember actually thrusting my head through one of the front windows. Fortunately, I went through to the other side without cutting myself. Coming out would be an entirely different matter— neurovascular bundles and all of that. I remember that I hung there in limbo with my head suspended out the window and stared across the street. Alberta screamed, "Don't move!" She grabbed me and held me motionless while Ginger ran across the street for help. Soon a small crowd had gathered, and they slowly began to extract me from the window. Happily for all concerned, John and I outgrew this sort of behavior with life and limbs intact.

Alberta worked from 8 a.m. to 5 p.m. on weekdays and from 9 a.m. to 12 noon on Saturdays. Before we started to go to school, we had the main meal at noon. Alberta could cook up just about anything. I remember most fondly her pies. She made the best chocolate and lemon meringue pies I've ever eaten. Her fried chicken was better than anything Colonel Sanders could serve up.

The night the movie house next door burned down Alberta was baby-sitting us at home. I think that she was the first person in the town to realize that the building next door was ablaze. We were terrified. She calmed us down by telling us that our parents would be along shortly and everything would be all right. I don't know why that has stuck with me through the years, but I have often thought back on that night during trying times and found consolation in my memories of how she comforted us.

John had a fundamental anatomical problem. He was born with an esophageal stricture. I got the migraine headache problem, and he got the swallowing problem. Identical twins are never truly identical since mutations do occur in development. Anyway, John was prone to having pain swallowing—especially with meats. It usually happened when he ate too fast or failed to chew meat properly, and the whole bolus hung up in mid-esophagus. Alberta always seemed to look after John more closely than Ginger and me because she was afraid that he might choke to death.

It's hard to imagine there was a time before automatic washing machines. I remember that Alberta scrub-washed much of our clothing. She then hung it all out on lines tied to trees. She let me help out, but I usually came out drenched. On one occasion Alberta and I were hanging out the clothes and sheets when an escaped bull came charging through the yard. I narrowly escaped injury or worse as Alberta pulled me out of its path before the animal ripped the sheets to pieces.

When we moved to our new house at 105 College Drive, Alberta came along as part of the family. She delighted in cooking on the new gas stove, which was a novelty then. I suppose that she wasn't well paid. I say that because that's the way it was back then. Domestics are not well paid today, and it was worse in the 1950's. The day finally came, as we were growing older, when Mom said we couldn't afford to keep Alberta any longer. I was fifteen years old and cried my eyes out.

Mrs. Hope Bell, who lived on Concord Road, hired Alberta. She worked for Mrs. Bell for several years and then moved on to become a cook at the Phi Kappa Alpha fraternity house at the college. When John and I graduated from North Mecklenburg High School in 1966, Alberta was right there on the front row to watch "my boys" receive their diplomas.

While I was a freshman and newly minted frat brother at Davidson College, I saw Alberta frequently as I made my way across the fraternity court to my meals at the Alpha Tau Omega (ATO) fraternity house. She always came out and hugged me, and we would stand outside a while and catch up on old times and the local gossip.

During my sophomore year at Davidson, Alberta had a stroke. She was hospitalized at Lowrance Hospital (now Lake Norman Regional Medical Center) in Mooresville. She was in a coma and obviously was not going to live much longer. John and I visited her just before she died. I kept thinking about the night the movie house burned down. I will always carry that with me.

Hope Bell, Mom, John, and I attended her funeral down in Smithville. Alberta was a pillar of her community, and the church was packed. It was the first and only service I ever attended in an African American church. After the funeral I stood before our old house on Main Street and tearfully thought about all that she had done for us. I have never met another person like her.

Some of my fondest memories of that old house on Main Street are of the Christmases we spent there. In 1953 I received a call from Santa Claus asking me if John and I would like an electric train for Christmas. Of course, Santa was Dad, and of course, he wanted a train as much as we did.

On Christmas morning that year we awoke to find the train set spread out on a ping-pong size table at the head of the stairs. It was an elaborate Lionel train, which actually belched smoke when the appropriate tablets were in place. The train came with a coupler device, small station, and huge water tank. We played with the train for about a year. When we started exploring centrifugal force by running the locomotive at high speed off the tracks and table, our parents relegated the train to a large box in the attic.

It has been almost fifty years, but I still have that old train boxed up in my attic in Asheville. It emerged briefly to the light of day in 1987 when I set it up for my six-year old son. Lionel had built it well, and it had sustained only minor damage from our reckless abuse of it years before. The thing actually worked—at least for a while before the transformer shorted out. I haven't been able to find anyone to repair either locomotive or transformer.

Throughout the 1950's Dad was developing the premedical program at Davidson into one of the best in the nation. On one tally it ranked first—based on the proportion of applicants admitted to medical school. Dad was particularly proud that eleven senior members of the 1958 Davidson College football team went on to become doctors. He had contacts with colleges, universities, and medical schools all over eastern America.

In the summer of 1953 Mom and Dad took us on our first real vacation—or at least one longer than a few days. They told us about their plans that spring after they had arranged to rent a cottage for two weeks at Pawley's Island in South Carolina. Pawley's, settled by the Pawley family in the eighteenth century, is one of many barrier islands that shelter the coasts of the Carolinas. Over the years it would become a popular beach retreat.

We were very excited about going to "Poison Ivy." We had eagerly awaited the day in June when we drove down the South Carolina country roads to the beach. Outside of Florence we crossed the long bridges over the Pee Dee River and swamps. I had never seen a swamp before and was fascinated by plants and water all receding into darkness. Dad said there were alligators and other reptiles in the swamp. When Dad mentioned "other reptiles," I knew that he was talking about snakes. He had a live rattler and a copperhead in cages in his lab.

I remember driving into Myrtle Beach for the first time and seeing the ocean. I had been to Atlantic Beach near Morehead City, North Carolina, when I was four years old, but I had virtually no memory of the trip. That day the ocean looked awfully big, larger than anything I had ever seen. We then drove down to the island.

Pawley's lies about twenty miles south of Myrtle Beach off U.S. 17. I remember seeing Spanish moss for the first time, and I thought that it was nature's way of drying clothes. We drove by the hammock shop, famous for its Pawley's Island hammocks, and then crossed over to the island.

Two causeways traversing a wide tidal marsh are the only approaches to the island. We rented a cottage on the northern end. It was a two story structure on the tidal marsh side of the island and had wide screened porches on each floor. The cottage rested on stilts, and there was room for parking and a shower underneath.

We spent two weeks there during each of the summers of 1953 and 1954. Though we were there only for a brief time, I remember those days fondly. We followed a daily routine. Dad was usually up at dawn and down at the seaside for surf or pier fishing. I accompanied him a couple of times, but getting up that early had not yet become a part of my lifestyle. I gave it up for the privilege of going down to the small store by the northern causeway later each morning to pick up a copy of *The Charlotte Observer*. By then Dad was usually back at the cottage—usually empty-handed since the Blues were never running. After breakfast Mom took us down to the beach before it became too hot. She was wise to keep us out of the sun as much as possible. I don't think I ever burned.

In those years polio was pandemic, and our parents were very concerned about our health. Mom decided that a good afternoon nap would help ward off the evil virus. From 2 to 4 p.m. each afternoon during those summers I learned what utter boredom was. I couldn't sleep, so I just lay there fuming over my loss of freedom. Having had a child, I can understand how Mom and Dad must have felt. The Salk vaccine finally ended the naps.

We made frequent excursions while staying on the island. I enjoyed going to the hammock shop over on the mainland to watch the ladies make hammocks. We bought a Pawley's Island hammock, and it remained on the porch of our farm cabin until that winter of 1960. They built them well. We punished it hard, but I never saw a thread out of place.

Just up U.S. 17 from Pawley's is Brookgreen Gardens. The gardens are a large sculpture park created from an old rice plantation by the famous American sculptress Anna Hyatt Huntington and her husband. I remember the ancient live oaks as the most beautiful I've ever seen. Dad walked us down to the Waccamaw River and told us about the tragedy that befell the owners of the plantation. He said that in 1813 Theodosia Alston, daughter of Aaron Burr and wife of South Carolina governor Joseph Alston, left the plantation dock for a journey to New York. She boarded the vessel *Patriot* at Charleston. She and all others aboard were lost at sea in a gale off Cape Hatteras. I asked Dad if Theodosia's ghost ever returned to haunt the gardens. He told us that over the years there had been numerous sightings of a woman in white walking the waves off Nags Head. Many thought this was Theodosia. He added that there were plenty of other ghosts afoot in this part of the South. This was the South Carolina Low Country, Edgar Allan Poe's favorite haunt.

My parents were friends of Archibald Rutledge, the poet laureate of South Carolina. I don't know the basis of their relationship, but they visited the Rutledge plantation near Georgetown on at least two occasions during those summers. Dad told us about a ghost named Uncle Henry, who haunted the old Rutledge mansion. He was no Amityville Horror—just the mysterious opened or closed window-door apparition. I wanted to go with my parents to get a glimpse of Uncle Henry, but they arranged their visits during our nap times.

I learned from Dad that there was a ghost much closer to Pawley's named the Old Gray Man. Since the eighteenth century inhabitants of the island had reported sighting an eerie man dressed in gray walking the beach in the face of an onrushing tropical storm or hurricane. It was intriguing that not everyone could see the apparition. Those that did see him found that their homes survived the storm unscathed. Those who weren't so fortunate found their homes washed out to sea or into the tidal marsh. Whenever a thunderstorm struck, I ran wildly to the beach to catch a glimpse of the Old Gray Man. Of course I didn't see him and had to wait anxiously through the storm to see if our cottage would be swept out to sea.

During each of those two summers we made excursions to Myrtle Beach. In those years the beaches were much more subdued than the crowded, frolicking resorts of today. There was a pavilion where the young people gathered for arcade type amusements. Further up the strip was an amusement park with carnival rides. I remember that Porter Halyburton, who lived on Lorimer Road in Davidson, looked after me one summer night at the park. We got into the same car and rode through the House of Horror. I was terrified, but Porter, several years my senior, kept reassuring me that it was all in fun. I didn't think anything could scare him. His courage would serve him well in Vietnam. More than a decade later, Porter, a naval flier, was a POW in North Vietnam—a harrowing ordeal he survived both physically and emotionally.

After the summer of 1954 we never returned to the island. Over the years I was in and out of Myrtle Beach and Charleston but never got back to Pawley's. In June 1998, my son enrolled in the North Carolina Governor's School in Laurinburg. He had a three-day weekend intercession in July, and my wife, Margaret, her mother, Jim, and I decided to spend the time at Litchfield Beach just north of Pawley's.

That weekend I resolved to go back to the island, knowing that everything would have changed over the years. Since Pawley's is a barrier island, wind and waves tend to rearrange the geography. We first stopped at the hammock shop, which is actually a collection of rustic buildings. A woman who had worked there for over fifty years was giving a demonstration on the art of assembling a hammock. She had probably been there making hammocks during those visits in my summers long past. I told her about my vacations on the island as a child. She was delighted to meet someone whose memories went back to a quieter time along the Grand Strand. She kindly gave my son a hammock rope sample as a souvenir.

We then drove over the causeway to the northern end of the island, which was much as I had remembered it. Margaret remarked, "There you go again, down memory lane." That's exactly what I was doing. Once on the island I turned left to explore the northern end. I knew that the old house had probably been destroyed by a storm, but after forty-four years there it rose, out of the mists, like Scarlett's Tara, unscathed by weather or time. For a moment I was transported to another time—before the tacky motels and condos that line the Strand today, before the enormous popularity of beach music and the Shag, and before the millions who flock to these shores in the summers and strain the balance of the marine ecology.

We took other memorable trips in the 1950's, always in a three-speed, white 1951 Ford Custom Victoria hardtop coup. In 1955 we drove to Washington, D.C. (The Smithsonian Institution and Mount Vernon were the highlights.), Colonial Williamsburg, Jamestown, and Yorktown. In 1958 we went to Williamstown, Massachusetts, where Dad ran the summer program in biology at Williams College, and where John and I did our first fossil hunting and began to collect baseball cards in earnest, starting what would become a more than 4000 card collection by 1960. Also in that memorable summer of 1958 we visited New York City, where we stayed with my mother's first cousin, Eleanor Straffin, and her family in Scarsdale. Eleanor drove us into the city where we ascended the Empire State Building, rode the Staten Island Ferry, and dined at an Automat. We spent a glorious mid-August afternoon at Yankee Stadium. To our immense delight we got to watch Mickey Mantle play, but the Yankees lost to the Baltimore

Orioles. In December 1959 Dad took us to Miami, Florida, where he spoke at a biology symposium. We spent Christmas with Cousin Eleanor's parents, Edwin and Lizzie Whitehead, and beheld the Fountainbleau, the Eden Roc, and other hotel marvels on Miami Beach.

A few wrinkled photographs survive from those trips, notably one of John and me on the front lawn at Mount Vernon. John's left arm is in a cast supported by an arm sling. He had fractured it when he tripped over our dog Gizmo and crash-landed on a sidewalk.

Back at the college Dad's reputation as a teacher grew. His teaching methods became legendary at Davidson. He helped develop plans for the new Dana Science Building on campus, personally designing the biology labs, leaving a legacy of numerous and intricately designed movable blackboards for his main lecture hall. He highlighted his lectures with many colored-chalk drawings, moving from one blackboard to another. It was mandatory that students bring colored pencils to his classes. Dad was the only man I ever knew who could draw with both hands at once.

My father was very religious, and he clearly saw God's handiwork in all of nature. Someone once asked him if he believed in parthenogenesis, the Virgin Birth. Dad replied whimsically, "Look around you. See the moon, the stars, the galaxies, and the broad expanse of the universe. Now couldn't the elegant hand that designed all of that make just one baby in all of history without a daddy?" He was a distinguished evolutionary biologist who would not discount the most scientifically improbable event imaginable. He often spoke of the *Bible* as a product of a particular time and place, and thought that it conveyed both symbolic and literal truths.

Davidson College had a superb religion department. Many of its students went into the ministry. Despite the theological talent on campus, the Men's *Bible* Class at the Davidson College Presbyterian Church chose Dad to be its teacher. He was that good. I think that speaks more of him than anything.

Dad had a *joie de vivre* and great sense of humor. He was often seen on campus whistling or singing old Gospel favorites, and he always had a hoard of jokes to tell. I remember as a child how my brother and I had completely demolished a paint job on the back porch of our house on Main Street. The painters had put down this awful gray paint, and we couldn't resist the opportunity to slide in the slime. Mom caught us and was furious. She made us pick out our own switches and let us have it. Our tears had hardly dried when Dad came home from work. There we were in our shorts and tee shirts all dripping with gray paint. Dad gave us the evil eye and sternly said, "If I had only moved this way or that or perhaps sneezed at the opportune moment, this may have never happened." It took me eleven years to figure out that he was referring to the moment of insemination.

Someone once asked Dad, "How do you tell those boys apart?" Dad stood us side-by-side and moved his arm back and forth until it rested on one of us. He replied, "This one, he's the pretty one."

On another occasion John and I brought home particularly bad report cards. We were incorrigibles, and C's in conduct were standard marks for us. This time we had flunked conduct. Dad took us behind the proverbial wood shed and explained, "The elevator to success is not running. You boys will have to climb the stairs."

We had lots of pets in our early years, always with Dad's blessing. Louise Martin picked deeply into her dog Jezebel's litter and came out with a mongrel that we named Gizmo. The dog became our constant companion. To our chagrin, Gizmo had a penchant for biting, which eventually led to his demise. As complaints about our dog mounted, Mom took matters into her own capable hands. One day when Gizmo failed to appear, she told us that she had given our dog to a farmer in Iredell County—which may have been her euphemism for having had Gizmo put to sleep.

Our next dog was Trigonometry or "Trigger" for short. Like many of our dogs, Trigger bought the farm in the middle of Concord Road, the victim of a four-wheeler. In time we had enough canine bodies buried in the backyard to qualify it as a pet cemetery. Other memorable dogs were the short-lived Cha Cha the Chihuahua and Gretchen the Dachshund. We also had cats.

The first cat we had gave birth under the big freezer in the kitchen of the Blake House. Dad named two of the kittens Electricity and Refrigerator. In 1951 we took in a pure white cat we named Tinker Bell. An unseen cat we called Captain Hook kept her perpetually pregnant through the six years she lived with us. We concluded that it was the same father since one litter after another looked about the same.

In the summer of 1957 Tink died defending her litter from Dr. Nelson Mebane's bulldog. We gave one of the survivors to the Shaw Smith family next door. That cat, Ramasses, inexplicably thrived on Rice Crispies. We kept the other survivor and named him Frisky. When I think of that cat, all that comes to mind is a ball of fleas. He ran off the following summer.

In 1965 a kitten showed up at our back door, and we decided to keep it. We named her Just Cat, but Mom called her Justine. Dad called Justine "Madame Ovary," to honor the multiple litters she presented us. Mom shortened it to "Madam," and she was Madam thereafter. We finally had her fixed. Justine had showed up for dinner one night and stayed for sixteen years. One night in 1981, Mom called me to say that Madam hadn't come for supper for several days. We never saw her again. Mom thought she might have gotten into poison somewhere. Of course, the cat may have just up and died.

Fate—or, I now think, good fortune—placed each of the Puckett siblings in Olin Puckett's college level general biology course. My sister was a student at Mary Baldwin College and spent part of a summer at home to take his class. I remember the day shortly after Ginger had completed the course. That afternoon she charged through the front door crying, "He gave me a B! My own father gave me a B!" Mom asked him, "Olin, what's this all about?" Dad replied, "She earned a B, and that's what she got!" His sons fared a little better, but we had to bust our butts to do it.

In 1966 Dad developed congestive heart failure. He had always been a heavy smoker. After he recovered, he went straight back to teaching and did well until the summer of 1969, when he had a stroke that took half of the vision in both eyes. I was a senior at Davidson College and was in Dad's last premedical class.

Each autumn Dad wrote letters of recommendation for his premedical majors. They said that his letters could make you or break you. A good word generally resulted in acceptance. Dad knew that the medical schools differed over what they considered an ideal candidate. Therefore, he wrote a separate letter of recommendation specific to whichever institution a premedical student was applying. He was an excellent two-finger typist who did all the paperwork himself.

That autumn of 1969, for the first time, Dad had to have some help. I can still see Mom and Dad agonizing through all of that. I asked him not to write any letters for me. I wanted to stand on my own merits alone. I felt that it would be too obvious and would give me an unfair advantage over the others. Dad insisted on writing all five of them since I had done very well in my studies and finished fourth in my college class. After much discussion, I relented. I later learned that some students in my class had applied to as many as ten or more schools. That was a lot of letters.

This was all very difficult for him. He became depressed, and I believe it affected his teaching. Someone in the administration (whose name I will withhold) told him that he was malingering. This upset him terribly. I marched over to President Samuel Spencer's office and protested the injustice. Dad and Sam Spencer were longstanding friends, and Dr. Spencer straightened out the situation, but the wound still lingers.

Shortly after that, Dad developed an expressive aphasia as the result of another stroke. He could comprehend spoken language but couldn't find the words to express himself. Despite considerable improvement with speech therapy, he had to withdraw from teaching. He never lost his interest and love for people and made his rounds of the college and town, speaking as best he could with practically everyone he met.

It was apparent that Dad had no immediate backup in the premedical program. Dr. James Fredericksen took over and did a fine job, but the program was not the same without Dad. In the summer of 1970, just before I left for my first year in medical school, Mom, Aunt Louise, and I took Dad up to Brevard in the mountains of western North Carolina. That was the last time I really knew him. Shortly after that he had another stroke, which took the remainder of his vision and his mind.

Dad spent the last months of his life in Huntersville Hospital under the care of some of the finest medical personnel I have ever met. They were truly loving and compassionate. Dad was totally blind and could do nothing for himself. It was heartbreaking to see him lose his personality and dignity.

Dad finally found his peace on June 3, 1972, while I was off at medical school at the University of North Carolina at Chapel Hill. Mrs. Adele Logan notified Dr. James A. Bryan, a Davidson alumnus and a popular professor at the medical school, who called and broke the news to me. I cried for a short time. It wasn't so much out of sorrow as it was out of relief and joy. I had mourned Dad's passing long before he actually died. Now he was alive in Christ.

Dr. Sam Spencer came by the house after the funeral and announced that Dr. David Deck and Dr. Charles Cook, two of Davidson's medical alumni, wanted to raise money to endow a chair at the college in Dad's name. Mom and Ginger convinced them that Dad would have preferred a scholarship fund. They agreed, and that fund today offers merit scholarships to Davidson students with an interest in science. Dad would be pleased.

Dad was formed from the clay of northern Mecklenburg County, and he would spend most of his life there. He loved the land and will forever be a part of it. More than the land, he loved Davidson. He devoted his life to Davidson College, and in the end, I believe, he literally gave his life for it.

A few years ago I attended a medical meeting in Boston. One evening I had dinner with several doctors. Upon learning that I was a North Carolinian, one of them commented that he knew a bunch of doctors who had attended a small liberal arts college in North Carolina. They frequently talked about a beloved professor of biology and his artistic abilities—especially his ability to draw with both hands at the same time. He asked me if I had ever known such a man.

An
American
Cemetery

Most small Southern college towns have somewhere tucked away among oaks or magnolias an old college burial ground. Davidson's most historic cemetery is a small plot on North Main Street situated among white oaks, surrounded by a black iron picket fence. The earliest graves date close to the time of the founding of the college in the 1830's. A lot of history is buried in this cemetery. Robert Hall Morrison, the first president of the college, lies here. Dr. Morrison had four daughters, three of whom married Confederate generals. One of those generals, Daniel Harvey (D.H.) Hill, later a professor at the college, is here. Dr. Morrison's daughter Mary Anna married Thomas "Stonewall" Jackson, and she was with him when he died near Fredericksburg in 1863. Mom said that Davidson descendants of the Morrisons possessed the Civil War correspondence between the Jacksons. These were sacred family treasures, which they never relinquished for historical scrutiny. Sadly, they were lost in a fire. Old Dr. Mark Sentelle, a firebrand of a theologian, and his sister, Agnes Sentelle Brown, who loomed large in my early life, are both buried here. It was here that I stumbled onto the strangest of gravestones.

I recall that it was a warm, gloriously golden, autumn Saturday afternoon in 1959. I had ventured into the burying ground to do some heavy thinking. At that time Sidney Small, a vivacious fifth grader who lived on North Main, was the object of my affection. She hardly knew I existed. The approaching sunset found me in the Rodin thinker mode on top of D.H. Hill's gravestone. Here were names that my maternal grandmother had emblazoned in my Confederate soul—Antietam, Gettysburg, and Malvern Hill, among others. After a while I concluded that old D.H. didn't have much to offer in the consolation line, so I decided to leave. On the way out an obelisk-shaped stone that I hadn't noticed before caught my eye—it was as if the sun had selectively illuminated it just for me. It marked the grave of a boy named Fred Hobbs, who drowned in 1900.

This aroused my curiosity, and I approached my father that night to find out what it was all about. He offered the following explanation. Around the turn of the century a student from Persia named Daniel Yonan enrolled at the college under the auspices of Presbyterian missionaries. One warm Sunday afternoon a group of Davidson College students from Hobbs' Sunday school class rounded up some horse-drawn wagons and headed out to the swimming hole at Beatties' Ford on the Catawba River. They invited the young Persian to go along with them. The river at the ford crossed the fall line, and the currents swirling around the rocks could be treacherous for the unwary swimmer. At this time the river was rain-swollen. Fred Hobbs, unfamiliar with the swiftness of the current, was swept downstream. He panicked and began to drown. The Persian student jumped into the torrent to save him, but tragically both boys drowned. The Persian never had a chance. Having grown up in the desert, he was a poor swimmer. Dad told me that students carried the bodies back to Davidson, where they were buried together in the college cemetery. The faculty authorized the headstones and felt it appropriate to place the biblical words, "Greater love hath no man…" on the headstone of Daniel Yonan's grave.

I have returned to the cemetery on three occasions in the past thirty years. There are two individuals accounted for on the obelisk head stone and neither of them is Persian. On neither occasion could I find the Persian's grave. Dr. Malcolm Lester recently gave me the explanation for what I perceived to be a discrepancy in Dad's story. He told me that the college president, Henry Lewis Smith, was with the party at the river. He went into the water after the two boys, but his efforts were futile. The party carried the bodies back to Davidson. In those years students who died while attending the college, if the family desired, were interred in the student section of the cemetery. Fred Hobbs was a student from the town of Davidson, and his family buried him in a grave that stands at the entrance to the cemetery. The Persian rests in the student section. My wanderings in the cemetery had never carried me back that far. Dad's "buried together" meant that they were buried in the same cemetery at the same time, but not side-by-side.

I still find it odd to think that with all the problems this country has had with Iran in recent years, something marvelously beautiful and peaceful from that tortured landscape rests forever in a cemetery in a small Southern town. Any animosity I have ever felt toward that country melts away when I think of that sacrifice. It taught me a great lesson about human love and compassion.

I revisited the old cemetery on that April morning in 1995 and made the rounds of the old familiar headstones. On the way out of the cemetery I paused before the grave of Dr. Mark Sentelle. He was the dean of students and taught biblical studies at Davidson College in the early part of the twentieth century. He didn't just come from the old school of biblical teaching; he *was* the old school. He is best remembered for his biblical trivial pursuits.

Grif Bowen (Davidson Class of 1970) passed on to me a story about his father Sumter (Davidson 1927). It demonstrates just how chilling a class under Dr. Sentelle could be. That afternoon in 1923 the professor was in a particularly dour mood. He ended his class with an oral pop quiz. He queried, "Mr. Bowen, Mr. Sumter Bowen from Belhaven, North Carolina; pray tell, Mr. Bowen, how many square cubits were in the left side of the Ark of the Covenant?" Bowen, from Belhaven scratched his head. "Four, Sir, I think." Sentelle replied, "Mr Bowen, if you take that number, divide by two, and add one fourth, you will have the correct answer." Then the hapless Mr. Bowen noted that Dr. Sentelle wrote a zero after his name in the professor's black grade book.

Dr. Sentelle asked one student to name the father of Methuselah. The student, obviously ill prepared, replied, "That I cannot do, Sir. That is known but to God." The old man sharply replied, "Good! God gets a hundred. You get a zero."

The most dreaded part of a Sentellean course was the final exam. This usually involved one question that required an expansive knowledge for a passing grade. One student had "spotted" (a college term for reviewing exams retained from prior years) the old professor and found a pattern. Every five years the question "Discuss the Kings of Israel and Judah" came up regular as clockwork. This was the pentagonal year. This student was determined to outfox the old professor and make an A. He spent the entire semester studying and memorizing the details of every king of the northern and southern kingdoms. He was often heard bragging on campus about how he was going to dazzle Sentelle with his knowledge of the *Old Testament* kings.

Exam time finally rolled around. The student, brimming with confidence, picked up Sentelle's exam. The question read, "Discuss the Major and Minor Prophets of Israel and Judah." One classmate in later years related that the failed essay began with "Far be it for me, mortal that I am, to discuss, distinguish, or in any other way express knowledge of the Major and Minor Prophets of Israel and Judah. BUT AS FOR THE KINGS . . ." There followed a disquisition of some thirty written pages. When the paper was returned, above the grade the student saw a little mark, barely discernable. The good professor had put a plus on his F!

I never knew Dr. Sentelle. I did have the great fortune to know his sister, Agnes Sentelle Brown, who was in her mid-seventies when I was born. We grew up in the old Blake House on Main Street, which our father rented from the college. "Miss Agnes" lived next door. She basically adopted my twin brother and me, and over the years we spent a lot of time at her house. I remember every room even to this day. Miss Agnes always had treats, and I specifically remember drinking Coca Cola from her early twentieth century Coke glasses.

In 1952 Miss Agnes acquired a television set, one of the first in Davidson. For the next several years children from the neighborhood would gather daily in her living room at 5:30 p.m. to watch *The Howdy*

Doody Show. For us Clarabelle the Clown was the quintessence of evil—his instrument of terror was a seltzer bottle. Every day things remained fairly calm until Clarabelle started hosing down Buffalo Bob Smith and the Peanut Gallery. Then all hell broke loose, and we, the Peanut Gallery at large, would join the screaming kids in the studio, jumping up and down, driving Miss Agnes to momentary distraction.

We were afraid we would lose our free run of her house when the James Southall Wilsons arrived from Charlottesville, Virginia, and took over Miss Agnes' upstairs apartment. Dr. Wilson, an emeritus professor at the University of Virginia, was the world's foremost authority on Edgar Allan Poe and was at Davidson on a special appointment. He and his wife were both in their seventies. They accepted us immediately, and we became regulars both up and downstairs.

Mrs. Wilson was President John Tyler's granddaughter. Her full name was Julia Tyler Gardiner Wilson, and she hailed from Gardiner's Island, off Long Island. She kept us entranced with stories from her childhood and tales of Captain Kidd, who reputedly hid his treasure on Gardiner's. Before Dr. Wilson returned to Virginia, he gave us his dictionary and an early edition Poe, both of which we still have in the family as treasured reminders of those events almost fifty years ago. I was pleased to learn that the English building at the University of Virginia is named in Dr. Wilson's honor.

As the years passed, we grew out of Miss Agnes' house. She provided us with shelter when the movie theater burned down in 1955—an event described in Chapter 6. I would continue to see her frequently throughout the next twenty years. In her mid-nineties she moved to a retirement home in Charlotte. When I last saw her, she was almost one hundred years old, still bright and spry. She died shortly thereafter and lies buried next to Dr. Sentelle in the college cemetery. I count Miss Agnes as one of the great blessings of my life.

One afternoon in a hospital in Asheville, I happened to run into Bob Smith of *Howdy Doody* fame. He had retired to nearby Hendersonville and was visiting at the hospital. We chatted a while. I told Buffalo Bob about those weekday afternoons in Miss Agnes' living room watching from the Peanut Gallery at large, and he seemed pleased and flattered. His song "Howdy Doody Time" was the anthem of an entire generation. Bob mailed me an autographed picture of himself with Howdy on which he wrote, "To Doctor Jim. From your friends Howdy Doody and Buffalo Bob." I framed it and put it in my den.

The Ghost
of
Chambers

The Cornelius sheriff was outraged, but the situation was out of his jurisdiction. The Davidson constabulary and white citizenry simply viewed the problem as a necessary evil and would not discuss it.

The problem dealt with the old North Carolina Medical College, which was on Concord Road in Davidson across the street from the old Davidson College Presbyterian Church. The Medical College was a part of the Davidson scene in the late nineteenth and early twentieth centuries. The Victorian-style building had a single tower that resembled a glue-pot top. In the 1950's it was no longer a science building but served as a duplex residence for Davidson faculty. A grove of oaks surrounded it, and my friend Herb Russell called the complex "a bowling alley for the squirrels and birds."

The building achieved national fame. Shortly after Roentgen discovered x-ray technology in Wurtzberg, Germany, investigators from the Medical College made the first radiographs in the Western Hemisphere. Some say these landmark X rays were actually made by the students who broke into Dr. Henry Lewis Smith's lab in Old Chambers. I've seen a picture of what they saw—just some medical instruments in a bag—and prefer the story relating it to the Medical College building.

Medical students took their basic science courses here for two years before their clinical training at a hospital in Charlotte. The basic curriculum at the Medical College included human anatomy. Cadavers were precious commodities and, in the years before more refined mortuary science, seldom lasted more than a few months. When fresh bodies became available, those students fortunate enough to have access to them had to work very quickly. Often a student would fall behind and find it unbearable to catch up by dissecting a rotting corpse. There had to be a source of fresher bodies. Some of the students found a temporary solution.

The solution lay beneath the sod of the old African-American burial ground at the north end of town, where the black community of Davidson buried its dead. Bodies were often not embalmed—simply buried in a pine box. The remoteness of the cemetery, located in woods far from the highway, made it easy for the medical students, under cover of darkness, to steal bodies shortly after they were laid to rest. They hid the bodies and did their surreptitious dissections in a barn behind what would become A.H. Whittle's house on College Drive and later serve as a backstop for our sandlot baseball games in the late 1950's and early 1960's. When the students had completed the required dissections, they reburied the bodies in the cemetery. I have no idea how frequent this shameful practice was, but town folklore avers that it did indeed take place.

My father told me an interesting and perversely humorous story of somewhat just desserts about some of the grave robbers. Sometime around 1900 a young man named John Alcorn enrolled in the medical school. He was forever behind in his subjects, and anatomy was no exception. Late one January day he realized that he had cut too many classes to be prepared for his semester exam. He needed to familiarize himself with the muscles of the arm and hand.

The cadavers had already been cremated, so this left Alcorn with no alternative other than to get his own cadaver and do the necessary work. Late that wet and cold winter afternoon Alcorn enlisted Monroe Potts in Cornelius to loan him his wagon and services for a nefarious job. Alcorn had heard that there had been a burial at the black cemetery that afternoon.

Shortly after dark Potts drove Alcorn up the muddy stubble that was Main Street in those years, then onto a rutted trail that led to the cemetery. They took out their shovels and left the wagon unattended to dig up the body. What they didn't know was that two medical students had overheard Alcorn discussing his plot with another student. When the Potts wagon arrived, they were hiding in a grove of trees out of sight. As Potts and Alcorn labored on into the night, burdened with heavy winter coats, one of the two pranksters crawled in under the tarp in the back of the wagon. The rain had turned to sleet, and the night was pitch-black. The two grave robbers hastily deposited the corpse under the tarp, not noticing that two bodies were now there.

The student under the tarp didn't realize how badly decomposed the body was. The funeral had actually been several days earlier. He quietly regurgitated out the back of the wagon. As the wagon was about to turn onto Main Street, Potts remarked to Alcorn, "Sure was mighty hot work back there." On this cue the livid cadaver, clad in white tarp, rose from the rear and proclaimed, "Not nearly as hot as where I've been for the past seventy-two hours!" Four eyes shot from four sockets as Alcorn and Potts blasted out of the wagon. The other student arrived, and the two rode off to the old barn with their newly acquired wagon and cadaver.

The Victorian building long outlived its usefulness as a school of medical science, but as a duplex, it retained its charm and was a very interesting place. With secret rooms and back stairways, it was a great place for kids to play hide-and-seek.

Arthur Link, a history professor at Princeton University and the world's leading authority on Woodrow Wilson, had married Margaret, the daughter of Dr. Douglas, who taught at the college. In his later years Dr. Douglas lived in a duplex there. The Links came down to visit in the summers and brought their son Stan with them.

I have two vivid memories of those visits. One deals with an employee who slaughtered chickens out in the backyard. I remember the first time I witnessed that activity. I was four years old, and the sight of a chicken running around with its head off was unsettling.

What was even worse was being invited to dinner and seeing the poor fowl dressed and ready to eat.

Another memory involves Stan and his water sprinkler. On a hot day in mid-July 1952, John and I were dressed to attend Pookie Morton's birthday party out on Greenway Road. We were playing in a nearby grove of oak and pine trees—today called the Village Green and in our time the Grove. When we saw Stan cooling off in his sprinkler behind the old med school complex, we stripped down to nothing and hopped right in. That's when we heard our mother calling for us. We panicked. We didn't know how to dress ourselves, so we dumped our clothes in our little red wagon and headed buck-naked through the Grove, in full view of the Main Street business district. Our sister, Ginger, and Mimy Martin were out roller-skating, and they saw us. No sibling rivalry here: Ginger ran screaming for Mom, who swatted us good for that one.

A brief epitaph: Dr. Douglas died shortly thereafter. In the late 1960's the college finally demolished the old building. The barn behind the Whittle house was taken down at roughly the same time.

***

Shortly before the outbreak of the Civil War, Salisbury textile magnate Maxwell Chambers donated $250,000 to Davidson College. This made Davidson the most richly endowed institution of private learning in the South. With it the college built the Maxwell Chambers Building, the finest college administration building in the South. The college invested the remainder of the funds in Confederate bonds. The Civil War would eventually all but bankrupt the college, but the Chambers legacy lived on in the building and land.

My father had all sorts of stories surrounding the old Chambers Building. Many of these went back to the days when the medical school was in operation. I don't know if the architectural plans for the original building have survived. I have in my possession a colorized photo (Dr. Sentelle's copy given to Mom by Agnes Brown), one of three in existence, of the building from the early part of the twentieth century. The large columns and cupola are apparent. I learned from my father that there was a ramp that led up to the cupola, and students often kept their mules up there.

Dad told me that one student bribed a janitor into keeping his mule tied up in the cupola. This student competed with another student for the affections of a young woman in Charlotte. He and his competitor loathed each other. Having finally won the young lady's hand in engagement, he left his mule in the care of the janitor and headed off to Charlotte to enjoy a prenuptial bliss over the spring vacation. The other suitor promptly headed over to Chambers to strike another deal with the janitor. For an appropriate sum he purchased the mule, led the beast over to his rival's dormitory room, which was vacated at the time, tied the mule to the bed, and then shot it. When the betrothed student arrived fresh from his courtship pleasures two weeks later, he found a reeking mess that took two weeks to fumigate.

The campus police force had its offices in Chambers Building. The campus cops had a lot to keep them busy. In the early part of the last century it became fashionable for upper classmen to haze freshmen. And things could get downright dirty. Mr. A. H. Whittle told me that one favorite trick was to take an unfortunate freshman over to the gym, blindfold him, and tie his hands with a rope thrown over a rafter at the top of the basketball court, about forty feet up. The pranksters actually pulled him only several feet off the floor. By carefully manipulating the rope, they would simulate an upward motion while the poor freshman dangled there helplessly. His tormentors spoke in low tones from a distance, giving the unfortunate victim the impression that he was up in the rafters. The gleeful upper classmen then dropped the rope, and the panic-stricken freshman fell three or four feet with a deadening thud. The victim tended to land very hard.

Upper classmen were particularly adept at terrorizing freshmen, and some brutal beatings took place in the dorms. Dad told me about one student from Cornelius who was a freshman at Davidson in the early 1920's. His father gave him a gun with the explicit instruction, "Shoot the bums, but don't you shoot to kill." Shortly thereafter a group of seniors cornered the apparently hapless freshman on the north end of Chambers. They said they were going to beat him to a pulp. The intended victim was carrying his handgun and began shooting for the legs. That was the end of hazing on campus.

Over time Chambers Building housed the administrative offices and most of the classrooms on campus. It also housed the town's volunteer fire department, a fact that would figure largely in the events of November 28, 1921.

Dick Richards, a member of the class of 1923, was my neighbor in Concord, where I practiced medicine for almost seven years. He was one of the few people still living who remembered the events of that night. Apparently the fire broke out in the central part of the building and rapidly engulfed the structure. Students living in the dorm sections evacuated without injury. The entire student body and town turned out for the conflagration, which was by all descriptions quite a show. There wasn't much that could be done since the edifice burned quite rapidly, and the fire department never got its equipment into action before its own cremation. About all that was left were four massive columns.

Plans were made to replace the building. Wrecking and construction crews came in to clear the devastation. When workers pulled down the columns, they found human skeletal remains. Various explanations arose about whose and how the bones came to be "buried" in such a place; the facts have never been discerned. A forensic study turned up nothing. Some believe that there were openings at the tops of the columns and that maybe medical students had taken a short cut in the disposition of cadaver parts. Others claimed there were no such column openings. They believed that there was foul play as the building was rising in 1857. Regardless, the remains gave rise to the legend of the Ghost of Chambers.

In 1929 the new Chambers Building opened. Today this is a splendid Georgian structure in the Jeffersonian style, and, I believe, one of the most beautiful college buildings anywhere. It fronts onto the vast openness of the front campus at the apex of the road that once transected the campus in the form of a "D."

A few years after its dedication, children began reporting to their parents that there were strange markings out in front of the building. On occasion students noticed the outlines of the columns that had once supported the front of the old building. When I was a child, we called the strange markings the Ghost of Chambers. Some locals believed that this was the revenge of the cadaver for having been deprived of his rightful grave.

I have fond memories of the building. As a child, I found it to be a great playground. When I attended the college, most of my non-science classes were held there. The main hall is over one hundred yards long, and in the winter months we used it to run wind sprints. Coach Heath Whittle laid out some specially built starting blocks, and we would race up and down the north-south hall. We had to alert everyone working on the hall about our training lest someone inadvertently walk out into a collision. It miraculously never happened. On rainy days we would go upstairs to Love Auditorium and run laps around the room—there were approximately eleven laps to the mile. It kept us in shape during inclement weather.

Chambers Building is partially modeled after the Rotunda building that Jefferson designed at the University of Virginia. Up in the dome there is a lecture hall. During my freshman year professors taught the humanities courses there. During one lecture a student had a grand mal seizure. I heard that Dr George Labban approached Dr. George Abernathy with, "George, don't you think we need to call the infirmary?" Dr. Abernathy supposedly replied, "I don't think so. He already has *eleven* cuts [absences]!" He particularly emphasized eleven because that number of unexcused cuts warranted an automatic dismissal from the class and a failing grade.

I returned to Davidson in April 1995 for my twenty-fifth reunion. As we dined on some lousy cold cuts out on the front campus, I mentioned to one of my classmates the story of the Ghost of Chambers. He said he had heard about it but thought it was rubbish. I asked him if he would follow me upstairs into the building. From up on the third floor we had a clear view of the front campus. At first I could make out nothing of the old outlines. He laughed and said that I didn't know what I was talking about—that I was resurrecting some childhood fantasy. Suddenly, the sun came through the clouds, and, clear as crystal, there appeared the impressions of the old columns and the outlines of the building that had vanished over seventy years before. It was my raising of the *Titanic*. He gasped and exclaimed, "Well, I'll be damned!"

Our Last
Picture Show

Our old house on Main Street stood next door to a building that after its tenures as a general store, garage, and laundry, became the Davidson Theatre. We called it the Picture Show, and it was the only movie house the town ever had.

The Davidson Theater was a rectangular, two-story, cream-colored stucco building. It fronted the sidewalk, and I remember that it had a tree out front and a porch, the sides of which were always festooned with colorful movie posters that were encased in glass frames. A ticket booth stood in the center of the porch, behind which was a narrow lobby and a small concession stand, which carried candy and greasy popcorn. The place always smelled of popcorn. The interior of the theater, which was perpetually dark, had an orchestra section, a balcony, and a Cinemascope screen (the latter installed in 1954).

The theater extended in a narrow but deep lot approximately 120 feet from the street; it could seat about three hundred patrons. The building was coal-heated in the winter, and it was a firetrap—oil from the garage era had seeped into the cement floor. The back of the place was a junkyard of rusted automobile parts, discarded film cans, and leader film. A tiny path led through the thicket that separated our backyard from this dump heap, and John and I used to pick our way through the trash. We would find all sorts of discarded boxes and crates and turn them into forts. One of our most memorable finds was a large wire spool, which we used as a make-believe dinner table. I remember once wandering into the back of the theater and the heater room. Coal was being fed into the furnace, and the size of the fire made an impression. There were oil stains on the floor and lots of discarded celluloid lying around.

One of my favorite childhood pastimes was going to the front entrance to view the trailer clips that bordered the main posters advertising the movies. These actually turned out to be almost as interesting as the movies themselves. And there were lots of movies. Some of them were for a mature audience, but none of the R-rated stuff so prevalent today. (Hollywood had censors back then.) John and I started going to the Saturday afternoon matinees as far back as I can remember. We received an allowance of twenty-five cents a week, which was generous for the times. Ten cents got us into the movie and another dime bought a box of popcorn. Cokes were a nickel. Usually the Saturday fare included *Tarzan*, *Jungle Jim*, and other adventure epics. The previews, often of movies that would never make it to a small town like Davidson, were particularly enjoyable. Every night throughout the week the theater featured flicks right out of *American Movie Classics*, except they weren't classics yet. It was a potpourri of Americana, 1930's through 1950's. There were all the Errol Flynn swashbucklers, every Western imaginable, and celluloid romances like *Ivanhoe*, *Wuthering Heights*, and *Elephant Walk*, the latter particularly memorable for its elephants tearing up the immense living room and staircase as a Ceylon tea plantation burned down around a screaming Elizabeth Taylor. We even saw film noir.

At the tender age of six I had a childhood crush on Linda Darnell, who starred in the feature film *Blackbeard*, and I thought she was the prettiest girl I had ever seen in a movie. *Gone With The Wind* made it to Davidson in the 1940's but did not return until 1953. All I remember of the latter showing is the burning of Atlanta and Scarlett's return to Tara—and that it was a fun way to spend a Friday evening with my family.

Early on I had a conceptual problem with the movies: I thought they were filmed from real life. For example, I remember seeing *Titanic* with Barbara Stanwyck and Clifton Webb. I cried for three days over those poor people flaying about in the water and those soggy lifeboats. In one film the intersection of main roads in a town vaguely resembled Concord Road at its intersection with Main Street in Davidson. In my naiveté I argued with my brother for weeks that it was an old film about Davidson. Finally my father enlightened me. Good thing. The movie that week was *The Thing* with James Arness as a murderous alien.

Growing up, my friends and I applied a three-stick rating system to country-town movie theaters. A one-stick theater meant that it took a stick to beat down the seat before you could sit down. A two-sticker meant one stick to beat down the seat and another to beat off the rats. A three-sticker meant a third stick to beat off the make-out artists who distracted the rest of the audience from the movie. Our Picture Show was a one-sticker—I don't recall any rats (although I heard that the Star Theater in Cornelius had them), and at the time adult opprobrium was sufficient to squelch petting in public venues.

At all events, the Puckett children got a few good years of movie going out of the place before that awful year of 1955. Some movie-minded people remember it as the year James Dean died, but for us it was the year the Picture Show burned down.

The date was February 14, 1955. I was in the first grade at Davidson Elementary. The day was clear and cold. Our parents were scheduled for the Lions Club Ladies Night that evening. At the college Louis "Satchmo" Armstrong was to appear in concert. Alberta Harvell, our baby-sitter, arrived around 7 p.m. John and I had finished what little homework we had, and around 8:30 p.m. we were watching television upstairs when the fire siren went off. The volunteer fire department was right across the street. We didn't pay much attention to it initially until we heard the commotion next door and began to smell smoke. Next we heard the pump truck. Then the doorbell rang—it was one of the volunteer firemen who announced that the movie house was ablaze (it was blatantly obvious by that time) and that we might have to evacuate our house. That was really scary. (In Chapter 3 how Alberta comforted us that night is described.)

At about 9 p.m. our parents were walking home across the campus and saw the flames over the trees. When they arrived, the firemen began hosing down the roof of our house. We were told to evacuate, and we went next door to Miss Agnes' house. At 9:30 p.m. I was settling down for bed and tearfully looked one last time at the Picture Show. As I watched, the roof collapsed, sending flames and sparks several hundred feet into the air. Then I fell asleep.

The next morning all that remained of the old movie house was the walls. Several of us children walked to school past the smoldering ruins. My first grade class was abuzz all day about the fire. Keith White announced that he had been in the theater when the fire broke out. He said that the movie was a boring Western. As he told it, some cowboys were seated around a large campfire, and at first the campfire looked strange, then strangely real; next the flames burst through the screen. The theater personnel directed a rapid and orderly evacuation of the building.

That afternoon the Junior Fire Department was organized with Jimmy Woods as chief. The volunteer firemen let him hose down the smoldering seats. It was a cold and bright February afternoon. I eagerly waited my turn to handle the hoses but was told that I was too young. I doubted I would ever have that chance again. I still can see Jimmy Woods working that hose.

The local authorities never determined the precise cause of the fire. The prevailing theory was that a burning cinder from the coal-fed furnace had popped out and ignited celluloid and oil on the floor. Shortly after the fire the theater owners held a fire sale in a vacant building across the street. All the solid concessions salvaged from the fire were on sale. I remember that awful smoke smell in the room; the popcorn was charbroiled, and the candy was thoroughly smoked. They would never get away with that stunt today.

Thus went up in smoke a significant part of our social life. We waited for news that someone would rebuild the theater. No one ever did. Archer's Gulf Station opened on the site in 1957. Mr. Archer had a grand opening, which featured a pathetic little merry-go-round that John and I, third-graders at the time, rode for an entire weekend. We were now relegated to going to movies at the State Theater in nearby Mooresville, the Davidson-Mooresville drive-in, the college union, and in later years the theaters in Charlotte. It would be almost forty years before another movie house would open in northern Mecklenburg County—but not in Davidson.

Pillars
of a
Childhood

Wonderful men blessed my life. All were neighbors who were intimate friends of my parents. I distinctly remember four of them whose influence I continue to feel almost daily. I have beautiful memories associated with each and his family. Here I include these stories.

James Baker Woods, M.D.

James Baker Woods was our town doctor. The son of medical missionaries in China, Dr. Woods graduated from Davidson College in 1918; from there he went to the Medical College of Virginia and later completed his surgical training at Bellevue Hospital in New York City. He married the daughter of Presbyterian medical missionaries to China, and together they returned there as missionaries. The Woodses were in China until the late 1930's, when the Japanese expelled all the missionaries. He returned to Davidson to be the town and college physician.

Dr. Woods' office was in a white-frame house on School Street, just across the street from the Davidson Elementary School. It occupied the first floor of the house. The top floor was an apartment for married college students. The downstairs living room of the house was his waiting room. He had a couple of steel filing cabinets, which were stuffed with manila folders containing patient records. Mary McConnell was his secretary; and when she was out, Elizabeth, Dr. Woods' wife, filled in. Salinda Mayhew was his nurse. Together they handled approximately one hundred patients a day. When I was growing up, the doctor bills were no more than two dollars per visit.

I recall Dr. Woods sitting at his big desk asking me questions, then taking my blood pressure and examining me as I sat in a chair. For more extended exams he had a room set up in what was once the sunroom of the house. I don't remember ever feeling more at ease with a person. There was something about him that commanded relaxation. It was a charisma I've never known in another person.

I once asked Dr. Woods how he managed to practice medicine so long and so hard. He explained that he paced himself. His daily schedule began early in the morning at the hospital in Mooresville, seven miles up the road from Davidson, where he made his rounds and did any surgery that was scheduled. Afterwards he returned to his office in Davidson, where he saw patients for the remainder of the day. After his office hours he made some house calls on any patients who were unable to come to the office. He always took Wednesday afternoons off and went to Concord, where he was a member of the country club, and played a round of golf. He worked on Saturdays until noon and held office hours 9-10 a.m. on Sundays for any emergent problems. Dr. Woods faithfully attended the college church, where he sang in the choir. He took two weeks off in the summer and often went with his family to Montreat, North Carolina, where he could relax in the mountains.

Dr. Woods was a general practitioner in every sense of the term. He did it all—surgery, general medicine, pediatrics, and obstetrics and gynecology. There were few problems that he couldn't handle. Of course, medicine was different in those days. We know a lot more now. But it was a simpler and kinder medicine; at the heart of it was a genuine concern and love for humanity. We can see that now in retrospect, but I believe we knew it was something special then.

Fate dealt cruelly with Dr. Woods. He raised three fine sons and a daughter. His oldest son, Dan, was a student at Davidson College in the mid-1950's when he contracted a rare strain of viral encephalitis. He was a student in one of my father's biology classes, and Dad said that Dan most uncharacteristically blanked a test. This and a series of other neurological problems led to the diagnosis. He eventually died in 1956 at Temple Medical Center in Philadelphia. I don't remember it, but my sister has told me that Dad went to Philadelphia with Dr. Woods to bring Dan back to Davidson. The Woodses were people of enormous faith, and it saw the family through that tragedy.

His son John was closer to my age and was one of our best friends. That friendship brought us into contact with Jimmy, the Woods' second son. Jimmy graduated from Davidson College in the early 1960's and went into the Army in the early years of the Vietnam conflict. He quickly attained the rank of captain in the infantry and was sent to Vietnam. I remember that Dr. Woods, Elizabeth, and Jimmy's wife went together to Hawaii to visit him on an R & R.

One cold Sunday morning in early February 1966, I skipped church and took off for Charlotte, where I visited my girlfriend Mary Whitton, a student at Myers Park High School. In the early evening I returned home. I thought I saw Dr. Woods' car out in front of a neighbor's house. When I got home, my father asked me to sit down for some bad news. He told me that Jimmy Woods had been killed in Vietnam. Dad said that Dr. Woods had spent part of the afternoon looking after the Roberts' little girl up the street. She had meningitis, and he had arranged for her to be transferred to a hospital in Charlotte. The Woodses had just received the news about Jimmy that morning.

My father suffered a stroke in the middle of the night during the Christmas holiday of 1969. At three in the morning Dr. Woods was at our house. I suspect he provided the same service to anyone in the town who needed him. I have been associated with hundreds of doctors in my career, but none finer than Jim Woods. He was the most Christ-like person I ever met.

Dad died in June 1972. Dr. Woods was going on vacation, and a few days before leaving, he visited my father in the small hospital near Huntersville. He knew that Dad had only a few days to live, and he went ahead and signed the death certificate. Before leaving that day, he stood by Dad's bed and sang all of the verses of "Abide with Me."

If there were an ideal role model for a young doctor, it would be Dr. Woods. I find myself even to this day addressing complicated patient situations with, "What would Jim Woods have done?" He set a standard I have never attained. I thought he would live forever—at least as long as he continued to practice. I sensed that when he quit, well, that would be his time to move along. In the end that's how it worked out.

Salinda Mayhew, his nurse, finally had to retire in her late eighties. That's when Dr. Woods, roughly the same age, called it off. He just couldn't continue to practice without her. A short time later he was diagnosed with a brain tumor. He declared that he didn't want anything done. I heard that he said, "I've loved and served Jesus all of my life, and now I am going home to Him."

I visited him at home on one of those final afternoons. Another Davidson alumnus who is also a doctor was there. Dr. Woods was in a coma. We talked about his life and how much he had given to both town and gown in Davidson. Frankly, I don't think Dr. Woods was there. Even though he still showed signs of life, we both thought that he had moved on to his greater reward. I'm glad I spent that afternoon with him. When he died a day or two later, I felt a great sense of loss, but also felt immensely blessed for having known him. In my memory he stands forever, black bag in hand, in front of the Roberts' house on that cold February evening in 1966. To my mind, his life and work bore the signature of God.

Colin Shaw Smith, Sr.

Our immediate next-door neighbors on College Drive were the Colin Shaw Smiths. They were remarkable and talented people. Mr. Smith joined the college faculty in the mid-1950's as director of the college union. He eventually expanded his family to five children, all of whom were immensely talented in a diversity of ways. My parents struck up what would become a lifelong friendship with the senior Smiths. They planned to build houses side-by-side on College Drive.

The Smiths moved in shortly after we did, and for years our families would be inseparable.

In those years there were few times when there wasn't a Puckett at the Smiths or vice-versa. The Smiths had a housekeeper named Julia, who was given charge of looking after all of us. How she bore all that I will never know. Julia had to endure a lot. I remember once when Shaw, Jr., dragged a hose into the house and shouted imperiously, "Cookie, take that!" He proceeded to hose down Julia and the kitchen. That action lent new meaning to the term "grounded." Shaw's mother had him in his room for days. Julia mothered her charges with affection, and fattened them up, too. She was a superb cook—she had to be, cooking for nine to twelve people at any given time, depending on how many of the neighbors happened to drop in for lunch.

Our first outing with the Smiths was a campout in our backyard on Main Street shortly before we moved into our new house. Shaw, Curtis, John, and I were jammed into a pup tent designed for one adult. It was a dreadfully hot July night in 1955. It was our first experience outside the safe confines of our parents' observation, and we were scared to death. Our trusty dog, Gizmo, crawled in with us. Huddled up in that sweaty space, we all finally got to sleep. In the morning we felt tremendously proud of our accomplishment: we had made it through the night without having to run back to the house.

Pattie Newell, the preacher's daughter, had it in for Shaw Smith, Jr. I don't remember how we hatched the plot, but one morning at the Newell house we bowed to Pattie's desires to poison Shaw. We concocted a devilish brew of Halo Shampoo, lemonade, Mercurochrome, and who knows what else. We telephoned Shaw and invited him over to have some lemonade. Shaw was no dummy. He knew lemonade when he saw it, and that definitely wasn't lemonade. When he wouldn't drink it, we doused it all over him. He left the house howling. About twenty minutes later a furious Mrs. Smith showed up sporting a wrath the likes of which we had never seen. She proceeded to call the mothers of the guilty urchins. Our mother used a whistle in those days to round us up when she wanted us home pronto, and now she was blowing it at the top of her lungs. Suffice it to say, Mom put a Bunsen burner to our fledgling careers in pharmaceuticals.

All the Smiths were musically gifted. Mrs. Smith was an accomplished pianist, who played a Steinway. Our mother decided that her boys needed to learn piano, and she sent us to Mrs. Smith for instruction. Vladimir Horowitz I was not. The fundamental problem was that I had all the musicality of a stick. Another problem was that I had not a hoot of interest for practice. Most of what I remember from my piano years is how to get the lid off the piano and find middle C. When I told Mrs. Smith I was giving up piano, she said wearily that I had made the right decision. The irony is that my son, Jim, is a superb pianist. Mrs. Smith would be the first to question his paternity.

The greatest talent the Smiths possessed was their ability to entertain. Big Shaw, as we all called Mr. Smith, was a professional magician who brought his entire family into the act. (He had toured with the USO in World War II using the moniker "Colin the Magnificent.") These were the years before all of that technical magic on television. Colin Shaw Smith, Sr., came from the old school of magic, where illusion was a simple handicraft. I don't believe I ever saw a finer magic act than the Smith family performers. The Smiths had all those wonderful magic animals in their backyard—cages of white doves and rabbits. I had names for all of them; they were Mystic, Prestidigitation, and Harry Houdini, to name but a few.

The Smiths' act got to be such a novelty that they received invitations to perform at colleges all over the country. They bought this humongous RV and traveled from one campus to the next during the summer months. We called the RV the "*Queen Mary*." The Smiths garnered so much fame from their program that they actually went on a European tour.

During the show little Smiths and their animals would be in constant motion—Big Shaw had them appearing and disappearing all over the stage. He worked his magic with a sprinkling of what he called "Woofle Dust." It was immensely good fun. John and I prodded and pried to learn how they did it, to no avail; the Smiths were bound by a magicians' code of ethics that would not allow them to divulge their wonderful magic secrets.

Big Shaw directed the Davidson College Union and its entertainment programs. For such a small college he had some heady contacts. I remember when Louis Armstrong came to town. How can I forget? It was the night the Picture Show burned down. Mr. Smith and Vincent Price (of those outrageous horror flicks) were friends, and Price was an occasional visitor at college functions in those years. Mr. Smith was instrumental in bringing Eleanor Roosevelt to the campus artist series shortly before her death. I still regret not going to that program. Over the years he brought all kinds of entertainment to Davidson. He told me once how he had to push a terrified young singer named Dionne Warwick onto the stage. It was her first college concert. He got the Kingston Trio in for one of their first college hitches in 1959. I think his biggest coup was the Supremes, who came in the mid-sixties. We also had Ray Charles, the Four Seasons, the Righteous Brothers, the Association, Chicago, the Nitty Gritty Dirt Band, Jay and the Americans—and the list goes on and on. .

My favorite memory of Mr. Smith involved my son, Jim, when he was five years old. We were living in nearby Concord at the time and came to town to visit my aunt, Louise Puckett. We went next door to see the Smiths. I asked Mr. Smith if he wouldn't mind showing Jim a little magic. Almost immediately coins starting coming out of Jim like a jackpot slot machine payout. He was howling with glee.

Eight or nine years ago Mr. Smith died suddenly while my family and I were on a trip to Europe. John told me about our friend's passing when we returned. Sadly, we had missed the funeral. He was a much-loved friend and neighbor, who is deeply missed. The "Woofle Dust" that was the life and being of Colin Shaw Smith, Sr., continues to work its magic on all of us who were blessed to have known him.

Andrew Heath ("Pete") Whittle, Sr.

When we were four years old my twin brother and I enrolled in Daisy Whittle's nursery school. The home that housed her little school stood on Concord Road in Davidson. I would spend two years at "Miss Daisy's" school. Attendance was a rite of passage for the young children in our neighborhood, and some of my earliest childhood acquaintances were made there. Though nearly half a century has passed since those days, I have some vivid, pleasant memories of the school.

I specifically remember the mandatory nap late each morning. We would all curl up on blankets on the living room floor and fake somnolence. Once, Randy Jones decided to make certain that I was asleep and clobbered me over the head with his toy six-shooter. I was coldcocked for about five minutes. When I came to, all the kids were standing around looking at me with puzzled faces. There was a hot debate among the adults present concerning whether or not to call Dr. Woods. Mr. Whittle came in and decided that I was all right, and the school continued as if nothing had happened.

The highlight of each nursery school year was the annual picnic. This took place in Johnsie Shelton's horse pasture, which started behind the Whittle house. We would pack up some PB & J sandwiches and soda pop and head off into the wilds of the countryside. I remember once eating on top of a water drain that would remain in place until the George Abernathy family built their house on that site several years later. The picnic was always held in May when the weather was warm and fair. I still can see Miss Daisy and those beautiful children who would become so much a part of my childhood in Davidson.

Andrew Heath Whittle, Sr., Miss Daisy's husband, was a graduate of Davidson College in the late 1920's, who returned to the campus to head up the track and cross-country programs. Pete Whittle was a former track star in his own right, having once tied the world record in the sixty-yard indoor hurtles. Though he never had a scholarship program, he cultivated some excellent running teams over the years.

One of the best runners he ever coached was Sterling Martin. Sterling, a waif of a boy who came to Davidson in the early 1960's, was clearly the best distance runner the college had produced to that time. He was short in height and didn't weigh much over a hundred pounds, but he could run! In the years before Lefty Driesell's superb basketball teams of mid-late 1960's, Sterling was the first athlete at Davidson to make an all-Southern Conference team in all three years of his eligibility. He was a standout in cross-country and the two-mile run indoors.

Once in a cross-country meet at the University of West Virginia in late October, it snowed heavily. Sterling told me things got so bad that he decided in mid-race to lie down for a spell in the snow. He fell asleep. A frantic runner, fearing Sterling was dead, roused him. Sterling won the race!

When the Army tried to draft him, Sterling decided he was not exactly Green Beret material. He knew that he was close to being too small for military service. A pound or two less and he would be underweight. He once told me that he ran for hours the day before the induction physical and neither ate nor drank. And he flunked the physical.

It was good for us that Sterling stayed in Davidson. I fondly recall seeing him riding about the campus on his unicycle. He would later be instrumental in getting John and me involved in cross-country and track. Following graduation, he accepted a position in the athletic department at Davidson and became the assistant coach under Mr. Whittle. During the glory years of Davidson basketball (described in Chapter 17), Sterling announced the home games. He always stayed in shape. I ran against Sterling in an old-timers meet at Davidson in 1986. He ran the hilly five-mile cross-country course in thirty minutes—not bad for a man in his mid-forties.

The Whittles spent the summer months in Montreat, the Presbyterian Church's retreat and conference center in the mountains of western North Carolina. In 1897 the beauty of these hills had drawn religious Presbyterian folk to a site deep in a cove just outside of the little community of Black Mountain. They built some rudimentary dwellings on a fast, plunging stream called Flat Creek. The creek flowed off a mountain called Graybeard, which is the southern anchor of the Black Mountain range and adjacent to Mount Mitchell, the highest peak in eastern America. In time these Presbyterians would build a dam on the creek and create Lake Susan. Around the lake they built Montreat-Anderson College, a beautiful hotel, and a conference center—all constructed from creek stone. Churchgoers from all over the South came here and built rustic homes for their summer vacations. The most famous denizen, Billy Graham, a Baptist, had his first headquarters here and built his current home high on a mountain overlooking the lovely cove.

In Montreat the Whittles helped establish a recreation program called the Clubs for children whose parents were vacationing or attending the summer conferences. Activities were designed for kids in grades K-12 and were supervised by college students who lived in assigned college housing for the summer. Most of the counselors came from Davidson College and Queens College in Charlotte. The daytime program operated weekdays and Saturday mornings, with an emphasis on sports and arts and crafts. Evening activities included, on different days of the week, roller skating, basketball, and square dancing, the latter involving folks of all ages.

I first visited Montreat in the summer of 1956. We stayed at the Lewis Schenck cottage, a three-story wooden edifice on Alabama Terrace. (Dr. Schenck taught in the religion department at Davidson.) That summer we spent a lot of time down in the town part of Montreat, which consisted of several ramshackle white buildings—a soda shop, general store, and post office. An old church building across the street was used as a community center for black laborers who worked for some of the cottage owners.

That summer we joined the club program. Mr. Whittle was interested in getting John and me involved in sports. I remember that he took us to nearby Camp Rockmont, a boys' camp located in the North Fork Valley of the Swannanoa River. The Montreat "primaries" played the Rockmont elementary-age boys in basketball. I had never played before. I remember someone throwing the ball to me; I stood there terrified, all the while being swarmed by the opposing players. I didn't have the slightest idea of what to do with the ball.

Perhaps my most painful memory of that summer in Montreat was swimming in Lake Susan. Fed by Flat Creek, which starts its run at an elevation of about 5,500 feet, the lake is frigid. The first time I ever swam there I launched myself into the water off a twenty-foot high sliding board, freezing on impact and unable to move or breathe. Mom had to fish me out, after which I shivered for about an hour.

We stayed at the Schenck's house for two weeks. Toward the end of the vacation, there was a Saturday night square dance at the wood-floor roller rink. I remember that my dad called the dance, and there was a large crowd present. As the last dance was ending and the participants were all circled up, one of the college students broke off and starting leading the line out of the building.. Without telling my parents, I perched myself on the shoulders of Bill Workman, a Davidson neighbor, and headed out the door with him. Bill carried me with the crowd all the way around the lake and eventually brought me back to the rink. My journey lasted forty-five minutes, and Bill and I talked with practically everyone in the line.

My family had given me up for lost. They had no idea where I was. A search party was already down at the lake looking for me or my remains and talking about dragging the lake. I remember someone asking Bill, "Have you seen Jamie?" That I was Jamie didn't register with Bill, and he replied, "I don't know Jamie." The folks were frantic when I finally showed up, and I caught no end of grief for my escapade.

The next summer we returned to Montreat for two weeks. The Schenck cottage was a wreck and we couldn't stay there this time. At the end of the preceding summer Dr. Woods' family had descended on the place. When the Woodses closed up the cottage to head home to Davidson, Jimmy Woods accidentally left the faucet running in an upstairs bathroom sink, with the plug engaged. The house flooded completely and was now in rehab. We rented the Croswell cottage on Texas Road, across the street from the Montreat-Anderson tennis courts. My only other memory of that summer is the campout up Mount Graybeard.

Eddie Booth and Sam Sloan, the latter nicknamed "Greasy" (his older brother was "Slimy"), who were students at Davidson, led the group of seven to nine-year-olds up the mountain. I lugged a sleeping bag that was on loan from the Whittles. We hiked up to the falls, at about 4,500 feet elevation. A huge log crossed the chasm just below the falls, and I was terrified when Greasy made me walk across it. We pitched camp in a clearing by the stream. Supper consisted of two cold hot dogs. Following a longstanding campfire tradition, Greasy told us a harrowing story called "Three Claws," about a genetically warped deer-bear which haunted these mountains and delighted in attacking youngsters on campouts, ripping up tents and sleeping bags and leaving its signature three claws posted on a tree, like Zorro. Just as Greasy finished the tale, a growling Eddie came up behind us with a flashlight positioned under his chin, illuminating a ghoulish grin, leaving us screaming at the top of our lungs. Later, just as I was drifting off to sleep, Bruce Loftis, a troublemaker, launched a rock that hit me in the eye. Boy, did I howl! Fortunately I only had a black eye and a bruised ego. Figuring that he needed to stay in good graces with

Davidson faculty, my father in particular, Greasy pulled his sleeping bag next to mine, and I finally got to sleep.

The next morning I ate another cold hotdog and washed it down with some water from the creek. Then we started down the mountain. About halfway down, Arthur Croswell fell off some rocks and knocked himself out. Arthur had to be carried the rest of the way. When we got back to the cottage four hours later, around 11 a.m., I threw up my hot dog and slept the rest of the day.

Our next trip to Montreat was the summer of 1959, when we stayed at the Gaither cottage on Mississippi Road. The Gaither place fronted the back of a house Billy Graham had built on Assembly Drive, the main road in Montreat, and once used as his headquarters. Our fourteen-year-old cousin, Anne Straffin, from Scarsdale, New York, was visiting my sister Ginger for the summer, and Anne came to Montreat with us. She was quite attractive, and secretly I had a crush on her. That was the summer John and I met the Douglas crowd.

Eileen Douglas and her brood lived in Clearwater, Florida. Her husband was an attorney there, and during the summer months he sent his family to Montreat, where they owned a cottage on North Carolina Terrace. There were four children—Eileen, the oldest, followed by Larry, Bruce, and Scotty in that order. The three boys were only two full years apart. John and I would be inseparable from them over the next several summers.

The Douglas boys were nothing but trouble that first summer of our acquaintance with them. A girl our age named Lynn Phillips stayed in her family's cottage across the street from the Douglas enclave. Lynn was the daughter of the dean of the law school at the University of North Carolina, Chapel Hill. After I gave up on Cousin Anne, I set my amorous sights on Lynn. Unfortunately she had eyes only for Bruce Douglas. Try as I might, I could never get her attention. Seeing pictures of myself at that age, it's hard to imagine that any girl could have been attracted to me. I was emaciated and sported a flat top stiffened by Butch Hairwax. Douglas wasn't much better; his head was all lathered up with Brylcreem.

When we weren't chasing for the hand of the lovely Lynn, we were up to mischief. Much of that involved the local constabulary, in the person of a mysterious night watchman known around Montreat as "Batman." He hailed from the neighboring town of Black Mountain, drove the "Batmobile," a battered yellow pickup truck, and had a mongrel dog that was locally dubbed the "Bat Hound."

We kids took great delight in seeing that the public bathrooms at the Assembly Inn remained depleted of toilet tissue. Our targets were the grand dames from Norfolk who came to social functions at the Inn. After a heist, we would follow the ladies down to the restrooms and giggle convulsively when they emerged appearing quite angry and uncomfortable. The great caper had the community abuzz. The innkeeper brought it to Batman's attention. One night during the Sunday hymn sing at the Inn, we slipped down to the ladies' room. Bruce Douglas opened the door and there was Batman, standing on a commode. The night watchman marched a shaken Bruce down to his truck, got his telephone number, and told him to stay put. He then came after the rest of us, but we had long since fled the premises.

There were rumors that Batman had moonshine connections. This would not be surprising as the liquor still was a common means of supplementing an otherwise meager living in that part of the state. Over the years I've stumbled onto the ruins of several stills during my ramblings in the North Carolina hills. U.S. 70, which passes through Black Mountain, was called "Thunder Road," a notorious avenue for the delivery of the illicit stuff. In 1965 Robert Whitton gave me a sample of some moonshine he claimed he had purchased from Batman. It was really awful.

Bruce Douglas showed up later that night, totally unruffled. Batman had let him off the hook. Bruce didn't say why, but I suspect he stumbled onto something embarrassing in the rear of the Batmobile. At all events, we desisted from further misbehavior at the Inn, and Batman left us alone.

Our family became regulars in Montreat during the summers from 1960 to 1965. Every year Mom and Dad rented a cottage for a month and turned us loose in the Whittle club program. The Douglas boys acquired drivers' licenses in Florida, where the driving age was just fourteen, or so they told us. We used to wheel around Montreat in their Jeep Scout and even go as far as Asheville with them. These were carefree times—I don't think I've ever felt freer. Yet it was also very dangerous riding in an open-air Jeep at forty-five miles per hour, on winding mountain roads without seatbelts. I'm sure our parents never knew the extent of our recklessness; otherwise, they would have prohibited it.

One summer, when we were sixteen years old, John and I became friends with Anne Graham, one of Billy Graham's children, through our association with the Douglases, who were friends of the Grahams. On occasion we would accompany Larry, Bruce and Scotty up to the Graham home at the top of Mississippi Road, about two miles from the center of Montreat, overlooking Black Mountain. I remember once being ambushed by Heidi, the Graham's huge St. Bernard; I escaped only to run into Peter, their snarling German shepherd. (A sign at the entrance to the Graham property announced that "Trespassers Will Be Eaten.") I remember our congregating in the Grahams' kitchen, where Anne's mother, Ruth, presented us with home-baked cookies. We also swam in the pool down the hill from the house; fed by a mountain spring, it was as cold as Lake Susan.

Anne Graham had a VW Bug. One night when she was visiting Mrs. Douglas, Bruce and I pulled the distributor caps off the engine. When Anne couldn't start the car, she called her father, who came down and immediately identified the real source of the problem.

The summer of my eighth-grade year is memorable for Howard Arbuckle and Phil Cramer's assault on Mt. Mitchell. Howard, a student at Davidson College, was the son of a federal court judge in Charlotte. Phil was also a DC student. I don't know who came up with the bright idea, but it was hatched one evening on Lake Susan. Why not take the "intermediate" boys up to Mount Mitchell on the Old Mitchell Road? When we learned about the plan, John and I eagerly signed on.

Built in the early part of the twentieth century, when automobile excursions came into vogue, the Old Mitchell Road was the original motor road to the top of Mt. Mitchell. It winds through the hills from Black Mountain; and before the Blue Ridge Parkway was built, it went all the way up to the top of Mt. Mitchell. In the early 1920's my grandfather lost the brakes on his Model T on that road.

By the 1960's the "Old Toll Road" was a rugged and rocky dirt affair, its condition having deteriorated from years of neglect. The Blue Ridge Parkway, created in the 1930's, had long since replaced it. The trail was useable only for off-road vehicles and hiking. There were several ways to approach it from Montreat. The fastest route was to go straight north up Graybeard Mountain to the flats below the falls of Flat Creek, and then to follow a trail due east to intercept the road as it wound up toward Mt. Pinnacle and the Parkway. The distance from Montreat to the top of Mitchell is approximately eighteen miles.

We left that warm day in August 1961 and headed single-file up Graybeard, loaded down with camping gear. After about three hours we reached the falls and found the roadway, eight or nine miles to go to meet the Parkway, all on relatively level ground. Late in the afternoon we arrived on the Parkway and began the walk up the winding road leading to the top of Mitchell, approximately five miles distant—a climb of approximately 1,500 feet. After walking for what seemed an eternity, we reached a Park Service sign that indicated we still had two miles to go. That was about all we could take; by our lights we were already above the death zone. Fortunately a truck came along and ferried John, some others, and me up to the restaurant, below the parking lot near the top.

We hadn't brought food along and were counting on being able to buy food at the restaurant. Our parents had given John and me each a dollar, which we all thought would be enough for dinner and breakfast. When we got there, however, we learned that burgers were fifty cents a toss. Famished, each of us purchased two burgers, and then we pilfered leftovers off tables that hadn't been bussed.

I don't remember if we got to the top of the mountain. I do remember that we camped out that night close to the Parkway, in the yard of a dilapidated cabin on the Old Mitchell Road. As we were hiking to the campsite, a commotion broke out at the front of the line. It was pitch dark on this moonless yet clear night. Somebody started yelling, "Moonshiners!" I thought my goose was cooked. We had heard all sorts of stories about what moonshiners did to innocent people who stumbled across a distilling operation. Taking no chances, I scrambled into the brush. As it turned out, Arbuckle and Cramer had been planning this hoax for days. Thoroughly frightened, I later pitched camp behind a big rock near the cabin and zipped myself into my Artic sleeping bag, which Dad had purchased from ROTC surplus.

The down bag was heavy, but I was glad I had brought it—the temperature dropped into the thirties, and everyone else was freezing.

The next morning some of the boys, including John, decided to hike to the top of Mt. Pinnacle, which was looming just above us. They climbed for about an hour through the brush and then stumbled into a nest of rattlesnakes that had come out of their den to sun on the rocks. Fortunately, nobody was bitten, but the snakes and a swarm of yellow jackets were enough to send the hikers scurrying back down the mountain. Eventually, a couple of large trucks showed up from Montreat and carried us home on the conventional roadways.

The following summer of 1962 is memorable for the basketball game with Camp Rockmont and its aftermath. We had rented a cottage on Assembly Drive for the last two weeks of July and the first two weeks of August. Camp Rockmont, over in the North Fork Valley, fielded teams in all youth age groups and took on all-comers. John, Bruce and Scotty Douglas, William Brown (the current director of the Davidson College Union), and I made up the starting five for the Montreat "intermediates." The Rockmont boys were undefeated for their season. That Saturday night in August we played a thirty-two minute high school type game. We gave them a pretty good run. I scored two-thirds of the points for our team. We came up short by two points at the end, but we were very pleased with our effort.

After the game we went to Pattie Newell's family cottage on Graybeard Road. Some of the kids got into it hot and heavy in the basement. I just stood there alone watching the action, feeling sorry for myself. Then I spotted a girl standing alone in a corner, and with nothing to lose, I introduced myself. She told me she was Anne Anderson from Lakeland, Florida, and her father was a Davidson graduate. She and her family had a place over on Texas Road, up from the Croswell house. We chatted for a few minutes and then started kissing. It just happened spontaneously.

I remember seeing Anne at church the following morning, Sunday, August 5, 1962. She ran up to me and excitedly announced that Marilyn Monroe had committed suicide. At that moment I felt the same sentiment expressed by Pat Boone when Elvis died fifteen years later: Who could imagine an old Marilyn?

I played putt-putt golf with Anne in Black Mountain the following day. That was the last time I ever saw her in Montreat. She was bright and industrious and worked throughout her high school summers. We struck up a mail correspondence, and she wrote me a letter about every two weeks, all the way through high school. I saw Anne during my freshman year at Davidson when she was visiting relatives in Charlotte. She had grown into a beautiful young woman. I invited her for a dance weekend the following year, but she couldn't arrange transportation. I suppose she used that as an excuse for having another beau. I never heard from her again. When I emptied out the attic in our house after my parents had died, I came across a stack of her letters. They remain a fond memory from my youth.

Another event from that summer which stands in memory is the Frankie Harrison (I have changed the name) incident. Harrison was a known troublemaker, a preacher's kid gone sour. Vowing to have fun and outsmart Batman at the same time, he began smuggling toilet paper out of Assembly Inn to "roll" the trees on Assembly Drive. I remember the night of August 9, 1962, vividly. That's when Batman beat the hell out of Frankie Harrison.

We had gathered at the Montreat soda shop around 8:30 p.m. and were listening to rock and roll on the jukebox, when Frankie came bursting though the door screaming, "Don't let him get me!" Close on Frankie's heels, an enraged Batman broke into the room. Frankie became hysterical and grabbed a pole supporting the roof and held on for dear life. All the while, Neil Sedeka was belting out his hit single, "Breaking Up Is Hard To Do." It wasn't hard for Batman. He broke up Harrison something terrible on the floor and hauled the kicking and screaming kid down to the Black Mountain police station. We never saw Frankie again. We heard later that he had left Montreat the day after the incident.

In the summer of 1963, Wilson Greene of Orlando, Florida, showed up in Montreat in a VW van that had its own water pump and dispenser. The accoutrement was great for loading up water balloons. In the early 1960's rowdies from Black Mountain would regularly come into Montreat to stir up trouble; they liked to catch "cottage boys" and rough them up a little. That summer Wilson declared war on them. On July evenings he would load up the van with anybody with a sense of adventure, hunt down the interlopers, and bomb them with water balloons.

One night the hoods spotted John, wearing a blue letter sweater, getting into the van. Later that evening as I emerged from a basketball game, six of the thugs accosted me saying they were looking for a kid in a blue letter sweater—something like mine, which was identical to the one my identical twin was wearing. I nervously explained that I had a twin brother and he was the one to blame. They said, "Sure you do," and started to punch me around. Fortunately, this happened in front of the gym and some of the older kids came to my rescue. By the time Batman finally showed up, the hoods were long gone.

I met my high school girlfriend Mary Whitton in Montreat in 1964. She was a lovely and brilliant girl, who stood near the top of her class at Myers Park High School in Charlotte. The Whittons had a summer home on Georgia Terrace, and I became a fixture there. That summer Mary and I attended all the club activities for high school students. I would spend hours in conversation with her on just about every topic imaginable. Occasionally, we would ride over to Asheville in her VW Bug for a movie, or just to take in the city lights. We whiled away hours on her front porch, swinging in the breeze. There was something magical about all that—the cool summer nights, the white noise of the creek tumbling down the mountain in the distance, and all of the creature sounds, including a guy and his best gal cuddling on a porch swing in the moonlight.

I courted Mary during our senior year in high school. The summer of 1966 her parents sequestered her and took their family on a trip around the world. Mary sent me some Egyptian sand from the area of the Pyramids. After that I saw her only infrequently. We went our separate ways in college; she had a full scholarship to Duke University, and I attended Davidson College. I did get her over for homecoming my freshman year, and she came to my graduation in 1970. I lost track of her after that. Mary remains, like Anne, embedded in my memory, and I'm grateful to both of them for helping me develop some arts of courtship that in time would help me persuade another lovely young woman to marry me.

I spent two summers of my college years in the North Carolina mountains. In 1967 Mr. Whittle helped me get a job at a summer camp near Brevard. My fellow counselors and I spent a lot of time over the six-week session hiking in the Shining Rock Wilderness in the mountains above Brevard. The Park Service was blasting an access road into the Wilderness; I felt this was a big mistake that would in time ruin the area, and history has since vindicated my concerns.

We spent several nights on top of Cold Mountain. I learned why the locals call it "cold." Summer nocturnal temperatures hovered in the thirties on the mountain. I also found how extremely steep the mountain is—you had to do your business clutching a tree and hanging on for dear life. Few people are aware that a World War II B-17 bomber crashed on Cold Mountain in 1945. The plane was cruising at 6,000 feet in foul weather—Cold Mountain is 6,030 feet high. The engines are still there, clearly discernible amidst the other wreckage. I carried off a small piece of fuselage as a souvenir.

After the six-week camp ended, I took a job in Montreat as a bellhop at the Assembly Inn until school started up again. I would return as a bellhop the following summer of 1968, the last one I would spend in Montreat.

The Whittles continued to go to Montreat each summer to run the club programs. Mr. Whittle was my track and cross-country coach at Davidson. I remember a valuable lesson he helped me learn. It was a spring afternoon in my sophomore year; the event was an annual track carnival called the Davidson Relays. That day I ran the anchor leg on the two-mile relay team. By the time I got the baton, I was at least twenty seconds behind the rest of the field, in a hopeless situation. I decided that an all-out effort just wasn't worth the price; we were going to lose badly anyway. So I dogged the race and finished the two laps in a desultory jog. Mr. Whittle was furious, and he berated me long and hard; I had insulted by teammates and thoroughly disgraced myself, he yelled. This embarrassing incident taught me a lesson about my fiduciary responsibility to the people I work with. I also learned, painfully, that giving less than my best effort is not how I wanted to present myself to the world.

Mr. Whittle had the greatest green thumb in Davidson. He loved horticulture, and he built a splendid greenhouse behind his house on College Drive. After he bought the old sandlot behind the barn, the last remnant of Johnsie Shelton's horse pasture, he and the entire neighborhood turned it into a large summer vegetable garden.

I was in Europe with the U.S. Army in 1976, when I received a letter from my mother telling me that Pete Whittle had died suddenly of a heart attack. I loved and respected him, and regret terribly that I missed his funeral. The college built an all-weather track at Richardson Stadium and fittingly named it for Mr. Whittle. Daisy outlived him by almost fifteen years. They are all gone now. All of their children married and moved away, and I've lost touch with them over the years.

James Young Causey, Sr.

Dr. James Causey taught Spanish at Davidson College. He and his family first lived in Davidson on Lorimer Road just across the street from the Woods family. He and his wife, Ruby, had three children—Joanne, Ruth, and Jim. They also had a mongrel dog.

One spring afternoon Viney Thompson, who lived nearby on South Thompson Street and drove like Cruella de Ville, ran over and killed the Causey's beloved canine; Viney didn't stop but kept right on speeding along. Viney drove so recklessly that my peer group called her "Road Hog."

John Woods told me that on the night after the dog died, he accompanied young Jim Causey down to the Thompson house and tied cherry bombs to all four tires of Viney's car. Her husband, Sam, knew who had blown the tires, but he never could prove it. The town policeman, Mr. Honeycutt, said he couldn't do anything without hard evidence.

In 1956 the Causeys built their new house across the street from us on College Drive. This put Jim, who was four years our senior, in our immediate neighborhood, and over time that spelled trouble for us.

Dr. Causey loved to play tennis. He taught Jim the game, and Jim grew into a muscular teenager and an excellent tennis player, among the best in the South. During his high school years he was three times North Carolina's state tennis champion in singles. The Causeys played tennis almost every day. Dr. Causey kept all of the practice balls in a large duffle bag. Almost daily I would see them walking over to the college's clay tennis courts, which were among the finest in the country.

Dr. Causey enticed John and me to play tennis, arranging to have the college tennis coach, Dr. Harry Fogleman, give us free lessons. "Fogey" drove a red Ford Thunderbird. He was both jocular and corpulent, and we called him "T-Bird Tummy." For an entire fall we were on the courts almost every day, smashing balls under Fogey's tutelage.

Our parents bought John and me Wilson "Jack Kramer" rackets. Jim Causey was a regular on the courts, and often ambled over to tease and bully us. He also taught us how to play tennis baseball. The game consisted of a T Ball-type format, with the field being the vastness of four consecutive tennis courts running east to west. Jim was the only player who could put a ball over the far-side fence.

In our fifth grade year Dr. Causey (we called him "JY" behind his back) took over our Sunday school class at DCPC. He was one of the best teachers of theology I've ever met. He always spent the first half of each class teaching from the *Bible*. The second half was what we enjoyed the most: Dr. Causey talked about life and used examples from tennis to illustrate his lessons in fair play, integrity, and sportsmanship. A devout Christian, Dr. Causey taught us to treat our bodies as holy temples of God. I suppose that's why I never took up smoking or alcohol.

As young Jim matured and started high school, he seemed to go out of his way to pick on John and me. He was big, and we scurried for cover whenever we saw him coming. When Dad put up a basketball goal in the backyard in the early 1960's, Jim, who loved the game, became an unwelcome regular at the house. He played a rough game and delighted in running over the smaller boys. We simply couldn't compete with him, and if we protested, he left us black and blue.

Jim won a full tennis scholarship to the University of Georgia in Athens. We were all proud of him despite our fear of what he might do to us if we got his goat. Then tragedy struck in 1965, during the spring of my junior year at North Mecklenburg High.

Jim was returning to Athens early one morning after a date in Macon. He ran off the road (the highway patrol thought he had fallen asleep), and he was pinned upside down in the front seat by his seat belt. He hung there for hours before somebody found him.

Jim was in a coma and was all but neurologically dead. The grief-stricken Causeys transferred him to the National Institutes of Health in Bethesda, Maryland, in the hope that the doctors there could help him. Jim remained in a comatose state for nearly a year, and then he miraculously regained consciousness. That's when his doctors learned that he had been "locked in"—aware of what was going on around him but totally unable to move and communicate.

The Causeys brought Jim back to Davidson and remodeled his room to accommodate his disability. In time Dr. Causey began taking Jim out in his wheelchair, and they became inseparable regulars on the college campus and about town. Jim's speech slowly improved with therapy, and he was able to carry on conversations. His partial quadriplegia and severe limitations persisted, however. Despite these dire problems, Jim seemed to grow spiritually as the years passed, becoming a warm, gregarious man. He was always genuinely glad to see John and me whenever we dropped by, always smiling, always trying to find out what we were up to.

Dr. Causey died in 1997 at the age of ninety. I last saw Jim twelve years ago. Recently I learned that his sister Ruth has looked after him since their father died. I also heard that a few years ago he told someone he couldn't imagine what life would be like without his disability. It had brought him close to God, and he looked upon his tragedy as a blessing.

I view Jim as more of a spiritual being than the severely disabled person that his accident made of him. I suppose that if angels walk the earth, he is one of them. In my mind's eye I can still see young Jim, a duffle bag full of tennis balls slung over his shoulder, and Dr. Causey walking together up College Drive, heading for the tennis courts. It's a very nice memory.

Profiles
of a
Town

Davidson was in many respects a country town in the 1950's, sustained by a rich assortment of small proprietorships located on Main Street. Bill Withers and his wife, Johnsie, supplied the town's electrical and appliance needs. Bub Cashion and Willis Reid operated the two service stations in town, and the town garage supported both of them. Warren McKissick was the town's cobbler and shoe repairman. Ralph Johnson and Hood Norton operated our two barbershops. Piedmont Bank and Trust (PB & T) handled our financial and legal affairs. A.D. Cantrell ran the Western Auto Store and provided Western Union services. Irving Johnson operated a grocery store next door to the Western Auto. Walter Henderson ran a clock- and watch-repair business. There was also "Pop" Copeland's "Jungle," a multipurpose store that sold hardware items, sports equipment, outdoor gear, and an array of oddball items. Pop's daughter Mary was the women's clothier, and Rush Wilson owned the fashionable men's store. Davidson even had a Southern Five and Dime Store; Fannie McConnell and her sister Lula were the proprietors. Cloyd Goodrum, the town pharmacist, had his drugstore at the northern end of the business district. Bill Mayhew was the postmaster of the "new" Main Street post office, which was dedicated in 1958. And, of course, there was the highly popular M&M Soda Shop, owned by Murray and Mary, who had a grudge against the Puckett twins. All of these people, and many others on Main Street, served not only the townspeople but also the college students. The whole thing seemed to be held together by the newspaper, *The Mecklenburg Gazette*, which was the town's advertising medium and perpetual source of gossip.

Ralph Johnson

There were two barbershops in town, both run by thoroughly honest and decent men, Ralph Johnson and Hood Norton, whose emporia were on Main Street. The town and college were able to support the barbering business in Davidson because the 1950's were the decade of the crew cut, short flattop, Mohawk, and occasional skinhead. I remember Hood and adopted son Kenneth in one shop and Ralph with several other barbers in the larger practice.

Our mother sent John and me on a regular basis to Ralph Johnson. Three other skilled barbers worked for Ralph, but Mom preferred him. I remember in my early years sitting on a board in his chair while he went about giving me a closely cropped crew cut. It was a proud day when we graduated from the board to real sitting status and Ralph told us, "Now, you are men!"

Mom sent us for haircuts on Saturdays. This was particularly inconvenient for us since Saturdays were generally reserved for television at Miss Agnes' house, playtime in the neighborhood, and Saturday matinees at the Picture Show. Mom always had her way, which meant that we had to endure two to three hours of boredom while we waited on Ralph to finish with the seven or eight customers ahead of us. Ralph was in demand, and there was plenty of business on Saturdays. Most of the students had haircuts once a month, and Saturday was a popular time. In those days Davidson was an all-male college, and after Saturday classes, many of the college boys would head over to Ralph's to spruce up for their dates. No matter how early we got there, we still had to wait. What was particularly galling was when a student with "urgent business" bumped us back in the line. Even worse happened when Mom didn't approve the length of the cut Ralph had given us. She would march us back across the street, and we would have to endure the whole thing all over again just to get a shorter trim.

Fortunately for us, Ralph purchased a television for the shop. I recall winter afternoons huddling around the heater, watching the Atlantic Coast Conference Game of the Week, sponsored by the Pilot Life Insurance Company and the National Brewing Company. (The tuneful jingles "sail with the Pilot all the way," and "brewed on the shores of the Chesapeake Bay" still play in my head.) It was in front of Ralph's heater where I remember first seeing Oskeegum, whom everyone called "Skeegum."

I never knew Skeegum's last name and had no idea where he lived. He was probably in his late fifties. Ralph cared for Skeegum and employed him to shine shoes for the college students for twenty-five cents a shine. Ironically, Skeegum and I became business partners—of a sort.

D.G. Martin, son of the college president, was a student at Davidson in the spring of 1962. I was fourteen years old. D.G. was self-employed as the window washer for most of the Davidson businesses that fronted Main Street. My father said he thought D.G. did it to support his social life. On Saturday mornings D.G. worked Main Street, scrubbing windows. He really seemed to enjoy camaraderie with all the people on the street. It was there one spring morning that D.G. told me he planned to give it all up and offered to sell his business to me. For five dollars he sold me his bucket, squeegee, brushes, and rags.

He taught me the ropes, and I was in business. Looking back on it now, it was one of the best experiences of my life. Here I was at age fourteen gainfully employed and thoroughly independent. Unfortunately, I was permanently short of cash—the job paid Great Depression era wages. I could work three hours on a set of windows and earn only a dollar. It was apparent that the storeowners were paying me lower wages than they had paid D.G. Part of the problem was my age, and another part was my technique. I would pour a quart of Sudsy Ammonia into a two-gallon bucket, and that mixture would create a horrid streaking mess on the windows. All I really needed was a drop or two of liquid Joy, and things would have worked fine. Anyway, I really enjoyed meeting with the folks on the street on Saturdays. That's where I got into business with Skeegum.

Skeegum would follow along behind me, offering advice on how I could improve and speed up my work. After I had finished a set of windows and received the miserly pay, he would beg, "How's about a little sumthin' for Oskeegum?" I was a Christian and a Presbyterian, to boot. I felt obligated to him and would generally give him twenty-five to fifty percent of my take. He said he used it to buy cigarettes and food, and I honestly thought I was doing the Christian thing in giving him the money.

On and on it went—Saturdays, poor pay, and the dole to Skeegum. At Christmas, Skeegum would make his rounds of the faculty homes in Davidson. He always came to the back door, and my sister Ginger would generally herald his approach with something like, "Lord, Daddy, Skeegum's here!" Dad would then load him up with Winston and Salem cigarettes. Dad held the R.J. Reynolds chair in the biology department at the College, so I suppose he felt obligated to keep plenty of RJR products around the house.

Late one Saturday afternoon Dad asked me if I had been giving money to Skeegum. I proudly replied that indeed I had. He then asked me if I knew why Skeegum was frequently asleep at Ralph Johnson's barbershop to which I replied that I didn't know. He then told me that Skeegum had a drinking problem and that by giving him money, I was only feeding his habit. I was angry and hurt; I felt that Skeegum had used me. The next week I told him what Dad had said, and he denied all of it. Then I told him that I couldn't give him any more money.

James Raeford, who worked at Johnson's Barbershop, fondly remembers Oskeegum. James related to me that Skeegum was a decent and honest man and always tried to maintain a good appearance despite his poverty and weekend drinking. Skeegum was particularly conscientious in his work shining shoes at the shop. He also was Ralph's official greeter at the door and always told the patrons how good-looking they were as he collected their hats. Skeegum frequented college alumni events to chum with former students who had known him in years past. He considered himself an honorary member of the Kappa Sigma fraternity at the college and frequently referred to himself as a "Kappa Sig."

I don't know what became of Skeegum. Over the years I saw less and less of him, and he finally disappeared all together from the Davidson landscape. In the strictest sense of the term, Skeegum was not a street person because he did have a home to go to at night. But for some reason, every time I see a street person, I'm reminded of him. When I visited Washington, D.C. over Thanksgiving a number of years ago, I saw a man on a heater exhaust wrapped up in a sleeping bag at the Department of Justice; he was enveloped in steam, which made the whole scene surreal. He looked just like old Skeegum. When I rounded a corner and looked back again, he had vanished.

In hindsight I know that giving Skeegum my money was the right thing to do. I sometimes even wonder if old Skeegum wasn't actually a manifestation of Christ wandering the world seeking out decent folk.

I also know now that my relationship with Skeegum was shaped by Jim Crow social customs. As a child in Davidson I was unaware of the social injustices or moral dimensions of racial segregation. I knew, of course, that black children attended the segregated Ada Jenkins School in Davidson and later the all-black Torrence Lytle High School in Huntersville. Among my peers there were occasional references to "niggers." And some of my friends on School Street helped organize football games that pitted black and white youngsters against each other. None of that behavior was mean or malicious; it was simply part of a social system we took for granted. We just didn't give these matters much thought. Social change moved slowly in Davidson even amidst the turmoil of 1960's. When it finally came, it centered on the barbering scene in the town, and it happened this way.

Ralph Johnson was a prosperous, light-skinned African American, who had enemies on both sides of the town's racial divide. Perhaps the black community was hardest on him. As far as his Main Street business was concerned, Ralph would only cut a man's hair if he were white; this was the custom of his establishment. That's why all those years I never saw a black customer in his shop. His employees apparently barbered for the local black community after hours in their homes or in private shops. I never learned for certain. Anyway, Ralph was adamant about not integrating his barbershop. Matters came to a head in the spring of 1968.

In April 1968, as I was completing my sophomore year at Davidson College, two black men, supported by student demonstrators, walked into Ralph's new establishment in the Thompson Building (the old Five and Dime), at the corner of Main and Depot streets and asked the proud proprietor for haircuts. Ralph said that he wouldn't do it. The two men walked out onto the sidewalk where a crowd was beginning to assemble. Some of them carried signs such as "Ralph Johnson, what color are you?" A picket line immediately formed. Police dispersed the crowd because the protestors didn't have a parade permit. The next day, armed with the proper permit, they were back in earnest. Students and townsfolk who disliked Ralph rallied to the site. Ralph was obviously disturbed and hurt by this. He dictated a heated speech about his predicament and played the tape in front of his shop continuously throughout each day of the demonstration.

The protest went on for several weeks. One afternoon I crossed the picket line, to the jeering of the crowd. I knew Ralph had his faults, as we all do, but I also thought he was being singled out unfairly. Meantime, Hood Norton, who was Ralph's maternal uncle, continued to make a tidy profit down the street. Hood discriminated against his own race just like Ralph, and I thought it very odd that no one said anything about that. At all events, the story made the local and national evening network news shows and newspapers as far away as Seattle.

Recently, I was leafing through an issue of *Our State: Down Home in North Carolina* and came across an article about a barber from Davidson who had written a memoir called *David Played A Harp.* Having been away from Davidson for decades, I assumed that Ralph Johnson had died years ago. But there he was, alive and well, and a published author at age ninety-six, to boot! Time had been kind to him. His picture was much as I remembered him.

I read Ralph's book with great interest. He had written the manuscript in the early 1970's but waited until 2000 to publish it. What I found in those pages was a revealing portrait of a side of Davidson that had eluded my consciousness as a child and youth. The maps of town that appear in my own book depict the eastern side of the tracks—the only side of Davidson I ever really knew. Ralph and the other blacks in town lived on the west side. Even the west side was divided: Griffith Street, on that side of the tracks, demarcated poor-white Davidson from poor-black Davidson.

Looking back through the lens of Ralph's memoir, I learned the details of the silent segregation that permeated my community. I also learned about the hardship and violence that had followed Ralph as this self-educated man built a thriving barbering business and acquired rental properties. Ralph describes the resentment both races felt for him because of his hard-earned prosperity.

In the boycott of '68 Ralph was caught between the proverbial rock and hard place. If he opened his shop to black customers, he would lose his white patronage, the mainstay of his business. On the other hand, if he didn't integrate the barbershop, his business would be destroyed by the effectively led student boycott. Either way Ralph's business was doomed.

I remember that terrible night in April 1968 when Martin Luther King was assassinated in Memphis. I was participating in a track meet at Lenoir Rhyne College when we heard the news. One of my Davidson teammates, Ken Hill, remarked, "Things are going to burn tonight!" This tragedy only put more pressure on Ralph Johnson.

The crowds assembled daily on both sides of Main Street. The Gastonia-area Ku Klux Klan even made an appearance, albeit without the hooded regalia; they drove up Main Street and catcalled the demonstrators. I had seen a Klan assembly once before in my life—in the early 1950's when we drove past a nighttime rally on the way home from visiting my grandmother in Wilson, North Carolina. Klansmen were burning a fifty-foot high cross. Dad told us not to watch it. I suppose that in 1968 the Klan was actually supporting Ralph Johnson. What an irony that was!

Ralph finally relented and opened his shop to black customers, and saw his business of almost fifty years dry up virtually overnight. Over the next three years neither blacks nor whites would frequent the place. Ralph finally had to close his barbershop in 1971. Over the years I lost track of Ralph and he faded in my memory.

Reading Ralph's memoir brought all these things back into focus. Now, more than ever, I believe he was unjustly scapegoated for the sins of Jim Crow—a social system he was forced to navigate against huge odds his entire life. I am also aware how insidious that system was and how misshapen social and economic behaviors some-times actually became, even in Southern college and university towns. The Davidson barbershop incident is a compelling example.

My lasting memory of Ralph Johnson is of a man cutting a small child's hair. My brother, John, is seated on a board in the first seat of Ralph's old barbershop sometime in the early 1950's. Ralph is reti-cent and quiet, oblivious to the banter going on between his other barbers and some student customers. He is wearing a heavily starched and spotless white barber's tunic. There he stands in my memory, thoroughly professional, thoroughly dignified.

Murray and Mary

The M & M Soda Shop stood on Main Street opposite the Grove. It was a constant part of my childhood. Murray Fleming and Mary Potts ran the establishment and served up burgers, shakes, soups, and sandwich fare. Murray was famous for his egg salad sandwiches. At lunchtime students and townsfolk congregated there. There were no freestanding tables, only wall booths, so there was a modicum of privacy.

John and I were drawn to the shop by its grand assortment of magazines. As children we would slip in through the front door and crawl along the floor and pull magazines off the shelves. Murray and Mary sold *Classics Illustrated, Superman*, and *Batman* comics, and these were usually our primary targets. This was highly irritating to the proprietors, and we were frequently rudely bounced from the establishment.

In time the M&M Soda Shop became a social hub of the com-munity. Virtually every student who attended Davidson College would, at one time or another, visit the shop for food and gossip. Some folks came so often that they virtually had seats reserved for them—what the Germans call a S*tammtisch*. I remember sitting in one of those privileged seats and being evicted when the reserved party arrived.

I began to visit the M&M less frequently as my rude ejections became more frequent. From time to time I would sneak in and catch up on some of the magazines. The problem was that I was growing up, and it was becoming harder to conceal myself.

Murray and Mary could be downright mean. I remember when we won our first Pony League baseball game one Saturday in the late spring of 1961. Our coach, Eugene Reid, took us to the Soda Shop for milkshakes and hamburgers. When the order was placed for fifteen burgers and fifteen shakes, Murray exploded! To this day I can't understand that. After about an hour we finally were served.

Matters had taken an ugly turn by the eighth grade. When my friends and I played softball in the Grove, we all wanted to put one across Main Street and through the window of the establishment, but, fortunately, none of us could hit that far.

It all came to a head in the spring of 1962. John, Doug Cantrell, and I went to the M&M after school for some Cokes. We got the customary evil eye from Murray. After we had finished, John and I departed, leaving Doug behind to look through the magazines. What we didn't know was that Doug had turned his ice-filled cup upside down on the table. My parents got a call later that afternoon banishing us forever from the Soda Shop.

There were other options in our small town. Up the street, near the corner of Depot and Main, stood Cloyd Goodrum's drugstore, which was a watering hole for some of the older college professors. Professor Earnest Beaty of the classics department had his own *Stammtisch* here, and he held court daily. Mr. Goodrum was far more tolerant than Murray, and he allowed us to read the magazines. Unfortunately, he only had a few—but at least he didn't throw us out. He also made fountain sodas the old fashioned way: ice cream, chocolate syrup and carbonated water. His drinks were great until the town converted to Lake Norman as its primary reservoir; the sodas were unimaginably foul tasting for a month.

Mr. Goodrum's brother-in-law, Hugo Sapp, ran an establishment midway between the drugstore and the M & M Soda Shop. It was simply known as Hugo's. Mr. Sapp was a large man who was quite permissive regarding activities in his shop. He is best remembered for his "Ice Age" milkshakes, which were almost as thick as the boxed ice cream from which they emanated. For years he had the only jukebox in town. So there we were, blasting out those 45's and chilling out on milkshakes. I remember sharing a shake with Pattie Newell there—two children and two straws attacking the frozen drink.

After Hugo died, Ralph Quackenbush took over his store, completely rebuilt it, and renamed it the Hub. For a number of years it was truly a hub of town and student activity, making a serious dent in the M&M's business. From the eighth grade on, John and I were regular customers there. Ralph had a grand selection of magazines and had no objections to our browsing. He made great shakes and burgers, and his grill cheese sandwiches were the best in town.

Ralph was a partner in the Tastee Freeze ice cream shop in Cornelius. He had an ice cream truck and would ride about town playing a jingle and drumming up business. We would frequent the Tastee Freeze after our Sunday night church youth meetings. One Sunday evening I purchased a butterscotch sundae and headed back to Davidson with some friends in a convertible. As we approached the intersection of Main and School streets, on a whim all of us launched the remains of our goodies at the stoplight. To our chagrin, the light turned yellow, the driver hit the brakes, and a gooey spray dowsed us all. The girls were furious that the stuff got in their hair.

Another memorable eatery was the restaurant run by the Deweese family. It stood on Main Street in the 1950's before the Hub came onto the scene. The Deweeses had a son, Jerry, who was always up to mischief, and a lovely daughter, Jeanette. She was with me in school from the first grade all the way to our graduation night at North Mecklenburg High. She was a regular part of our gang, and we often attended the Teen Canteen and dances with her.

Jeanette married Jimmy Honeycutt, who lived in Davidson. I learned that Jimmy died suddenly in his mid-thirties of a heart attack. His dad, who had operated a meat market on Main Street, had died at almost the same age. We were in the second grade then, and townspeople, assisted by the Charlotte television stations, put on a benefit for the American Heart Association in Mr. Honeycutt's memory. I saw Jeanette from time to time over the next several years after Jimmy's death but lost contact with her after my graduation from medical school.

An eatery that appeared on Main Street around 1968 was Lefty's Wildcat Den, a pizza parlor of sorts. Lefty Driesell was the head basketball coach at the college, and he made extra money from a television show on Davidson basketball at Charlotte's WBTV station. I suppose he used that money to get a lease on the building and set up his restaurant. He made my old friend and fellow college student Bill Adams his manager. Lefty's business suffered terribly in the first year. It was set up as a nightspot, and it was poor competition for the beer joints just across the Iredell County line. Indeed, until 1969 the town of Davidson was dry as a bone, so all of the evening business went "up the road" to wetter climes. Never mind that Lefty finally got a beer license; his restaurant couldn't overcome the inertia of local habit. The only business he got was a late-night smattering of students wandering over from the college library. In no way did this first failure deter Lefty's culinary ambitions. I visited the University of Maryland in the early 1970's when Lefty was the head basketball coach there. On the main road into the campus I spotted a restaurant with his name on it.

Throughout my childhood and college years, any attempt at a successful night establishment in the town of Davidson was doomed to failure. All the business went where the beer flowed. That's where the Widow Morgan and Hattie's enter the story.

In the years during and shortly after World War I, Hattie and my father attended school together in Cornelius. Hattie married someone named Morgan, and after he died, she opened a beer establishment just north of Davidson in Iredell County. Complying with the town's ordinance against alcohol, the college prohibited any drinking by faculty or students. So, everybody went "up the road" to Hattie's. The Widow Morgan had some competition from the Anchor Grill just down the road, but the majority of students favored her.

During our high school years John and I occasionally went to Hattie's, bumming rides with some of the college students. We always ordered hamburgers and washed them down with soda pops. The Widow Morgan had pinball machines, and we would play until our change ran out.

In time Hattie's place became the largest cross-county beer distributor in North Carolina. Her best seller was Budweiser. People flocked there day and night for beer. Sometime in the mid-1960's when we were having a great deal of trouble with the railroad crossings north of Charlotte (Chapter 16), the student body at Davidson took things into its own hands. Students would take their dates up to Hattie's, get plastered, and then hurl beer cans and verbal abuse at the trains passing north. The Southern Railroad lodged a complaint, and state officials threatened to revoke Hattie's license even though she wasn't directly involved. That was enough for the students, and things quieted down.

A final note: Once I became a college student I returned to the M & M from time to time, although the Hub remained my regular haunt. That I was no longer a pesky kid seemed to mitigate the animosity Murray and Mary had held toward me. We actually got to be on good speaking terms. I always complemented Murray on his egg salad sandwiches, which were easily the best I've ever tasted.

Withers' Electric

Bill Withers was the town's electrician. He and his wife, Johnsie, ran an electrical appliance store that stood catty-corner across the street from our old house on Main Street. Bill was an electrical genius, but one would never guess this from the disheveled appearance of his work area. The front end of the building, where they sold General Electric appliances, however, was in better shape.

Bill and Johnsie had six children, and at least one of them was always present helping with the business after school hours. We thought Bill and Johnsie must have done very well because they had a lovely home on Grey Road, just outside town. In order of age, the children were Elizabeth, Mary, Nancy, Billy, Richard, and David. Nancy and Billy were my contemporaries. All of the Withers children were extremely intelligent and did very well in school.

Some of my earliest memories of Davidson are tied to the Withers' first home on Walnut Street, not far from the Mimosa Cemetery and town ball fields. John and I frequently visited Nancy. She had a horse named Skipper, and her mother let us ride with Nancy—always a treat. During our teen years Nancy hosted parties in the large basement of the Withers' Grey Road home. She always invited a horde of young people, and these were, by our standards, elaborate affairs.

Nancy and I went through all twelve years of our public education together. During our sophomore year at North Mecklenburg High School in 1963, our homeroom class chose Nancy and me to organize the homecoming project, and we went at it with a vengeance.

North played the East Mecklenburg High School Eagles at homecoming that year. Nancy and I built a mock-up launch pad for a space rocket, which was an elaborate setup called Cape Carnivorous and themed "Orbit the Eagles." We won second place.

Nancy and I competed academically at North, but we still remained close friends. In the end she went to Queens College in Charlotte, and I went to Davidson. During our sophomore year Nancy arranged a blind date for me with a fellow "Queenie" named Teresa Caton, from Anderson, South Carolina. She was lovely, witty, and very musically talented. I dated her more than any other girl during my college years. We had good times together, and I fondly remember her for rescuing me from the doldrums of monastic Saturday nights on campus.

After college Nancy studied library science at the University of North Carolina, where I attended medical school. We would get together occasionally. Nancy married Philip Dishman, and they have a home out on the Kannapolis highway near Davidson. She works today as the town librarian and continues to tend to her horses.

The Jungle

William "Pop" Copeland was a retired Presbyterian minister. His wife ran a boarding house next door to the building that was once the Helper Inn, and Pop ran a multipurpose store on Main Street. It was in such disarray that the college students called it the "Jungle."

Mrs. Copeland was arguably the best cook in Davidson. During the school year she and her daughter Nancy ran the boarding house, and in the summers she and Nancy went to Montreat, where they initially ran their cottage as a boarding house and later combined that business with the management of the William Black Home, a hotel owned by the Presbyterian Synod of North Carolina.

A visit to Pop's emporium was an adventure. It was like so many family-run hardware and multipurpose stores of that era. We couldn't find a thing, but Pop knew where everything was; somehow he had a system. A pipe wrench might end up next to a fireplace screen. Somewhere in that entire jumble I found a baseball glove that I liked. My dad bought it for me for fifteen dollars, which was a tidy sum for a glove in those days. Pop told me he gave me what he called a "team price."

The store was filled with ropes and hammocks. Upon entering one had the notion that this might be a Chinese brothel—with all the rope and lanterns hanging down. Somewhere in all that mess was Pop Copeland.

Everything had a set price, but everyone knew that Pop loved to bargain. He had the distinct ability to make the customer feel as if he or she had gotten the better end of the deal.

I remember my summers in Montreat with the Copelands. Mrs. Copeland prepared the meals for all of her guests—both in the Copeland summer home on North Carolina Terrace and at the William Black Home. During our summer vacations in Montreat, Dad would occasionally take us to the Copeland home for the evening meal. It was served family style, and we would stuff ourselves to the gills.

My brother worked for Nancy Copeland at the William Black home for two summers in college. He and our Orlando, Florida, buddy Wilson Greene did all the dishwashing and maintenance work. During those summers I worked as a bellhop at the Assembly Inn, and I would come over to the Black Home during my off hours.

The kitchen had two doors for the dinning area—one in, and one out. One night Nancy came up short on help and enlisted me. John and I had on the same red butler outfits, and wearing the same style of aprons, we looked like the same person. Simultaneously, as John would swing into the kitchen, I would come out into the dining area. You could hear a murmur in the dining room; it took a while for the patrons to catch on. One of the cooks was so thoroughly vexed that he started crying.

After I graduated from Davidson, I rarely returned to Montreat. When my family moved to Asheville, I took my wife and son over to see Nancy. Mrs. Copeland had died in her nineties, and Nancy was running the William Black Home. Mrs. Copeland was no longer there to oversee the operation, and the meal we had didn't compare to those of my youth.

Nancy later died from cancer, and I'm not sure who runs the Home today. I still go back to Montreat from time to time, but it's just not the same. It's still beautiful, but I no longer feel any real connection to the place. The town's status as a major conference center for the Presbyterian Church has diminished. Gone are the wonderful Copeland eateries that supported those conferences. Also gone are the people I knew who sat around those tables chattering aimlessly, all the while gorging themselves on Mrs. Copeland's country-style cooking.

Frank L. Jackson, Sr.

Frank Jackson, Sr., was the Davidson College treasurer and mayor of Davidson in my childhood. He lived in a house on Concord Road. Mr. Jackson had a reputation for being a miserly man; everyone called him "Cash." I suppose that's a prerequisite for both a treasurer and a mayor. Ralph Johnson's book paints a darker picture of him, one that is contested by his family.

The senior Jacksons had three children—Frank, Jr., Neena, and Susie. Growing up, I knew Frank, Jr., and Neena. Frank, Jr., ran a dry cleaning emporium on Depot Street. He later moved into the building across the street from Bub Cashion's Gulf. In my window-washing years Frank hired me to do his windows every month. He had a lot of window space, so it would take me two to three hours to complete the job. I was a monument to inefficiency. Usually I got thirty-five cents for the job, but on occasion Frank would feel sorry for me and give me a dollar. In the autumns John and I cleaned up the leaves for Frank Sr., and the pay was even worse.

Frank's sister Neena married Tom Northcott, and they lived on Thompson Street. Neena worked for years in the college registrar's office, where she always greeted students warmly and provided impeccable service. Tom taught us in Sunday school during my early grade years. He was a remarkable person. Tom was on Corregidor in the Philippines on December 7, 1941, and when the Japanese overran the islands, he became a POW. He somehow survived the death camps and the war. Tom was also a corpsman in the Korean conflict and participated in the Inchon landings, for which he received the Silver Star for heroism.

Tom was obviously a very strong person, and this came out in his *Bible* lessons. He was very kind and gentle and seemed to have a very genuine love of Christ—a strong faith that saw him through that terrible ordeal in the Philippines.

During my eighth grade year Bill Bondurant, Neena, and Tom organized an Easter excursion for our Sunday school class to Winston-Salem, where we were guests of the Moravian Church in Old Salem. To my knowledge, we were the first outside group to be allowed to stay overnight since the inception of the building in the eighteenth century. That night we attended the Love Feast and the orchestral-choral rendition of the "Seven Last Words of Christ." Afterwards, Bill led a contingent to a local drive-in theater to see *Your Cheating Heart*, but I stayed behind to ramble through the old Moravian village. That night the boys in the group slept in the men's room of the church, sacked out on the floor. With all the comings and goings, we got no sleep whatsoever. Regardless, I remember the Easter sunrise service as the most beautiful religious event I have ever attended.

Bub Cashion

Our beloved movie theater burned down in 1955. Two years later Mr. Archer built a Gulf service station on the site. I remember the opening festivities. Archer brought in a clown and a small merry-go-round and gave out treats to the kids. We didn't care for any of this in the least because it was apparent that no one was interested in rebuilding the movie house.

We called Archer's "The Slaughter House" because all the wrecked autos involved in highway fatalities in northern Mecklenburg County were brought here for public display. I remember one grisly lesson in human anatomy.

There was a blind intersection on U.S. 21, less than half a mile above the western boundary of our farm. One rainy night an inebriated driver coming over the hill passed a car and hit another head on; the drunk's speedometer was frozen on 120 miles per hour. His car was towed to Archer's and left for display. The inside was splattered with blood, and then and there, I vowed I would never be an apostle of speed.

We often played in the rear of Archer's station among the wrecked autos, which were cannibalized for used parts. The service station workers took a disliking to us and would repeatedly chase us off and complain to our parents. All of this was before Bub Cashion bought the station from Mr. Archer.

Bub's station became a center of social activity. We often gathered there to watch Bub and his assistant "Doodle" Wally work on cars. Bub let us do the windshield work and run the pumps. He was one of the most service-minded people I've ever met—a man who loved to work with customers and enjoyed it so much that it almost ran him out of business.

Bub let just about anybody run up a credit account. He once pulled a stack of bad credit bills from a drawer and showed them to me. Bub never chased after his unpaid bills; he just trusted that they would be paid over time.

In 1969 my brother-in-law, Bill Grizzard, in Roanoke Rapids fixed up an old 1963 Plymouth Valiant for me. It was my first car, and it cost all of $250. It had 77,220 miles on it when I left Roanoke Rapids; and when I sold it for scrap six years later, it had 77,227 miles on it. The odometer-speedometer cable broke seven miles outside Roanoke Rapids as I was driving it back to Davidson. I was destined to drive that car for six years without ever knowing my speed or mileage. I just winged it and went with the flow.

I took Nellybelle (I named my car after Roy Rogers' jeep) to Bub to see if he could repair the cable. He said that the repair job would cost almost as much as the car and advised me to let it lie. At Nellybelle's first yearly inspection, Bub told me that there was a gaping hole in the floorboard that I hadn't noticed. He fashioned a piece of steel to cover it and told me not to worry about it.

I had to bring the car back to Bub's station every year to get it inspected because his was one of the few service stations in the state that would pass me without charging rip-off prices. I owe him a lot. Outside of Nellybelle, I had no transportation. I estimate that Nelly went almost 70,000 miles during her tenure with me. We went all over the East Coast together. Sadly, her steering began to fail during my intern year at the Medical College of Virginia, and I had to sell her for fifty dollars for scrap. It was like losing a member of the family.

I heard that Bub was forced out of business. The state required that he install new fuel tanks, since the old ones from 1957 were breaking down and leaking. Bub apparently didn't have the resources or the desire to close down temporarily and comply with the new, very expensive regulations. He then had to close permanently.

I haven't seen Bub in recent years. His old station came down about the time the college moved the Blake House to clear land for a grocery store that has yet to materialize. It's a shame that we no longer see his kind of service for our cars. Bub Cashion's Gulf station was one of the last places where a driver got full service as a matter of routine.

Warren McKissick

Mr. Warren McKissick, an African American, was the town cobbler and shoe repairman on Main Street. He was a kind man and was the best leather worker I've ever met. He could do just about anything with leather.

Mr. McKissick kept us in shoes for most of my childhood and adolescent years. We wore leather heels and soles in those years. Over time they would wear down, and we would take them to the shoe shop, where he would put on new parts while we watched. His machinery entranced me. This man had full command of everything in the shop. He moved rapidly and efficiently and did his best to please every customer. And his prices were very reasonable.

We looked forward to taking our shoes to Mr. McKissick for repairs. He always shined them up for us after fixing them, and in this manner shoes could last for years—at least after our feet stopped growing. He kept us looking cool. It was fashionable to have steel taps nailed onto the heels of our shoes, which we used to slide down the slick hallways at Davidson Elementary. We loved the loud tapping sound they made. In our early adolescence John and I wore Bass Weejuns, purchased at Rush Wilson's mens' store. We spent a lot of time spit-shinning them to a high gloss, and Mr. McKissick supplied us amply with polish, brushes, and shine cloths.

During our baseball years Mr. McKissick helped us string our gloves and taught us how to oil the leather properly. I still have my old Rawlings glove from my Pony League days, and when I bring it out, I am always reminded of this special man who gave so much good service to all the folks in Davidson.

Piedmont Bank and Trust (PB&T)

Frank Capra's film *It's a Wonderful Life* depicts the small town of Bedford Falls and its memorable Bailey's Savings and Loan. Piedmont Bank and Trust was Davidson's only financial institution and in many ways it reminds me of Jimmy Stewart's bank in the movie.

As a child I knew that the large vault at the bank held a U.S. Savings Bond for $1,000, given to me by my paternal grandfather for my college education. I also knew that my life savings of six dollars were earning an interest rate of six percent. By grossly miscalculating the compounded interest, I figured that I would be a millionaire within a few years. I frequented the bank just to make certain my savings were intact. I always was a little uncomfortable whenever I saw the huge, antique vault open.

PB & T issued real bank checks (the only name was Piedmont's), which were honored by the merchants on Main Street; in fact, the merchants would provide the checks—I did a lot of business with Ralph Johnson that way.

The bank welcomed children and placed great emphasis on teaching us to save our money. In those years PB & T had stacks of blank checks freely available, and the tellers allowed us free access. John and I pretended the checks were real money and made a game of doing our own banking, taking our "hard earned" cash to Frances Justice's mother, one of the tellers, who allowed us to negotiate our checks at the counter. Of course, we got nothing back for this.

The bank was open 9 to 5 weekdays. In those years there were no ATM's to withdraw money for the nights or weekends. There really was no nightlife in Davidson anyway. People did all of their financial business during the week and took out only as much as they absolutely needed for an occasional weekend outing. There were no such things as credit cards. Without ATM's and credit cards, folks generally were financially responsible—a rapidly disappearing trait in today's society. All business was done either by check or cash.

I remember that overdraws were handled differently in those days by PB&T. Usually the offender received a phone call, and unless an inordinate sum was involved, the matter was quietly dropped. This happened to me when I was in college; I received a call with a reminder that overdrawing was technically illegal. At all events, the bank didn't charge me anything.

One can still find friendly and attentive service in the small branches of the mega banks of today. Indeed, the ones I have frequented over the years remind me in some ways of PB&T. Unfortunately, behind the shade of the small branches looms the consolidated behemoth, and that definitely has changed the approach to service. A few years ago I was made acutely aware of this.

The problem surfaced shortly after Aunt Louise died in 1997. My siblings and I were her only survivors. She had always been like a second mother to us. She was a meticulous planner and years before had entrusted her will to the trust office at PB&T. She named the bank as her executor, and the trust officer assured her that the bank would honor her will.

By the time of Louise's death, First Union Bank had long since swallowed up tiny PB&T. I didn't believe that would change any arrangements that had been made many years before. When John, Ginger, and I went to the bank to begin settling her estate, we were confident there would be no problems. We went directly to the bank trust office and were served by a pleasant young woman who said she lived in Charlotte. When we told her about the bank's arrangement with Louise, she said she would have to call the main bank in Charlotte for approval. I assumed that this was just a formality. After forty-five minutes, however, she returned and announced, "First Union will not approve this. We don't handle estates this small." She insisted that this was bank policy. Furthermore, she had no idea where the will might be. We then began to seek out an attorney to handle the estate and track down the will.

Needing advice about an attorney, we dropped in on Russell Knox at Knox Reality and told him about our dilemma. Russell had for a number of years managed our farm on Bailey Road. He directed us to John R. Cunningham, grandson of the late Dr. John R. Cunningham, who had done so much for Davidson College in the 1940's and 1950's. John is a Davidson graduate and former valedictorian; he also graduated from Yale University School of Law.

To my mind John is what a good lawyer should be. Specializing in estate law, he maintains a small office that faces the intersection of Concord and Main. His office is mostly empty space—John does all of his own work by computer. He is a monument to efficiency and has a paralegal in Charlotte who does a lot of his legal legwork—which has cut his overhead to a minimum. We were very impressed.

John took the case. He went to the bank to open Louise's vault box, but there was no will. The bank did cough up some evidence that there was once a will on record there, but it had left the premises in the buyout by First Union. John reminded the bank's officers of their fiduciary obligations and asked them to locate the will. Sometime later it emerged in a First Union Bank in Concord, eighteen miles distant. After that, John closed the estate in a thoroughly professional and efficient manner. Having him handle this matter was one of the best decisions we ever made.

I miss the old PB&T with its Bailey's Savings and Loan approach. The new Mr. Potters of huge conglomerate banking have taken something beautiful from the system. Ed Crutchfield, at the time CEO of First Union, is a graduate of Davidson College. I thought about writing him a letter of protest, but I decided it would probably never reach his desk.

A. D. Cantrell, Sr.

Mr. Alvin Douglas Cantrell and his family lived on School Street right across the street from the McEver home. A.D. and his wife, Eileen, owned and operated the Western Auto store and Western Union on Main Street. Their son, Doug, was my contemporary.

John and I were frequent visitors at the Western Auto. The Cantrells sold all types of utility and sports equipment. Dad bought our first baseball gloves and our favorite Louisville Slugger bat, "Old Faithful," from Mr. Cantrell. A.D. and Eileen sold football uniforms and helmets, two sets of which Dad purchased for us for Christmas in

1954. I had a Charlie "Choo Choo" Justice jersey, honoring a great football player at the University of North Carolina.

The Cantrell Western Auto was the only hobby store in town. It had all types of car, ship and airplane models. As soon as we had enough money, we would go there to buy a new model. The glue smelled good. One of my classmates at Davidson Elementary came up with the idea of putting an opened glue tube in a bag and sniffing it. Fortunately, the rest of us thought that was a bad idea, so glue sniffing never really caught on with my peer group.

I remember one Christmas Eve at a remote time in my childhood when the Cantrells had their store open late. Theirs was the only toy store in town. That night a small crowd had assembled in and about the store. Dad told me that the Cantrells were donating toys to poor people in the town.

Doug Cantrell and I went through all twelve years of school together. We played baseball together in Little League and Pony League. When Mr. Cantrell died suddenly of a heart attack in the early 1960's, it was a terrible blow. After that Mrs. Cantrell continued to run the Western Auto and the Western Union service. John and I continued to visit the store frequently, but it was never quite the same without A.D.

Doug went on to become a career Army officer. I learned that he was in Germany during my two year Army posting time there. I tried to reach him several times but, given Army efficiency in Europe at that time, had no luck.

Miss Fannie's Five and Dime

The Southern Five and Dime Store stood at the corner of Main and Depot streets. "Miss Fannie" McConnell and her sister Lula ran the store. Miss Fannie was a slightly corpulent, short woman who appeared to be in her early sixties. She was a shrewd trader who qualified as an organized Pop Copeland. She had an abundance of goods, all of which were clearly marked and easily located.

We spent a lot of time in the store looking around and spending our measly savings. The most coveted articles were play money, baseball cards, and, on one occasion, a special chemistry set called the

"Fannie Special," which consisted of nothing more than a small test tube filled with baking soda, to which was attached a small vial of vinegar. We mixed the two and waited for the universe to explode. This upset our mother, who believed Miss Fannie had gypped us.

In the 1950's much of what Miss Fannie sold was made in Japan. "Made in Japan" signified the incredibly cheap goods that were typical of the post World War II economic restructuring of Japan. At one point "Made in USA" began appearing on cheap goods. My father was quick to point out that they were made in Usa, Japan, and not in the U.S.A.

Our parting with Fannie McConnell came one Christmas in the mid-1950's, when Mom gave John and me thirty-five cents to buy Dad a Christmas present. We told Miss Fannie we were shopping for a present. She learned what we had to spend and made some helpful suggestions. However, a large "Classics Illustrated" comic book caught our eye. It sold for exactly thirty-five cents. We forgot all about our Christmas mission and purchased the comic. Mom had a fit. She blamed Miss Fannie, and even though we were the responsible party, she declared the store off limits for us.

After several years we started going back to the Five and Dime. By 1959 we were purchasing baseball cards there on a regular basis. A short time later a fire damaged the building, forcing Miss Fannie out of business. Ralph Johnson later purchased the Thompson Building and completely overhauled it for his new barbershop. In my memory it is the place where I was shorn of both money and locks.

Those Staid Couriers of the Mail

The Davidson post office (the PO) of my early years, 1947-1957, was in a two-storied brown brick building that stood on Depot Street. The actual PO was on the first floor. Business was transacted out of a small caged window that was located on the left side of the rear wall of the facility. The right side of that wall was entirely filled with individual mailboxes. The facility had a large supporting pole in the middle of the floor, and when we came to the PO, we always flung ourselves around it before trying to figure out mailbox combinations.

Of course we had no success. The Pucketts' was box 386, and in time I did learn to open it.

In 1958 the U.S. Government opened a new post office on the corner opposite the Thompson Building, next door to the old Helper Inn. We were all proud that President Eisenhower himself had authorized the construction of the building. Many of us remembered his hand-waving pass-through on the train in 1952 (see Chapter 16 for details).

The new PO became a social hub of Davidson. When either or both of our parents announced that they were going to the PO, we knew they would be gone awhile. Folks just naturally congregated there, and there was something awry if they didn't get there even for a few minutes each day.

In the early 1960's I became a regular visitor at the PO. The purpose behind my frequent visits related to my infatuation with Georgeanna Mayhew, the daughter of the postmaster, Bill Mayhew. I thought that getting in on his good graces would somehow bring me to his daughter's attention, but it did no good at all. The Mayhews did take me bowling once—I suppose out of sympathy.

A torrent of criticism has been levied at the postal system in recent years. The Seinfeldian character Newman has not helped that image at all. During my years as town resident and student, the service was impeccable. The PO was open six days a week, and the service was friendly and courteous. The only malfunction during my entire experience with the Davidson postal service occurred during my college years.

My freshman roommate at Davidson College was Harry Truman Goldman, III, from Waterproof, Louisiana. Harry and his family invited me down for Christmas vacation in Waterproof in 1966. That's where I met his first cousin, Kathy Goldman, and we struck up an instant friendship. I told her that I would write, and she promised to write me back. As no response to my letter arrived in the mail, I decided that Kathy had no real interest in me. Her letter arrived at my box 1588 three years later.

The government built yet another new PO for the town in the 1980's. It is a beautiful building, located behind the Main Street row and fronted by a garden on the lot where Miss Hattie Thompson's house once stood. The building merges well with the brick decor of the town.

Mail delivery in Davidson is not what it used to be. I recently mailed a letter to John Cunningham and addressed it to his Main Street office. The letter was returned with a stamped message disavowing any such person or address. That seemed ridiculous since practically everyone in town knows John. The same thing happened to a letter I wrote to Mrs. Nancy Smith. I learned later that the post office accepts only box numbers and not street addresses. There was a time in the not so distant past when a letter addressed "Aunt Minnie 28036" would have found its way to the right box.

Miss Louise Sloan

"Miss Louise," as we called her, didn't own a business in town, but she was such a part of the Main Street scene that I include a sketch of her in this section.

Herb Russell told us that Miss Louise kept her millions boarded up in the walls of her house on South Main Street. Whether she was a millionaire or not, Miss Louise was clearly an eccentric woman. We saw her as a composite of Silas Marner, the bird lady in Disney's *Mary Poppins*, and the Mad Woman of Chaillot. Not a few in the town regarded her as the Mad Woman of Davidson.

On any given Saturday morning during my window-washing years Miss Louise, Skeegum, and I formed a motley trio. I worked the windows, old Skeegum followed close behind, tapping into my wages, and Miss Louise followed not far behind him, rummaging through trashcans both on the street and behind the businesses.

Some folks said she was looking for discarded valuables. Others thought she was looking for old newspapers; she was, after all, an educated woman. I believe she was looking for something deeper.

My father once told me that Louise Sloan was a graduate of Trinity College in Durham in the years before it became the nucleus of Duke University. She obviously loved newspapers—she became a fixture at the college library's periodical room. Dr. Chalmers Davidson, the librarian, knew she was harmless and gave her free run of the facility.

Miss Louise died years ago. The old house on South Main is today a legal office located beside the town hall. I never learned if she had any money hidden in those walls.

Louise Sloan still walks the Main Street of my memory—always in a black suit and matching hat, always carrying a large black bag, and always rummaging through trashcans. No one ever knew for certain exactly what she was looking for. My own opinion is that she was an astute observer of the human condition and believed that there was more to learn about a civilization from what it discarded than from what it created.

Inquiring Minds

There were two newspapers in Davidson. *The Davidsonian* was the weekly college-sponsored paper dealing with campus life. The rest of us read *The Mecklenburg Gazette.* There really wasn't enough news or gossip in Davidson to warrant a paper, but with news and literary contributions from the other communities in the northern part of the county, the paper prospered.

The *Gazette* was special to the young people of the area. It gave deserving children a chance for recognition in print. The smallest achievement could be elevated to the status of a Nobel Prize contender. All of our ball games and school activities, along with our names, found their way into the newspaper.

In those years a Charlotte newspaper ran a detailed Sunday society column. It dealt primarily with the well-to-do's who lived in the fashionable Myers Park district of Charlotte. During the summer months the paper described in detail the travel plans of the rich and famous. For example, a column might begin with, "Dr. and Mrs. John Simpson of 25 Posh Place are planning an extended two-month tour of the Continent accompanied by their children and their spouses." The announcement would be followed by a detailed itinerary of the trip. Those of us of more meager economic means weren't the only ones who read the society page. The "Home Alone" crooks also had their eyes on it. In those summer vacation months Charlotte crime, particularly in Myers Park, soared. Over time fewer and fewer people disclosed their travel plans, and the society page merged into the wedding section and later disappeared all together.

This was not the case in northern Mecklenburg County. Each small community had its designated contributor to the *Gazette*. This, in effect, gave each town or village its own gossip page.

Dr. Woods' wife, Elizabeth, wrote about the news in Davidson. Her writing was about as down-home Southern as it could get. It was more than a few rungs down from William Faulkner and Tennessee Williams but was thoroughly entertaining and often enlightening. Elizabeth wrote about birthdays, parties, weddings, travels, and occasional gossip tidbits. An Elizabethan line might read, "Rumor has it that Mary's [last name] parents soon will announce her engagement to John [last name]." Most of the time she got it right, but when Elizabeth missed, there was hell to pay.

I always enjoyed reading Elizabeth's weekly commentaries. She had an easy and appealing style of occasionally non-grammatical writing. She always ended her column with her signature statement, "And a good time was had by all." Elizabeth was one reason the old *Gazette* was a very special newspaper.

When Dad died in 1972, the *Gazette* ran a lengthy front-page article on his life and achievements. It described him as "a legend in his own time in northern Mecklenburg County." It said of Dad, "Gladly would he learn…and gladly teach." There were some beautiful things written in that article about Dad that I had never known. I will always be grateful to the *Gazette* for its expression of kindness in publishing that tribute to my father's life. The only thing I might add would be, "And a good time was had by all."

The

Reverends

The Southern Presbyterian Church supported Davidson College. The center of college life up through the 1960's was the Davidson College Presbyterian Church, located at the corner of Main Street and Concord Road. The current building was completed in 1952, at a cost of $1.7 million. During my childhood and youth in Davidson, several pastors served the church.

John R. Cunningham

The first minister with whom I had an association was not the college minister or chaplain. He was Dr. John R. Cunningham, and he came to Davidson in 1941. Much of what Davidson College is today has roots in his presidency.

Dr. Cunningham did not believe that the then existing College Presbyterian Church fully served the needs of either town or gown. The old building had been constructed facing away from the campus. Dr. Cunningham launched a building fund and razed the old structure. The steel frame took shape, and from it a grand new church rose. The building was completed in 1952, and I remember Oscar Thies' "chimes" ringing for the first time from the steeple at 6 p.m. that spring evening. The student body dubbed the church "The Cathedral of Slick John the Divine," and it became a showcase for the college and remains as such at the opening of the twenty-first century.

My fondest memory of the Cunninghams dates to 1954. Dr. Cunningham was away raising money for the college and was flying into the newly-opened Douglas Municipal Airport in Charlotte. Mrs. Cunningham asked John and me to go with her to meet him. We piled into her Cadillac and headed to Charlotte. Dr. Cunningham flew in on a propeller-powered plane, which taxied close to the only gate there. That was the first airplane I had ever seen up close, and I remember how sleek and shiny it was. Dr. Cunningham seemed an imposing figure coming off the plane.

The Cunninghams lived in the President's Mansion on campus. Dr. Cunningham raised chickens in the backyard. When we played with Jack McGeachy next door, we would often go over to the Cunninghams' yard and chase their hapless rooster. I suspect this annoyed the owners to no end. That tortured rooster would have his revenge in time.

A magician, named Birch the Magnificent, was performing at the college in 1957. He was quite good. He did magic the old fashioned way, and it became very personal to me one November evening during my third grade year. Birch was performing in Love Auditorium in Chambers Building, and he picked me out of all the kids on the front row that night. I went onstage wearing the slickest garb I owned, a gray windbreaker with black bands on the sleeves. Birch asked me a few questions, and I giggled through most of them. Next, he pulled a string of popcorn out of the back of my jacket. Then I felt a terrible rustling emanating from the same place. Finally, I heard a screech accompanied by a dreadful, scratching sensation on the back of my neck. Dr. John R. Cunningham's horrid rooster emerged. I was thoroughly perplexed. Fowl revenge! The audience was cheering wildy. In hindsight, it was one of the finest magic tricks I've ever witnessed. How in the world did Birch ever manage that? There was no indication of any avian presence until the last moment. I'm certain that the Cunninghams were pleased. I was featured in a spread in *The Char-*

lotte Observer the following day entitled, "Davidson Child Steals Show."

My first pastor at Davidson College Presbyterian Church came to Davidson during Dr. Cunningham's tenure as president. This was Dr. Carl Pritchett, and he became the first minister to preach in the newly dedicated DCPC in 1952. He had four lovely daughters—Dorothy, Betty, Mary Anna, and Peggy Jane. They were all older than John and I, but my sister's friendship with Betty opened up their living room to us. The Pritchetts had one of the few television sets in Davidson. After watching *Boston Blackie* and *Howdy Doody* next door at Mrs. Agnes Brown's house, we would run over to the Pritchetts' house for the start of the *Early Show*, usually some B rerun film. It was never long before Mom blew her whistle to get us home to dinner.

Dr. Pritchett left Davidson to accept the pastorate of a church in Bethesda, Maryland. We visited the Pritchetts there in 1955 during a trip through Virginia. When I worked in Washington in the summer of 1971, I visited Carl's church and heard him preach. Later, after he retired, he and Mrs. Pritchett moved back to Davidson to live at The Pines, a retirement home. I saw Dr. Pritchett occasionally until his death.

With strong Presbyterian foundations, an ongoing religious heritage, and a foremost preministerial program, needless to say, one often felt the reverend influence well beyond the church doors. For instance, one of my first playmates was Barbara Wilson, daughter of Professor Iain Wilson, who taught in the religion department at the college. Dr. Wilson was a rough and tumble sort who had managed to survive Omaha Beach on D-Day in 1944. Barbara was a lovely companion, and we often went to the movies together. I remember seeing *The Greatest Show on Earth* with her in 1955. She had an older brother named Colin, who assumed the leadership role among the kids in the neighborhood. Colin enticed us to play "chicken" out in Concord Road. That behavior lasted all of one afternoon and ended with a swatting from Mom.

Barbara was always very kind to me, and I remember her fondly for that. One afternoon Pattie Newell popped me on the head with a curtain rod. I ran home crying and dived under the covers of my bed.

A few minutes later Barbara was at the front door asking about me. Mom took her to me, and Barbara rubbed my head and swore revenge on Pattie. I remember Barbara's comfort as one of the most compassionate things anyone ever did for me.

Barbara's family moved to Baltimore after her second grade year. We later sadly learned that Colin, aged twelve, had been killed in a sledding accident after running into a concealed pipe. I saw Barbara again once during my seventh grade year; she was as beautiful as I had remembered her. Sadly, I haven't seen her since.

Dr. Wilson was one of many fine professors Dr. Cunningham brought to Davidson. My father was one of those professors. During Dr. Cunningham's tenure at Davidson both faculty and college underwent a major transformation. Dr. Cunningham knew how to raise money and went at it with a vengeance. I suppose he did more for Davidson College than anyone since Maxwell Chambers.

Samuel W. Newell

After the Pitchetts left for Bethesda, Dr. Cunningham was a guiding light in the call to Dr. Samuel W. Newell, a Davidson graduate (Dr. Samuel Spencer's college roommate) and minister in Mullins, South Carolina, to assume the pastorate of DCPC. He and his wife, Martha, had three lovely daughters, Pattie, Scottie, and Meg. John and I practically moved into the Manse with the Newells in 1953. Pattie and Scottie became two of our best friends.

I had the habit of climbing up the piping in the hall opposite the Manse's kitchen. One morning—I was six at the time—I found myself hopelessly wedged between pipe and wall, stuck and going nowhere. Mrs. Newell was frantic; she couldn't get me untangled. Actually by that time I wasn't trying very hard to help her. Somewhere up there twixt wall, ceiling, and pipe I stumbled onto my manhood—my first moment of sexual awareness. No power on earth, not even Martha Newell herself, could have extracted me from that pipe at that moment—I was transfixed by the luminous vision of her giggling daughter, Pattie.

I adored Pattie, who was one of the prettiest young girls in town. Her mother was quite a looker too, having appeared years before in

Look magazine as one of the loveliest college women in Georgia. Pattie was bright and always came up with imaginative games for us to play including the previously described ill fated plot to poison Shaw Smith.

Pattie grew into honorable pre-womanhood, and she grew quickly. By the sixth grade, she was fully pubescent, at a time when my own adolescence was barely discernable—perhaps a stubble or two. Lord knows I had sexual desire, but I had absolutely no idea about how or when to use any of it. I yearned for Pattie's lips but knew they would never be mine.

In the late 1950's and early 1960's we attended dances out at Erwin Lodge, a two storied stone structure located in the deep woods at the eastern boundary of the college property. Professor Edward J. Erwin had built the lodge as a memorial to his two sons who had died in combat in World War II, within six weeks of one another. Their pictures hung on a wall on the main floor of the lodge.

The lodge was a perfect place for teen socials. Add a record player spinning out Elvis, Johnny Mathis, and the Shirelles; throw in a few liberal chaperones; and we were set for a three-hour blast. I confess, it usually wasn't a blast for me. I could dance *very* slowly, but that was about all. I had never kissed a girl and had absolutely no way of knowing where to begin. The way it began for most of my peers was via "Spin the Bottle."

The chaperones at one of these soirées decided it was high time for the kids to learn the physical side of puberty. Out came the bottle, and to my horror they were actually doing it (kissing)! I couldn't get into it, using the lame excuse, "I'll only kiss the girl I marry." The truth was, I was scared silly by my own inadequacy. Pattie participated and broke my heart. That was all before our backyard cookout.

In the early 1960's the hottest things going were the Twist, white deck-pants (cut off just below the knees), white socks, and boys' grease-ball hairdos. Mom lined up a cookout for the neighborhood kids. Kristi Scott, Pattie, Jane Withers, and some of the guys on the block were invited. We were in the prime of cool—white socks and white cutoffs. Our pimpled faces were splashed with English Leather, and our heads bore the requisite flattops, replete with the stiffness applied from a jar of Butch Hair Wax, a standard aphrodisiac of that era. We were ripe, and we were hot. For the first time my confidence was brimming.

I don't know how it all got started, but we found ourselves immersed in the bottle game. Looking back on that, I believe that those girls actually felt an obligation to instruct us sexually. We certainly weren't attractive, looking like something ready for immersion in a frying pan. Dare I say it was an act of love (agape, not Eros)? Regardless, the bottle landed on me, and Pattie was in the batter's circle. She planted a whopper on my kisser. It was a short, hard, and desiccated affair. The track to romance that lay before me would be rutted and rocky, but at least I was out of the starting gate. Thus began my odyssey into sexuality—one that would always be modulated by the exigencies of my moral upbringing in the Southern Presbyterian Church.

In the seventh grade, disaster stuck: Dr. Newell accepted the pastorate of the River Road Presbyterian Church in Richmond, Virginia. Pattie would leave Davidson in the summer of 1961, just before our eighth grade year. I was crushed because she was among my dearest childhood friends. I don't think John and I ever completely got over it.

Over the years we would frequent the Newell house in Montreat during our summer vacations there. I last saw Pattie when I was an intern at the Medical College of Virginia. She had married a doctor in Richmond. We reminisced about the old days in Davidson. She joked about the time she and Mrs. Newell had to help pry me loose when I somehow got wedged between a pipe and the wall in the Newell's kitchen—and scared the daylights out of Mrs. Newell.

Will Terry

Curtis Harper, a Davidson graduate and a grand person, was briefly our pastor after the departure of Dr. Newell. I think he was perhaps the most personable minister I ever had. He left after several years to take the pastorate of a church in Raleigh. I have since seen him on occasion at Davidson affairs and am always delighted to see him. He was a marvelous pastor.

After Mr. Harper left, Will Terry, the college chaplain and a man of Irish demeanor, became the pastor of DCPC. I remember my trip to the beach with Will and my Sunday school class in 1964, when the church rented a cottage for a weekend at Myrtle Beach. Some of the parents and Will came along as chaperones. We set up a volleyball net on the beach and got into a vigorous game. Going for a ball, Will stumbled and stumped his right big toe, mangling it badly. It certainly looked broken, and we took him to a local emergency room where it was officially declared broken. He obviously couldn't use the foot. Then came the problem of what to do with his car—Will couldn't drive in his condition. None of us had ever driven a car any distance. Will paid me one of the finest compliments I have ever received by choosing me to be the designated driver. He agreed to sit in the front seat and supervise. I had a license but was very inexperienced. At all events, I drove the 250 miles back to Davidson without any problems. My self-esteem grew exponentially that day.

Will would later leave the pulpit and become dean of students at Davidson College and be enormously popular, especially with the Davidson Class of 1970. Esteemed as a friend and trusted counselor, he had a devoted following among my classmates and all the classes that followed. In time a scholarship would be established in his name at Davidson College.

Tom Clark

Although he never anchored the pulpit at DCPC, Dr. Thomas Clark stands tall in my memory among the ministerial elite at Davidson College. He taught our Sunday school class during my sixth grade year 1959-1960. He was a riot.

I remember particularly the church pageant we performed on the *Book of Ruth*. Dr. Clark came up with the idea for the production in the spring of 1960. We dressed in biblical fashions and performed scenes from the book as Dr. Clark recorded them on film for slides to later be shown to the church congregation. Sidney Small won the coveted role of Ruth. She was the closest thing we had to a Moabitess—she was Jewish (her family attended DCPC for lack of a local synagogue) and was the one of the sexiest girls in town.

For a short period I forgot my infatuation with Pattie Newell and had eyes only for Sidney. To me it was obvious that I was the dead-on choice for the role of Boaz—I had it in the bag. After all, I had been brownnosing Dr. Clark the week preceding the tryouts. I was stunned to see the role go to Bruce Parker. I was dying to get close to Sidney, and I pestered Dr. Clark for a good role—I told him I would even play the threshing floor just to get close to the action.

The show went off well. I vividly remember the slides. It actually was fairly good for an amateur production; at least the congregation gave us a lot of praise. Somewhere, perhaps buried deep in the church archives, is a folder containing some photographic slides from some long ago youth production. Among them is a picture of a young girl in biblical dress standing in what appears to be a field. There is behind her, wearing a huge grin, a boy dressed in garb that faintly resembles a sheaf of wheat.

When I was in the ninth grade, Dr. Clark helped with the Pioneer Department at the church. Newt Burns, a college student and Pattie Newell's cousin, assisted him. By that time Dr. Clark had starting driving a red Ford Thunderbird, and from then on we called him "T-bird Tommy."

Dr. Clark and Newt sponsored a weekend retreat at the Newell's cottage in Montreat. We drove up into the mountains one warm spring Saturday in 1963. I remember the song "Mother-in-Law" had just come out and was blaring over the radio; the stations all along I-40 kept replaying it. The highlight of the weekend, however, was Janet Godfrey and her short-shorts.

William Murphy spent the next two days drooling over Janet. There was plenty to drool over. She was magnificent! In fact, all of the boys were chasing her that weekend. On the way back to Davidson Janet was wedged into the back of Dr. Clark's Thunderbird convertible between Murph and me. She had on those wonderful shorts. Murph couldn't get enough of it. This only served to force her over onto my lap. I got a lap full for almost 100 miles! I just sat there, enjoying every moment of it.

Dr. Clark was my Religion 101 (*Old Testament*) professor at Davidson College. He was the most thoroughly entertaining teacher I ever had. We used Bernhard Anderson's *Understanding the Old Testament*. Thirty-two years later I completed teaching a five-year course on the *Old Testament* for my Asheville Sunday school class, based in large part on what I learned from Dr. Clark and his use of Anderson's material.

Dr. Clark was a talented sculptor as well as a professor. I remember watching him working on a bust under the west grandstand at the football stadium. I jokingly told him he ought to go into the sculpturing business. He did just that.

A member of my class at Davidson, Joe Poteet, later went into business with him, making the hand-sculpted Gnomes for which Tom Clark has gained worldwide fame. I hated to see him leave academics for the world of commercial enterprise—he was such a splendid teacher. Dad said that T-bird Tommy didn't need the money because he was independently wealthy long before the Gnomes. I also heard that he always gave back his salary to the college. Creating Gnomes and other lovable characters became his passion. I cherish my memories of his classes and count myself blessed to have had him as a mentor and friend.

Freaking Jesus (FJ)

FJ was a student at Davidson College in the early 1960's. I don't remember his real name, but his nickname has endured. At the beginning of his Davidson career FJ seemed normal enough, but things soon took a sinister turn.

FJ enrolled in one of the religion department's *New Testament* classes. One morning the professor was discussing one of the miracles of Jesus when FJ raised his hand and told the professor that the story wasn't like that at all. The professor asked him to explain himself and cite his authority. FJ replied, "I was there." From that day on everyone called him "Freaking Jesus."

In his senior year FJ announced that he wanted to produce a movie as a class gift to the college. He had absolutely no background in filmmaking other than home movies. At all events, he began to make plans for his cinematic extravaganza. FJ decided to locate the film along the shoreline of Lake Norman where Davidson has a plot of land known as the Davidson College Lake Campus. Students had named the beach area "Sun-No-Vah Beach," claiming preposterously that the name belonged to a long dead Catawba Indian chief. Out in the lake near the beach is a scraggly runt of a rise everyone called Goat Island. We often swam out to the small island to get away from the crowds on the beach. I cannot to this day imagine that it had any use for anything other than a wacky movie.

FJ called his masterpiece *The Battle of Goat Island.* He enlisted several hundred students and townies to be his extras. He directed all aspects of the film—costuming, grip work, lighting, and filming with his 8-millimeter motion picture camera. FJ had originally wanted to make a film on the life of Christ. Having recently studied the movie epic, *King of Kings,* which he considered an unimaginative, literal interpretation of Gospel events, he decided on a more adventurous approach: he chose the theme of Jesus at Armageddon.

The filming took place one Saturday afternoon in the spring. It was a crystal clear day, and the water was warm and calm. FJ had carefully arranged the costuming. He planned to portray the final battle between the Forces of Light and the Forces of Darkness. Little eight-year-old Conrad Snyder, decked out in a Keystone Cops outfit, commanded the Forces of Light. A student now lost to memory, arrayed in Chinese black pajamas, was the Anti-Christ.

FJ had "borrowed" approximately ten gallons of catsup from the college union dining hall. He assembled his entourage on the narrow beach of Goat Island and with megaphone in hand delivered instructions. When he had everyone in position, he yelled, "Lights, camera, action!" And thus began *The Battle of Goat Island.*

Students were clothed in costumes ranging from Vietnamese Peasant to Knight in Shining Armor. The standard issue weapon was a large bow that shot a plumber's friend. The battle raged for approximately fifteen minutes. When it was over, the lake near Goat Island was awash in catsup, and hundreds of bodies floated on the water. In the finale, from the far reaches of Goat Island, Freaking Jesus, arms lifted to Heaven, walked out upon the water. Actually, he sank, mortal that he was. At that point a great resurrection occurred as the floating bodies rose out of the water and followed him over the crest of the island. All the while a loudspeaker from shore belted out the "Hallelujah Chorus."

I attended one of the early showings of *The Battle of Goat Island*, which was held on the terrace of the college union. This film wasn't released; it escaped. It was the funniest short movie I've ever seen and was the stuff of Oscar, but no awards were forthcoming—someone apparently later absconded with the film and negative.

I doubt that many of us who participated in or watched the filming of *Goat Island* will ever forget one of those rare moments of truly comedic genius emanating from the mind of one of the most unique characters I've ever known. I wish you well, Freaking Jesus, wherever you are.

Miss Mary Black

She resembled a stern and stocky nineteenth century schoolteacher with her hair in a bun, stood no taller than five feet, wore thick black glasses, and pulled hair to discipline her young charges. We called her "Miss Mary," and she was my first Sunday school teacher.

John and I graduated from the DCPC nursery into Miss Mary's class when we were four years old. We were obstreperous, and on that first Sunday our new teacher leveled our crew cuts by several millimeters. That smarted and left a lasting impression.

Mary told us *Bible* stories, and I first learned the great *Old Testament* sagas and the stories of Jesus from her. She lived across the street from the college on Concord Road, and every time she saw us walking by, she reminded us to be on time for her class that coming Sunday.

Mary wanted all of us to begin to learn verses from the *Bible*. For every acceptable recitation, she placed a silver star by the scholar's name on the class bulletin board roster. A gold star was awarded for winning ten silvers. I had no interest whatsoever in trying to memorize scripture. This four year old earned only two silver stars. Mary gave me grudging credit for "In the beginning God created the heavens and the earth" and "Jesus wept."

On occasion Miss Mary took her charges to "Big Church." This was very exciting and made us feel like grownups. She paraded us into the main sanctuary for the 11 a.m. service and seated us on the front row, on the left side facing the pulpit. Fearing for our scalps, we were as silent as death. After the opening liturgies and before the sermon, she led us back to our classroom for playtime.

I have taken several Sabbaticals from religion since leaving Miss Mary's class, but I did rise to the occasion during my college years under Drs. Clark, Polley, and Arthur Buttrick. Those good professors rekindled my interest in biblical study. I have regularly attended church with my wife since my medical school years, but it has only been in the past ten years that I have intensely restudied and taught the Good Book.

Miss Mary helped lay the foundation blocks of my faith. It has taken almost fifty years for me to awaken to that fact. She was the first to introduce me to those wonderful *Bible* stories, to which I have added my own understanding of biblical history, archeology, and literary criticism.

The *Book of Exodus* says that Moses' face shone with the radiance of the glory of God when he descended the mountain. Miss Mary pushed me off my own Sinai with my hair standing on end all the way down.

Be
Prepared

My mother was one of the founding matrons of the Cub Scout movement in Davidson. Mom and Joy McEver were the den mothers for the pack. We met every Thursday afternoon during the school years 1957-1959—I at the McEvers and Brother John at our house. I believe I got the better end of the deal. The McEvers had this wonderful Lionel train pike laid out in the attic, and we spent hours up there running the rails. When we tired of that, we moved outside to the huge sandbox filled with the McEvers' hundreds of toy soldiers. We would set up command posts and strong perimeters and then stage elaborate war games. To add to the realism we put up trees (in abundance from the train sets) and added rivers by flooding areas of the box. This went on for hours until it was judged that one of the command post positions was untenable, at which point victory or armistice was declared. I learned almost as much about military tactics there as I would in the Army.

I still have some of the projects we worked on in those years. There is an old picture glued to the base of an ashtray, which was a Mother's Day project in 1958. It includes several members of our pack. I'm pictured with Nyko Trakas, Bruce Parker, Jim McEver,

Ted Thompson, twin John, and Craven Stowe. Of our group I remember especially Nyko and Jim.

Nyko's father, Pedro, taught Spanish at the college. The Trakas family lived in a two-storied white brick house on Concord Road next to the small house where I spent the first two years of my life before the Pucketts moved into the Blake House on Main Street. The Trakases were a lovely family. Nyko was very athletic and artistic. I remember the wonderful murals he and Jim McEver put together at the back of Mrs. Barnhardt's classroom during our second grade year at Davidson Elementary. Nyko painted the solar system, and Jim painted the three Wise Men at Bethlehem. I was envious of their artistic abilities.

I spent many afternoons at the Trakas home. We were understandably disappointed when Dr. Takas accepted a position on the faculty at Florida Presbyterian, the college that Frank Lloyd Wright designed. They moved to St. Petersburg. A year or two later we learned that Nyko had accidentally walked out in front of a car going fifty miles an hour. It was a miracle that he lived. I haven't seen or heard from him since, but I think of him often.

The other member of that den who stands out so vividly in my memory is Jim McEver. He was one of the most talented and well-rounded boys I knew in my childhood. He was bigger than any of the other boys in our gang. Jim could be in a moment my best playmate or my worst bully. He was artistic and articulate, and he had a consuming interest in science, which was contagious.

In the third grade Jim found an ancient chemistry text in the elementary school library. Jim had the book perpetually checked out. From that text we learned the rudiments of chemistry and some of the field's most notable personages. Jim got into the college library and pulled out some books on Albert Einstein's theory of relativity, and he would lecture us in the afternoons on light as a particle-wave and the relativity of time. We always looked to him as the strongest and brightest of our contemporaries.

During that school year of 1957-1958 Jim found some discarded chemical equipment, including an old Bunsen burner, outside the chemistry labs at the college. That piqued my envy. Pleased at my newly acquired scientific interest and knowledge, my father gave me access to the basement supply room in the Martin Science Building. The man who managed the stockroom let me have all of the broken, but still useable, discarded chemical glassware. I filled up a large box and proudly paraded home.

Morris Griffin, my across-the-street neighbor on the Lorimer Road side of our new house, several years my senior, saw me with my newly acquired treasures. He checked out the material and then offered to teach me some real chemistry. On that nearly fatal afternoon Morris, John, Jim, and I gathered in our tiny upstairs bedroom to learn some heavy chemistry. We hooked up a glass distillery to distill water. We whipped up some muddy water with large chunks of dirt gathered from the backyard and then set it boiling on Morris' portable stove. We over boiled it, I think, and a clot of dirt formed in the tubing. The pressure built up, and the flask exploded its muddy contents onto the plaster ceiling. Mom was furious. Jim and Morris bolted out of the house. When I revisited the house in 1989, the brown spot was still faintly visible on the ceiling after more than thirty years.

Jim McEver was not only a chemistry expert. He was an expert in all matters worldly and biological. He taught John and me how to cuss. That didn't last very long. One Sunday morning not long after we had blown up our room, we were sitting in our usual pew at the church, just two rows short of the pulpit. I couldn't find a hymnal, so I tried to get John to share one. He refused. I then blurted out, "If you don't do it, I'll knock the [expletive deleted] out of you!" Our mortified mother smacked me right then and there and hissed," Don't you ever, ever say that again!" Dr. Newell paused in his sermon briefly, looked sternly at me, and then continued. When she asked me later where I'd learned that awful word, I told her truthfully: Jim McEver.

By the seventh grade Jim had fully mastered the physiology of sex, technical knowledge that he imparted to the rest of us. He was also a model practitioner. Every day during ninth grade year we had to catch a bus for the thirty-minute ride down to John McNitt Alexander Junior High School, halfway to Charlotte on Route 115. Jim and his girlfriend from Cornelius would cuddle up in a bus seat and smooch all the way from Davidson to Huntersville each morning in full view of the rest of us riding what we called the "Love Bird Express." In those days high school students drove the school buses. They always got a full view of Jim and his girlfriend through the rearview mirror—and they occasionally ran off the road. The good mothers of Davidson and Cornelius finally got wind of this and put a stop to it. Jim and his friend were forbidden to ride in the same seat together, and that was the end of that.

Jim had a wide circle of friends that included Eddie Beam, who liked to cut up on the bus. The prison system in North Carolina used chain gangs to maintain the roads in those years. Outside Cornelius or Huntersville the bus would pass one from time to time On these occasions Eddie took great delight in pulling down his window and yelling, "Daddy, it's me, Junior!"

In the spring of 1960 John and I joined Troop 58 of the Mecklenburg Council of the Boy Scouts of America. That's where we got to know Grover Meetze, Sr., and Jr.

Grover Meetze, Sr., was administrator of the physical plant for Davidson College. He was a tall, lanky, good-natured fellow. Mr. Meetze dedicated himself to Troop 58 and was widely supported by the membership of the Davidson College Presbyterian Church. His son, Grover, Jr., was a horse of another color. Grover was a ninth grader at Davidson Elementary (in the years before the consolidated junior high school was built) and was a cocky character who spelled big trouble for me. Behind his back I called him "Little Grover."

The scouts met punctually at 7 p.m. on Friday nights during the school year at the Scout Hut, which was located in the woods behind the college's soccer field. We went down to Charlotte and bought spiffy new Scout uniforms for our first meeting that spring night in 1960. Ernie Patterson was particularly proud of his. Had we known what was coming, we would have probably gone naked.

As we proudly arrived at the hut, each of us was escorted down into the woods by one of the senior members, sent on a snipe hunt, and hazed. Some of the older boys went off to take a pee, and some of the initiates, including Ernie, were pushed into their line of fire. Meantime, I was bribing Little Grover as hard and fast as I could not to submit me to the same abuse. It cost me three weeks of allowances and the use of my chemistry set. Thus began Little Grover Meetze's reign of terror, which would last until one dark, rainy night the following summer at Scout camp.

After that first night of initiation, we fell into a more stable and safer routine. Charlie Lloyd, who was a high school senior and five years older than me, was the senior scout leader for the troop. He was a grand fellow. Charlie kept Little Grover and some of the other bullies at bay. We began each meeting with the Pledge of Allegiance, the Scout Oath, and the Scout Law. Next came a brief business meeting during which ten cents dues were collected from each member. Recreation time followed the formalities.

During the warmer months this usually consisted of "Capture the Flag" out on the soccer field, and in the colder months, we played "Steal the Bacon" in the hut. The hut was very small, and things could get quite rowdy. The floor was hard, but not as hard as the walls at either end. I only remember one of us getting cold-cocked.

As the big event of the year, Mr. Meetze arranged for our troop to go to Camp Steere, the Mecklenburg County Council's camp on Lake Wiley, which is in the Catawba River lake system south of Charlotte. That week, which I will forever remember as "The Terror," began innocently enough on a hot Sunday afternoon in June 1960, with our deposition at the camp infirmary, where we were all questioned by the camp medic and then dispersed to our campsite areas. My brother and I were assigned to separate cabins.

The cabins were enclosed on three sides and open completely on the fourth; doubled bunks lined the three walls. I unpacked my gear and dutifully made up my bed. There were two empty bunks by late afternoon, so I dumped some of my belongings on the one nearest my bed. To my consternation, Jim McEver and Little Grover walked in and announced that Jim was "The Colonel" and Grover, "The General." They then demanded to know who had desecrated Little Grover's bunk. I thought I was dead meat; I started to cry. Little Grover came over and punched me while Jim pulled out a towel, wetted down the tip, and taught me about rat-tails.

I was getting homesick very quickly now. At supper, which I hardly touched, Little Grover announced that I was going to regret greatly ever coming to Camp Steere. That night I found out just how much. The camp supervisors turned the lights out at 9 p.m. each night and played Perry Como's rendition of "The Lord's Prayer" over the P.A. system. That was the McEver-Meetze call to arms. Using the song to drown out the yelling, these two went about rat-tailing the first year Scouts in the cabin. This happened every night for four nights (it has taken me years to learn to enjoy that beautiful hymn). Then on the fifth night I rose from the status of tortured lackey to local legend.

That Thursday night a line of thunderstorms moved through the area, and it poured all night. Sometime around midnight, in a somnolent stupor, I dragged my welt-covered body out of my bunk and wandered out toward the latrine, getting soaked in the process. I returned to the dark cabin and started to crawl into what I thought was my bunk. I had mistakenly stumbled onto Little Grover, and he woke up hollering. In hindsight I believe he thought I had whizzed all over him and his bed.

All of this startled me into a more alert state where I realized that my life expectancy was now measured in milliseconds. Suddenly, John Hufford and Mike Gant bolted from their bunks to my defense, and the three of us started to pummel Little Grover. There was so much commotion coming from the cabin that Mr. Meetze and Charlie Lloyd were drawn from their cabin to break up the melee.

After hearing about the rat-tailing, Mr. Meetze announced that there would be no further hazing in Troop 58. Little Grover took his father's message to heart, but it didn't seem to faze Jim McEver. The next night Jim was sharpening his rat-tails. Grover told him he had better cut it out. Jim then popped Grover, who tore the towel from Jim's hands and began to rat-tail him all over the cabin just as Perry Como opened up with the "Lord's Prayer." At that most reverent of Camp Steer moments, Jim was howling, "Oh, goddamn! Oh, goddamn!" Thus ended hazing in Troop 58.

The following winter we went on a campout at Hugh "Fungi" Barger's farm where the troop had a campsite named Camp Barger. It was a cleared-out area in the woods just off the Davidson-Kannapolis highway. Escorted by Grover, Jr., with whom I now was on good speaking terms (I think he respected how I had handled myself at Camp Steere), I hiked the two and one-half miles from town to the campsite.

When I arrived, the others had already set up camp. We cooked dinner as a group and then in the fading twilight took turns firing Mr.

Meetze's 22-caliber rifle at tin cans on a makeshift target range. We adjourned for marshmallows and ghost stories around the campfire.

The excitement started around 4 a.m. the following morning. The temperature dipped into the low teens. Bill Adams was in his tent and had been freezing for hours. He hadn't bothered to tell anyone. He decided to build a fire in his tent to warm things up. I remember waking up with a searing sensation, thinking the sun had been up a while. I smelled smoke and darted out of my tent. The western end of the camp was ablaze. By that time everybody was out of his tent. Fortunately we were able to get the fire out before we had a full-scale forest fire on our hands. Bill's tent and sleeping bag were charred beyond recognition. He stood there pitifully among the ashes while the rest of us glared at him with contempt.

By the eighth grade I had failed to get beyond the First Class part of the merit badge program. John and I gradually lost interest, and we started skipping the weekly meetings.

Our last hurrah with the scouting program was Mr. Meetze's trip to Kings Mountain National Military Park, in South Carolina, about forty miles south of Charlotte. The troop drove to Kings Mountain on a brilliant October morning in 1961. We hiked up to the campsite, pitched our tents, and had a bag lunch. Next we went up to the battle-ground site, near the top of Kings Mountain. A walkway encircles the hill, which is heavily wooded with thick underbrush. Currie Johnson, an eleventh grader, was in charge of the Scouts on this trip. He first set us rambling through the thickets in search of Major Patrick Ferguson's whistle. He told us the following tale.

Legend has it that the British commander of the Tory forces used a whistle to rally his troops. When the Over Mountain Boys shot Ferguson off the top of the hill, the whistle went flying, and over the years it had been an object of dedicated search for generations of park visitors. Currie knew there was no whistle—it would have long since rusted away. Anyway, his tale was so convincing that we naifs spent three hours of utter futility in the woods looking for that whistle. To some avail, I did learn a lot about the battle and its role as a turning point in the Revolutionary War in the South.

We were bone weary by late afternoon, but my enthusiasm was at fever pitch. Currie took us over to a yellow jacket nest he had found, and we lured some jackets into cola bottles. To our delight Currie taught us how to slowly roast them—we probably scorched a hundred or so. After that, I was so tired that I crawled into my tent for a nap.

The next thing I remember was the cry, "Timber!" A fairly sizable white pine tree came crashing down on my tent. I had dozed off and didn't hear all the commotion it took to bring the thing down. My friend Will Brown, for reasons still unclear, took a notion to chop down the tree and enlisted a few of the other Scouts to help him. The result was an accident. The tree had me pinned in, but fortunately I was uninjured. That's when I had decided to play dead.

Currie ran over to what was left of the tent, screaming out, "Puckett!" Not a sound or movement from my direction. He started to pull the mess off of me but couldn't manage by himself. By that time the entire camp had arrived on the scene. They finally began to extricate me from the thicket. Again, no sound or movement came from my direction—I was about to crack up. Finally they were down to canvas, which they pulled off my immobile body. They thought I was dead. At that point I jumped up, laughing. Everyone else, except Currie, joined in. He was livid. That's my last memory of being a member of Troop 58.

In the summer of 1970, before entering medical school, I returned to Camp Steere to work as the camp medic. Gene Grimes, the patriarch of scouting in Mecklenburg County for a generation, employed me and arranged for the Mecklenburg Council to apply my $100 weekly stipend to a scholarship fund set aside for me at the UNC School of Medicine.

At the camp Gene was immensely popular among the scouts. Someone went down to Grimesland, South Carolina, stole the town sign, and plastered it up over the entrance to the dining hall, where it hung for years. All of the camp's leaders respected Gene and sought out his good advice on a variety of matters.

Besides Gene, another character is particularly memorable from that last summer at Steere. He was Zeb (no one knew his last name), the camp maintenance man. Zeb sported a mouth stuffed with Copenhagen snuff, and he was known to take a drink or two now and then.

One night in mid-July, Zeb wandered down to the infirmary and woke me up in the night saying that he had banged himself up. He was bleeding profusely from a cavernous scalp wound. I managed to get the bleeding stopped and bandaged him up as best I could. Mr. Knox, the assistant camp director, and I bundled Zeb up in the back of the camp maintenance truck and drove him to Memorial Hospital (now Carolinas Medical Center) in Charlotte. We spent the rest of the night and a good part of the next day with him as one of the interns sewed him up and gave him three units of blood. Had Zeb not shown up when he did, he might have bled to death.

On the way back to camp we found Zeb's truck wrapped around a tree at the bottom of an embankment. He had all of his Copenhagen in that vehicle and seemed more upset about that than the loss of his truck.

The great irony of that summer for me was my election to the Boy Scout honor society, the Order of the Arrow (OA). I knew that Gene Grimes had arranged it. In a way I felt ashamed because of my extraordinarily poor performance as an active Scout. Shaw Smith, my next-door neighbor in Davidson, ran the rifle range at Steere that summer, and he was also tapped into the Order. I don't know that Shaw was ever a Boy Scout. At all events, I was honored that night, and I have faithfully kept my OA sash in a cedar storage chest in my home.

Shortly before leaving for medical school, I sat down in Gene's office and reminisced about my only week as a camper in the summer of 1960. I told him about the Meetze-McEver reign of terror and the events of that stormy night in our cabin. Gene broke out laughing and said, "So you were the kid who pissed all over his cabin!"

On the occasion of my twenty-fifth reunion at Davidson College, I ran into Mr. Meetze at a service station in town. The years had been kind to him; he had changed very little. We talked about the old days in the Boy Scouts. I asked him what his most memorable moment was. He said, "That's easy. The night Bill Adams burned down Camp Barger."

The Game
that
Binds

Tom Stevens was the baseball coach at Davidson College during most of my childhood. I remember his kindness in letting John and me help out with the home baseball games each season. He instilled in us a passion for the game.

We were nine years old when Coach Stevens enlisted our help as ball-and-batboys during the season. John, C.W. Stacks, Jr., and I were the chosen few for this coveted work. After every game Coach Stevens gave each of us an old ball and any cracked bats from the day's game. We took the bats home and repaired them with small nails and athletic tape. They were as good as new to us. Since the bats were oversized for our age, there was little chance that we would damage them any further.

In the late-1950's we began to play sandlot ball behind the Whittles' yard in a vacant lot that was bounded by Johnsie Shelton's yard in left field, Oscar Thies' garage in center field, and Nelson Mebane's yard in right field. Right field had a wire fence that would become a symbol of futility for me. Our backstop was the old barn that had been used by the medical school grave robbers at the turn of the century.

We played ball virtually every dry day throughout the spring and summer. We could always drum up a game—usually seven or eight showed up. We exchanged players and used ghost runners to keep the game going. No one kept score.

I was a left-handed hitter. My goal in life at that time was to put a ball over the right field fence. I had little chance—there just wasn't enough power in my scrawny arms. Hoping to help, Dad went up to the Western Auto and bought us a new bat, a #28 Mickey Mantle-autographed Louisville Slugger, which we named "Old Faithful." Even with Old Faithful, I still couldn't reach that fence.

Most of the boys had their own bats, and if we didn't have enough, we simply supplemented the supply with some of Tom Stevens' repaired bats. Anytime a bat broke during a game, we stopped play, assessed the damage, and if the bat was beyond repair, we sawed it in two. We would call off play temporarily and hold a brief wake before hammering the broken bat's handle into the ground. After several seasons we had a sizable bat graveyard. My greatest fear was that Old Faithful would wind up out there. We took great care to keep that bat away from the bigger boys.

I had visions of Yankee Stadium in those years. My goal, after clearing the right field fence, was to become a major league player. Mom grieved over this because I gave up piano—much to Nancy Smith's relief. We spent so much time playing baseball that our grades, which were already bad enough, began to slip further.

My dream of baseball immortality would not be realized unless I moved from sandlot ball to more organized league play. That opportunity came when an exceptional community organizer brought youth baseball to the town.

Gene McEver was a tower of a man. He gained notoriety at the University of Tennessee, where he was an All-American football player in the late 1920's. His love of the game brought him to Davidson College, where he coached for a number of seasons. During WW II he coached football at UNC and VPI. After that he coached the Charlotte Clippers, whose home field was Memorial Stadium. He and his wife, Joy, had four fine sons—George, John, Jim, and Tom. They lived on School Street, just below the elementary school.

In the spring of 1958 Mr. McEver helped organize a Little League program in northern Mecklenburg County. He and Kenneth Caldwell held tryouts for us on a large sandlot that was located just across the railroad tracks on Griffith Street, west of the college campus. (Davidson's only shopping center stands there today.) I loved baseball, but I had a fundamental problem—I was scared to death of a fastball. The first time I stepped up to bat, Moe White hit me with a fastball. John and I knew we had little chance of making the team— we were skinny kids who could hardly field or hit. Still, Dad had faith in both of us. He bought us new gloves at Cantrell's Western Auto and encouraged us to try out for the team. Mr. McEver organized a practice game with Cornelius, which was the town next to Davidson. That game would determine the final cut before the season started.

The teams played on the American Legion Field at Cornelius under lights. When I finally got in the game, I was sent out to right field, the dead zone of youth baseball. My troubles started at the plate, where I had to face a big left-hander named Ronnie Barnhardt, who had a ferocious fastball. He also had no control. Barnhardt decked me with a pitch I barely saw. More ignominiously, I let two homeruns slip past me in the outfield. The next day the coaches cut both John and me. We would spend that summer in Williamstown, Massachusetts, where Dad was invited to direct a summer biology program.

Still loving the game and wanting desperately to improve, we took our gloves and Old Faithful up to Williamstown, where we played baseball on the huge field near the Williams College gymnasium. One morning in July, John and I were playing ball with some of the boys from our apartment complex. One of the bigger ones wanted to try out Old Faithful. It had survived Jim McEver and Doug Cantrell back home, so we saw no harm in letting him have a swat or two. On the first pitch we heard a sickening crack. He had broken our beloved bat in two. I was grief-stricken; I think I cried for two days. We lovingly wrapped the bat up in an old towel, and in August we carried it back to Davidson for burial. All the boys in the neighborhood came to the wake. Doug Cantrell, keeper of the bat cemetery, pounded Old Faithful's handle into the ground, and shortly after that we gave up sandlot baseball for good.

The following spring, 1959, we were back into organized base-ball again. This time we were put to work building a field. It was down at the end of School Street just below the Mimosa Cemetery and several hundred yards above the town sewer treatment plant. We helped clear and level the field, which at that time had no grass. It became a beautiful sandlot with real fences, with Mr. McEver direct-ing all aspects of its construction. A crew of townspeople pitched in.

That year brother John lost his confidence and didn't try out. I somehow made the team. The coaches had only a limited number of uniforms, which were paid for by local businesses. Instead of a num-ber, each of us wore the name of a sponsoring business on the back of his jersey. It was hit or miss if the uniform fitted. I proudly advertised for the Anchor Grill, a beer joint just over the county line in Iredell County. Mom was mortified, and Dad, appreciating the humor of it all, called me, "Beer Joint Puckett."

I spent the summer of 1959 on the bench. It was one of the low points of my athletic career. The team was simply awful—we lost every game. I carry several images from that ill-fated season. One game was miraculously tied 3-3 going into the last half of the sixth and final inning, when with two down and a Cornelius man on third, the batter lofted a high fly to the infield. The ball hung there in the lights interminably. Finally Vic Blackwell (Nancy Blackwell's son), our short-stop, waved off everybody else for the catch. He was never close—the ball bounced off his glove and dropped at his feet. The run scored, and we lost again. Vic walked two miles home crying his heart out.

The next game I remember was down at West Mecklenburg on the west side of Charlotte. This game was highlighted by Bruce Parker's encounter with a beanball—pow, right off the head protector. In that game we actually had the lead for a while. J.P. Stowe, the coach, told me I might get in some playing time. Of course, I didn't. Anyway, it was tied going into the sixth inning until Moe White out in right field dropped an easy fly to let the winning run in. My butt was getting sore sitting on the bench.

Mrs. Nelson Mebane told me, "You really deserve to play. You should get a sportsmanship award or something for keeping that bench so warm." Inside I raged. There was no reason Coach Stowe shouldn't let me play. His son Craven was the author of most of my misery. I thought he was the worst player on the team, yet his father continued to let him start at second base.

We played the final game that season at Huntersville under lights. We were winning this time. Huntersville tied it up in the bottom half of the sixth inning. They had a man on second with two out. That's when I got the nod from the coach. "Puckett, get out there in right field!" I had to hunt around for my glove. There had been some games where I didn't even show up with it. I prayed I had it with me. Happily, I located it and sauntered out to right field as Moe White came in and muttered something to the coach like, "What? Are you crazy or something?"

There I was—score tied, last inning, last game, two down, and a Huntersville man on second. The scenarios whipped through my mind. The next batter took a ball and a strike. He lined the next pitch to right. Here was my moment at last. Peg that guy trying to score from second, and I'll get to lead off the extra inning (I was the next batter in our lineup). I knelt down on one knee and neatly fielded the ball. The runner was rounding third and heading for home. Johnny Cashion, our catcher, had home plate blocked, and I intended to nail the runner. I fired as hard as I could. It was a perfect peg—one hop and Cashion had it. Or so I thought. The Huntersville man went into a slide, and when the dust had cleared, the ump gave a big "safe" signal. Our catcher had dropped the ball giving Huntersville the victory. Regardless, it was a good toss.

The 1960 season looked brighter. Gene McEver had expanded the field. Volunteer work crews added bleachers and spruced up the dugouts. That year "A" and "B" teams were formed in northern Mecklenburg to give more boys the opportunity to play. This was the Little League equivalent of major and minor leagues. I started out on the B team.

I was in Heaven. This was slow pitch baseball and a lot more fun than collecting splinters. Even though we didn't have the uniforms, we did get a nifty T-shirt with a Little League emblem. We dressed out in a Davidson baseball cap, T-shirt, Levi's, and cleats (usually spit-shined). We thought we were real slick dudes. We were the class of the B League and didn't lose a game. I played third base well and was the clean-up hitter in the batting order.

A highlight for me came in the opener against Cornelius on a sultry night in May. I came to bat with two men on and one out in the top of the first. The pitcher served up a surprisingly fast pitch. It was the sweetest and hardest ball I had hit up to that time; it landed about two hundred feet out and probably rolled another fifty feet. For a twelve year old it was quite a clout—and a sizable advance since my flailing days in the neighborhood sandlot. I doffed my cap to the sparse, cheering crowd as I rounded third. Unfortunately a thunderstorm came up, and the game was called one inning later, so the home run didn't count. Regardless, the moment lasts a lifetime.

Our next game was at home against Huntersville. In the second inning Huntersville managed to get runners on second and third. Their cleanup hitter was a big ugly fellow who liked to pull balls down the third base line. He tagged one hard right over third base. I dove to my right, grabbed the ball, and touched the bag to double off the runner there. I heard Bill Guerrant, our second baseman, screaming at me. I looked over in his direction and saw the runner on second halfway down to third base. I threw the ball to Bill, and he stepped on the bag, eliminating the third runner. It was the only triple play up to that time in Davidson youth baseball.

We were 8-0 in mid-June when I got the call to join the A team. Craven Stowe had left the team, perhaps because he turned thirteen and lost his eligibility. Whatever the reason, it freed up second base for me. The rest of the season was a struggle for me; the A team faced tougher pitchers, and I was an anemic three for fourteen at the plate. Two of my hits came in a game against Huntersville, both singles up the middle. In another game I hit a home run. A .214 batting average—at least I got to play.

The following year, 1961, Mr. McEver organized a Pony League program. He and other community leaders set out to build the finest field in the Southeast. That first year they carved out a field on the red-clay terrain just below the Little League field (John and I worked as volunteer youth labor to build the fences). Left-handed batters were hitting toward a right field fence that consisted in part of the backstop of the Little League field, looming about 250 feet from home plate, up a steep embankment. Left field was approximately 250 feet to the fence, all this on level ground. Dead centerfield was a preposterous

310 to 320 feet from the plate; the fence consisted, in part, of a swinging gate that allowed a tractor and dragging apparatus onto the field. The fences were too far out for most of us thirteen year olds to reach. Still, we had our own field.

Mr. McEver selected Eugene Reid to be our coach. Gene Reid, whom we nicknamed "Snoopy," had grown up in Davidson across the street from the elementary school. He was twenty-eight years old and taught math at East Mecklenburg High School in Matthews, near the South Carolina line. My aunt, Louise Puckett, also taught there, and she and Gene were good friends. Gene would get to practices around 5 p.m. Mr. McEver, Doodle Walley, and assorted dads would supervise the team until Gene arrived. He would then take over and coach practice until we finished up at around 6. Some days the assistant coaches couldn't get there. Mr. McEver scoured the college dorms for a reliable assistant and discovered "Baseball Bob."

Bob Gregory, from Deland, Florida, was a student at Davidson College. He answered Mr. McEver's call and came down to help out with the team, and we took a liking to him immediately. In time he would become the assistant coach and even head coach in Gene's absence. I think he did more for the town than any student who ever attended Davidson College. We affectionately called him "Baseball Bob," and we practically lived in his dorm room. I suppose his grades suffered for all the attention he gave us, but after four decades, that becomes irrelevant, at least to my mind.

Bob headed a delegation up to Washington, D.C. for the March on Washington, which Dr. Martin Luther King, Jr., organized in August 1963. He invited John and me to go with him. Our folks said no. To this day I regret not being a part of that great event. Bob would go on to organize and coach Pop Warner football in Davidson. At his graduation ceremony the town and college honored him with the Sullivan Award for his contributions to the community. No student ever deserved it more.

That first summer of Pony League was a disaster. Most of us were thirteen year olds, and we were lousy. I played every position except the battery. Brother John, who had found his way back to baseball, also rotated between the infield and outfield. Dad had taught him to hit right-handed, and he did well at that. Unfortunately, we lost most of our games that first season.

Two of our May games were with Cook Memorial, a team that represented the Long Creek community of northwest Charlotte. Nothing in our experience prepared us for Cook, whose players were mostly big fourteen year olds. They had two hard-throwing pitchers named Beard and Pagota. In the third inning of the first encounter, a Cook batter flattened our pitcher, Winston Reid, with a line drive off the thigh. The whole afternoon went like that. Brother John, playing third base, was so intimidated by the hard-hitting Cook team that he made five errors, which is probably still the town record for ineptitude at that position. Cook annihilated us with hit after hit, including a barrage of home runs. Mercifully, the coaches called the game after five innings, with Cook up 18-0.

When Cook Memorial came back the following week, we were better prepared. This time they won 10-4, with another display of homers. I almost got a hit off Beard—I dragged a bunt in the second inning and was called out at first in a disputed play. We still had a third game to play. This one would be on their home field.

We played them on a clear, hot, Saturday afternoon in June 1961. We only had eight players; several players, including John, were out sick with a stomach virus that was making the rounds. Gene Reid recruited Tommy "Wormie" Honeycutt to join the team for one afternoon. (Wormie had played on the 1960 Little League team but had opted out of Pony League.) The game took place at a crossroads park called Cook's Corner. As the field had no fences, we were able to adjust our outfielders to the range of their homerun hitters. They didn't hit any that day. Inexplicably, Cook's pitching fell apart, and we won 8-2. We were ecstatic over the victory. Looking forward to the 1962 season, we were certainly glad to be done with Beard and Pagota, who moved on to junior high school ball. The following year we would face an entirely different and more daunting pitching situation.

By the spring of 1962, the Pony League field in Davidson had been completely revamped. We had an entirely new field—fences, backstop, lights, and bleachers. The configuration of the park was entirely different. Home plate was now located below the embankment in what had been right field. Mr. McEver directed every aspect of the park's construction, and again townspeople and youth labor pitched in. We had never seen anything like it.

Davidson and Cornelius had both gone baseball crazy. Cornelius had Ronnie Barnhardt, the same pitcher who had conked me in my only game in our infant Little League season four years earlier. Barnhardt was big and mean, and he had the fastest arm we had yet seen—even faster than Beard and Pagota, who had at least been predictable (fast and over the plate). Barnhardt was fast and wild. You never knew where the ball would wind up. I suppose the thought of what that hard white pill traveling at warp speed would do to your face is what made him such an effective pitcher.

We lost to Cornelius in our home opener. We couldn't touch Barnhardt. It was hard to judge his release, and no one could tell where the ball might go. My first at bat came in the second inning. I remembered the first time in Little League when he had decked me, and I wanted him to pay for that. The next thing I knew I was in the dirt with a searing pain in my chest. Barnhardt had flattened me again.

We won the next two games in league play. At Mount Mourne I tried to score from second on a bunt and put the Mt. Mourne catcher in the hospital. I got some bumps and bruises from the collision and a tongue lashing from Gene Reid for running over the catcher. Our next game at Huntersville was a rout. We clobbered them 31-0, and the game was called in the fifth. I had a homer and four RBI's in the first inning. Next came the Cornelius game and the worst thing that ever happened to me in organized baseball.

Our second Cornelius game was the first game played under lights at what was becoming known as McEver Field. A substantial part of the populations of both towns turned out. I had never seen so many fans at a youth game. The Davidson crowd filled the bleachers behind the backstop and first base, and the Cornelius crowd filled the third base side. People who couldn't find seats straddled the fences.

Barnhardt walked me in the second. The game was scoreless until the third inning, when after Barnhardt walked the first two batters, Doug Cantrell, our third baseman, stepped up and walloped a high fastball way out over the left-center field lights. It went out like a cannon shot. That made it 3-0 and remained the score as we began the seventh and final inning. Cornelius was coming to bat.

With two down in the top of the seventh, Cornelius had runners on first and second. The next batter singled sharply to left where I was roaming the outfield. I charged the ball at breakneck speed to try to head off the runner on second base before he scored; to my dismay the ball zipped under my glove and rolled out to the fence. I frantically retrieved it and threw with all my might for home plate. Except for the detour into the bleachers behind third base, it wasn't such a bad throw. At least it ricocheted toward the catcher. Two runners scored, and the score now stood 3-2 with a Cornelius runner on third. Gene Reid was destroying the dugout, and the Cornelius fans were doing the same to me in left field. They threw uncooked spaghetti at me screaming, "Spaghetti arm!"

The next Cornelius batter was Sandy Lowrance, their shortstop, one of the best players in the league. Wayne "Buddy" Caldwell, our pitcher, got two fast strikes on him. The next pitch was a curve ball, low and inside. Badly fooled, Lowrance bit at it and missed, just as the ball grazed his foot. The ball bounced past Tom McEver, our catcher, and Lowrance ran to first on the passed third strike. The runner from third trotted home, tying the game. I could already see the gallows rising behind the Davidson bleachers.

Next came the bizarre ending of the game and my deliverance. The home plate umpire called both coaches and Mr. McEver for a conference at home plate. The umpire ruled that the ball had hit the batter's foot as he was swinging. A swinging strike and a ball ruled dead. The batter was out, the game was over, and the bragging rights were ours. The Cornelius coach, Red Gannon, protested the ruling vehemently, but the umpire stood his ground.

The ump was Mason Lowrance, the batter's father! Had he let the play stand as a passed ball, no one would have known the difference. But this wasn't about baseball. And it wasn't about winning or losing. It was about fair play and integrity. We all learned a lot that night. Mason also probably saved my neck since the Davidson crowd would have surely lynched me had we lost.

Eight years later over the Thanksgiving holiday my father had a severe seizure that was related to a stroke he had previously suffered.

The man who was driving the ambulance for the North Mecklenburg Rescue Squad that night was Mason Lowrance. Mason came to the house to take Dad to Memorial Hospital in Charlotte. He offered us words of reassurance and comfort. I've always been grateful to him for doing that. And I'm also thankful for the example he set on that spring night back in 1962. It's a powerful memory.

The ball field continued to grow. Mr. McEver and the town added grass and built a "green monster" around it to replace the old fences. In the summer of 1963 the Southeastern Pony League playoffs came to Davidson. That season after my eligibility ran out, the North Mecklenburg All-Star Team made it to the finals by beating a solid Greensboro team—on the heels of a miraculous home run by light-hitting Shaw Smith, my next-door neighbor. Our team lost in the finals to a team from Columbia, South Carolina. By that time the field was officially known as McEver Field.

* * *

Gene McEver's contributions to Davidson didn't end with the building of baseball fields and programs. He and his wife, Joy, had a deep interest in youth development. They helped establish a "Teen Canteen" at the old Helper Inn. The Canteen opened in the late 1950's. The McEvers chaperoned a Wednesday session from 3:30 to 5:30 p.m. and a Saturday night session from 7 to 10 p.m. each week during the school year. The main hall of the building became the dance floor. We paid a ten cents admission fee for each session. The place had a large jukebox, three pool tables, and two ping-pong tables. Smaller rooms were for socializing and card and board games. Bottle sodas were the six-ounce variety and were a nickel each. There was also a television set, which we watched only on Saturday nights. John and I were regulars from the sixth through the eighth grades. We learned many of the social graces there.

Before each visit to the Canteen we would grease ourselves up with Brylcreem or Vitalis. We sported flattops initially and later long greasy hair. We spent hours spit-shining shoes before venturing out on Saturday night. There was something magical about it—I can still feel it today. We were young and had our whole lives in front of us.

On Saturday nights we would arrive shortly after the doors opened. We usually headed straight for the pool tables. The girls drifted in later. Around 8 p.m. we would wander into the dance hall. There would have already been a few couples dancing, and the floor quickly filled with swinging teens. The McEvers kept up with the Top 40, and we never lacked good music. I danced mostly with the older girls, usually Kristi Scott, Jane Withers and the Barnhardt twins.

As I mentioned previously, Georgeanna Mayhew was my seventh-grade girlfriend of short duration. Why she dumped me became apparent one night at the Canteen when I spotted her dancing cheek to cheek with William Dowdy, a smooth-talking new guy in town, who had a cowlick in his greasily coiffed hair. Georgeanna added insult to injury when she presented a ring and announced that she and Dowdy were going steady. I was devastated. Brother John teased me no end about it until I socked him in the jaw and sent him sprawling.

Saturday nights came and went. We didn't realize it at the time, but this was how the town kept us off the streets and out of trouble. I can only remember one time when Mr. McEver had to get physical with a kid. An older boy came in inebriated one rainy Wednesday afternoon. He was a high school dropout with serious issues. When he started turning over chairs and tables, Mr. McEver, who had tried on other occasions to counsel him, grabbed him and pushed him out the door. Apparently the town had done about everything it could to rehabilitate this youth. That Gene McEver couldn't help him suggested to me how far the boy had fallen from grace.

Both Gene and Joy McEver are gone now. I visit the Canteen in my mind's-eye from time to time, where the old jukebox still turns out the tunes. I'm back playing ping-pong, shooting "eight-ball pool," and sipping nickel sodas choked with package peanuts. I see myself slow dancing with Georgeanna Mayhew.

Olin, Lonnie, Louise and Molly Puckett, ca. 1912

Dad and my paternal grandmother, Molly Washam Puckett,
ca. 1932

Mom and Dad victory gardening,
Princeton 1942

Mom and Dad in the yard at
Markam Road house,
Princeton 1942

Aunt Louise Puckett and my
maternal grandmother, Virginia
Hale House ("Now-Now"),
Pawley's Island 1953

Blake House

I am holding Gizmo, "the wonder dog" next to John and Mom, Blake House, 1955

I am to the right of Ginger and John, 1951

Nancy Withers and Skipper, ca. 1957

I am seated just behind Stewball's head, Blake House, 1951

Pattie Newell introduces her parents, Dr. and Mrs. Sam Newell, to Davidson society, DCPC, 1953

"They had to laugh at Daddy Shaw's jokes every night." C. Shaw Smith and the Smiths' "Saucy Sorcery."

Miss Daisy's nursery school, spring 1953. Jim McEver (third row, second from right) is the dominant male.

Kristi Scott, Davidson's littlest cheerleader, 1957

My first date, Georgeanna Mayhew

Diane Neil, North Meck. High classmate, 1966

Jim McEver, 1966

Cub Souts, 1956 (left to right): Nyko Trakas, Bruce Parker, James Puckett, Jim McEver, Ted Thompson, John Puckett, Craven Stowe

Murderer's Row. Pony league baseball, 1961

Francis Justice and Eddie Bean, 1961

Diane Neil and John, the thirty-minute
Junior-Senior Prom, 1966

1965 State Champs—North Mecklenburg Principal W.A. Hough,
right fondles the state cross-country championship trophy his
school claimed last week. Men responsible for winning the Rebels'
second state title (l-r) are coach Bill Cochran and runners James
and John Puckett. (Charlotte Observer photo by Philip Morgan)

Dad teaching one of his biology classes, spring 1969

"In holiness and purity will I pass my life and practice my art."
Dr. Jim Woods embodied the Hippocratic Oath.

James and John Puckett—Davidson College, 1966

Baseball Cards

In the summer of 1988 I took a week off and returned to Davidson to help clear out our house on College Drive and make it ready for sale. My parents were deceased, and my father's sister, Louise, who had lived with my family for over thirty years, was in her eighties and was moving into a retirement home nearby. I spent the better part of that week clearing out the attic. I first attacked boxes and boxes of old documents. I had a delightful romp through my maternal great-grandmother's genealogies, which traced her ancestry through seven family lines back to the seventeenth century. All that week I kept eyeing an old *World Book Encyclopedia* box looking forlorn in one corner of the attic. I knew that it was stuffed full of old baseball cards, but it would have to wait until everything else was finished. Finally I worked my way over to it. I was in for a memory rush.

My brother and I had sealed the box shortly after Roger Maris hit his sixty-first home run in 1961. By this point we had been collecting cards together for several years and our interest in the hobby had started to wane. Several weeks shy of our fourteenth birthday, we sorted our cards by teams, bundled them in rubber bands (a modern collector's taboo), stacked them in the box, and, on our mother's orders, hauled them to the attic. The box sat untouched under the attic eaves for nearly twenty-seven years.

When I opened the box that day in 1988, I knew it was a time capsule. I had no idea what all I would find there. It was as if I were opening all of those cards all over again. In my mind's eye I could see each card in its own individual wrapper—each protected by a flat rectangle of jaw-breaking bubble gum that left a signature gum smell that filtered through the years. I felt like a latter day Howard Carter about to unseal a crypt of precious treasure. There were 4,500 objects in my Tut's tomb and each would require meticulous cataloging. I would spend much of my spare time over the next few months doing just that.

The cards evoked a flood of baseball memories from my childhood. I had here something very unique—and the opportunity of hindsight. When we sealed the box, we had no idea what the future held for the then-living players represented in our collection. There was Joe DiMaggio before Marilyn Monroe and the Simon and Garfunkel song. There were Dizzy Dean and Pee Wee Reese before those weekly Saturday afternoon broadcasts of the Game of the Week, which they called from a makeshift booth next to the press box, all the while blasted on Falstaff Beer, and Dizzy uttering such priceless boners as "He slud into second!" There was Mickey Mantle in the prime of arrogant youth, decades before we learned he was a drunk. From the time I opened my first Topps baseball card, the Mick's was always the most sought after and difficult to find. Small wonder his 1952 rookie card is worth so much. And there was Henry Aaron, who with 120 career home runs to his credit, was well short of the improbable record he would later set. And Carl Yazstremski as a rookie in 1961, completely unknown to me then, now his great career entirely behind him and his achievements enshrined in the Hall of Fame.

In those years we collected simply for the fun of it. We loved baseball, which was truly a different game then. For starters, it was a game! There were no outrageous salaries, free agents, designated hitters, strikes and lockouts, and the servitude of the game to television networks. We bought cards at a penny a throw. These were the years when "mint," "very fine," and "show" were terms that applied only to numismatics. We had no thought of collecting as a form of investment.

We did things to cards that would mortify collectors of today. We traded them, slept with them, pinned them to bulletin boards, toted them to school and church, stuck them with scotch tape to scrap books, and made fans out of them for the spokes of our bicycles. Over the years I have seen cards at flea markets bearing the marks of affectionate misuse and abuse—furrowed edges, inked-in mustaches, brown pieces of Scotch tape, and tack holes. Such was the innocence of baseball card collecting in the 1950's.

My brother and I invented a game back in the summer of 1958. We would take down the card box and from it each of us would choose a team of nine players. We would spread the cards out on the living room floor to make a playing field. The fireplace screen made a high left-field wall; assorted chairs served as the right- and centerfield fences and grandstands. From a shoebox we would draw pieces of paper on which we had written particular words or phrases to direct our play—such as, "strikeout," "home run left field," and "ground out to third." We simulated the action of a real game by moving a tiny ball of cotton from card to card, according to the directions on each slip of paper. One of us would call the game with loud exuberance: "It's a high fly ball to left—that ball's outta here!" We kept score on facsimiles of real score cards. In this fashion we whiled away summer afternoons. A few years ago I was surprised to find *our* game in a toyshop, fully patented by someone else and selling for twenty-five dollars!

Each card (there are many duplicates) has its own story. I can remember opening many of them for the very first time. Collecting these cards brought players like Mantle, Aaron, Mays and Williams into our daily lives; through our fantasy game we experienced vicariously their superhuman feats on the diamond and even created some new ones. Now, after more than forty years, I look back with great nostalgia, yet also know just how human those players really were.

I have several cards of Hoyt Wilhelm. My favorite is the Topps 1958 issue. Wilhelm was probably the greatest knuckleball pitcher to ever play the game. A knuckleball doesn't spin; it goes on a wild ride of unpredictable gyrations. It's like a huge pill with a bad case of vertigo, exceedingly hard to hit and to catch. Hoyt's catcher, Gus

Triandos, had to wear an oversized mitt—Gus still got cuts and bruises from those confounding "flutter balls." Hoyt has the distinction of being the only pitcher in major league history to hit a home run in his first time at bat as a rookie.

Hoyt made it to Cooperstown and the Baseball Hall of Fame, primarily on the strength of his distinguished record as a relief pitcher. He was from Huntersville, a small town seven miles south of Davidson. Our father knew Hoyt and liked him. Dad, John, and I watched the Game of the Week one Saturday afternoon when Hoyt, in a starting role, pitched a no-hitter against the 1958 New York Yankees, who would win the World Series that year.

One of my favorite cards is Bobby Richardson's. Richardson played second base for the Yankees in their glory days of the late fifties and early sixties. While he was a superb fielder and a bulwark of the Yankee defense, he was a light hitter. That changed dramatically in the 1960 World Series, when he broke the back of the Pittsburgh Pirates in the third game, launching a grand slam home run over the left field fence at Yankee Stadium. I can still see it—and feel my pain. I had bet fifty cents on the Pirates.

I had all but effaced that memory until one Saturday morning in 1989 when I ran into my neighbor ninety-year old Dick Richards and a friend of his in a diner in Concord. Dick, a forever youngster with a passion for baseball, invited me to join them, and he introduced me to his friend, whose name was Bobby Richardson. It took a few moments for that to register as I rummaged through my memories of a man who had been thirty years younger. Once I realized that this was really *the* Bobby Richardson, I entered into one of the strangest conversations of my life.

I asked Bobby if he had fifty cents to spare to repay me for what I had lost on his home run almost thirty years earlier. I wasn't even going to charge interest! He laughed and said that he had caught nothing but grief over that from Pirate fans ever since.

Richardson's homer would undoubtedly have been the high point of the 1960 Series had it not been for Bill Mazeroski. "Maz" was one of those Warholian miracles—a man who enjoyed no great public notice until one fleeting moment of glory that would last him and all of us a lifetime. For sheer drama his feat certainly rivals Bobby

Thompson's "shot heard round the world" in the 1951 National League playoff or Don Larsen's perfect no-hitter in the 1956 Series. Maz's defining moment came in the final game of the 1960 World Series.

To say that the underdog Pirates were outgunned in this World Series is extravagant understatement. The Yanks routed the Bucs in three of the games by appalling scores 16-3, 10-0, 12-0. Bobby Richardson hit his improbable grand slam and drove in six runs in the 10-0 shellacking. Yet somehow the Pirates managed to stretch the awesome Yankees to seven games.

I was a seventh grader in the fall of 1960. World Series games were actually played in the afternoons of that era—and early enough in October to take advantage of Indian summer. Game seven of the Pirate-Yankee Series was played on October 13, a warm, sunlit afternoon, both in Pittsburgh and on the lower playing field at Davidson Elementary, where we listened to the game at recess on transistor radios. We were all pulling for the Pirates—we naturally hated the Yankees because they always seemed so indomitable. The spectacular finale of that famous game, as fate would have it, occurred just as Miss Winnie Potts, our teacher, started to wave us in off the playground. We didn't care. The fat lady was about to sing at Forbes Field.

The score was tied 9-9 in the bottom of the ninth inning, and the Pirates were at bat. Mazeroski was the leadoff hitter. Winnie Potts was hollering now, "You boys come on in right now!" We were pinned to our transitors and NBC radio. "Just a minute, Miss Potts," a visibly agitated Jim McEver retorted, as if he were swatting a fly. A minute is about all the time Maz needed to hit the second pitch thrown by Yankee reliever Ralph Terry, a high slider, out toward the left field wall. In ecstatic disbelief, we heard NBC Radio's Chuck Thompson make the call: "A high-fly ball going deep to left, this may do it! Back to the wall goes Berra. It is over the fence. Home run!" The playground erupted.

A sad epitaph to this jubilation is the fact that the Pittsburgh city fathers sold Forbes Field to the University of Pittsburgh for $2 million. The wrecking ball arrived after the 1970 season to make way for the Forbes Quadrangle. A plaque on the ground floor of one of those buildings marks the exact spot of home plate at Forbes Field. For those of us who were on the lower playing field of Davidson Elementary on October 13, 1961, that plaque is sacred ground.

A card that has a special place in my heart is Marv Throneberry's. Marv was a reserve first baseman for the New York Yankees in the late 1950's. What the Yankees ever saw in him remains a mystery. Undoubtedly, Marv would be long forgotten had he not been traded to the fledgling New York Mets in the expansion year of 1962. The Mets were just about the worst thing that ever happened in baseball. Even though the legendary Casey Stengel was their manager, they lost more games, gave up more hits and more runs, and made more errors than any team in history. Despite it all, their fans adored them. Setting all sorts of attendance records, Met fans poured into the Polo Grounds, the team's first stadium, by the tens of thousands. Marv was the first baseman for those howlingly inept Mets, and he became an emblem of Met futility.

My 1958 Topps card of "Marvelous Marv" Throneberry shows a ball in his glove. This is a stretch from reality. No two objects in the cosmos were more mutually repulsive than Marv's glove and a baseball. Sportswriters calculated the distance between them in galactic terms. Marv ranks as one of the worst first basemen to ever play the game. Yet he is immortalized because of his ineptitude. Met fans swarmed to see him and the other Met bunglers play.

Marv taught us that just about anybody can play baseball and have a good time at it, to boot. He left baseball over a salary dispute. He claimed the Mets weren't paying him enough. He should have counted his blessings that they didn't pay him what he was worth. At any rate, Marv went on to make a string of popular Miller Lite Beer commercials and established himself as a TV celebrity in the 1980's. It's no exaggeration to say that we won't ever see anything like Marvelous Marv or Casey Stengel's Mets again. Small wonder Mets fans dug up and toted home the Shea Stadium turf when their beloved underdogs won the 1969 World Series.

Another one of my favorite players was Roger Maris. When I went through my collection, I found two cards of Maris in his 1958 rookie year with Cleveland. I had no idea we had ever collected those cards. Certainly no one could have anticipated then what would happen to Roger Maris in the summer of 1961, when he would challenge the most celebrated record in baseball.

In that surreal summer a greatly stressed Maris came within one home run of Babe Ruth's record of sixty dingers in 154 games (Ruth had set his record in 1927 in a 154-game season). Although Roger had won the American League's Most Valuable Player Award in 1960, he didn't stack up in the press as a worthy successor to the Babe. Perhaps it was because his line-drive home runs offended old guard sportswriters who longingly recalled the Sultan of Swat's majestic blasts. Perhaps it was because Roger lacked the Babe's panache and *joie de vivre*. As matters stood, Maris had fifty-eight homers going into Game 154; the final game for his chance at Ruth's record was played in Baltimore, the Babe's hometown. John and I watched the game on television.

In his second at bat Maris hit homer number fifty-nine off Baltimore pitcher Milt Pappas. His chance at number sixty boiled down to his last at bat, when he faced a knuckle-balling relief pitcher. Maris hit the first pitch far into the right field stands—a towering shot we thought was a sure dinger—then watched disconsolately as it veered foul. On the next pitch Maris grounded out, and that was the end of it.

Roger Maris fell short of Babe Ruth's record, but he managed to hit sixty-one homers in 162 games that season for the modern record. The relief pitcher who robbed him of Ruth's 154-game record was Hoyt Wilhelm from Huntersville, N.C.

The short summer of Roger Maris' life ended in 1987 when he died of cancer. For his season in the sun in '61 Ford Frick, Commissioner of Baseball, awarded him an asterisk by his name in the record book, lest anyone mistakenly believe that Maris had broken the great Babe Ruth's 1927 home run record while setting the modern record in an extended season. Maris would bear this stigma for the rest of his life.

In the summer of 1998 the nation watched as Mark McGwire, in one swing of his mighty bat, effaced that asterisk forever. In that moment Maris' family and the millions of us who had followed Yankee jersey Number 9 through that glorious season finally found absolution. The very long summer of 1961 had ended at last.

I still connect to my long ago era of the game. One of my favorite baseball memorabilia is not a card but an autographed photo of a player named Henry Boney. You will not find him on a baseball card. A few years ago I struck up a conversation with an elderly gentleman at one of the hospitals where I worked. I asked him what he had done for a living. He said that he was in his nineties and had started life as a baseball pitcher. Thinking that he had probably played industrial or company ball, I politely kept the conversation going. I asked him what team he had played for. He said, "The New York Giants."

I absorbed the shock and impulsively grabbed his arm. I said, "You played for John McGraw!" Henry told me he was the great Carl Hubbell's reliever. He also said, "I wasn't very good." I told him, "You were good enough to make a great major league team, and you are alive and here!" He was the only living Giant player from that era. We spent the better part of an hour talking about the Giants of old, the Polo Grounds, Carl Hubbell, and Babe Ruth.

Shortly afterwards, Henry returned to his permanent home in Florida. I don't understand why, but for several years thereafter at Christmas, he sent me a box of Florida oranges and grapefruits. One year they stopped coming. I have a feeling that Henry Boney, like Archie "Moonlight" Graham, moved on to the Field of Dreams.

Finally, there is Mickey Mantle. My brother and I have nine cards of the Mick in our collection. Our most treasured card is the 1958 Topps, for which we traded an old tobacco card Babe Ruth to a five-year-old shrewd bargainer named Midge Fox in Williamstown, Massachusetts.

In the mid-1990's I was stunned to learn that Mantle had hepatitis C and cirrhosis of the liver. He then developed a hepatoma, a lethal liver cancer. His subsequent liver transplant sparked enormous controversy and criticism directed at his surgeons who may well have known that the tumor had metastasized beyond the liver at the time of the transplant. Such were the stature and reputation of the man.

What was the mystique of Mickey Mantle, who in 1995 appeared so frail and wasted—this champion of my youth? Why did my brother and I consider Mantle's 1958 Topps card, which was incredibly hard to find that year, among our most prized possessions? Was it because he was the consummate player—hitter, fielder, and base runner? Some baseball commentators say he hit the most prodigious home run in history—a monster shot to the far pavilions of right field at Yankee Stadium, which failed to clear the stadium by a Gillette razor's edge. Despite all of his remarkable achievements, I recall that Mantle only set one major league record that still stands today—most home runs in World Series play (18). He also struck out more times than any player in history—at least until Reggie Jackson passed him in that ignominious category. With Mantle it was all or nothing, slugfest or strikeout, boom or bust, and downtown or the dugout. But what is it about him that makes him such a venerable figure for my generation?

Mantle, the son of miner in Spavinaw, Oklahoma, was born into the Grapes of Wrath that was Middle America of 1931. Perhaps I'm drawn to the fact that the Mick and I share the same birthday, October 20. Or was it the very name of the man, whose father had prophetically seen his greatness even at his birth, naming him Mickey after the great Hall of Fame catcher, Mickey Cochran?

I saw Mantle in person only once. It was at Yankee Stadium, August 11, 1958, the year the Yanks beat the Braves in the World Series. Our father wanted us to see "The House that Ruth Built," a Victorian cum art deco monstrosity in the Bronx at 161st Street. The awkward shape of the stadium and its beautiful parapets and steel valances enthralled me. I asked my father which players were represented in the bronze statuary in deep center field. He answered, "Babe Ruth, Lou Gehrig, and some other fellow."

That day Art Ditmar pitched and Elston Howard caught for the Yankees. Mantle was in center field, and Yogi Berra was platooned in right. Marvelous Marv Throneberry (with his commercial fame a quarter of a century in the future) played first base, and, yes, Bobby Richardson was at second base. The Orioles won 3-2, notwithstanding Yank Moose Skowron's wrong-way dinger to the right field pavilion late in the game.

After I learned that Mantle was terminally ill, I determined to return to New York to search for the Mickey Mantle of my memory. I wanted to understand the hold Mantle had on my imagination. On a trip with my family to the city in May 1995, I took my son to Yankee Stadium to see George Steinbrenner's Bronx Bombers. I had little interest in the game—my memories carried me back to better times for baseball. I was here to relive a touchstone experience of my childhood, the game I had watched nearly thirty-seven years before—and to recapture the sense of awe and rapture I had felt watching Number 7 in centerfield.

Sadly, the new Yankee Stadium bears only a faint resemblance to the Yankee Stadium of my youth. Gone is the majestic façade, which the Yankee faithful said bore the dent of Mantle's prodigious shot. All that is left of that wonderful architectural structure, which once overhung the third-tier grandstand, is a simulacrum façade that forms a backdrop for the low-lying left- and right-centerfield bleachers. Gone are the wonderful disparities of the old ball yard's outfield fences—296 feet at the right-field pole, 470 feet in straightaway center, and so forth. Gone is the bonze statuary of Ruth, Gehrig, and that other fellow, Miller Huggins, Ruth's manager—banished to an ignominious warren far behind the low left field wall.

This is a sacrilege. The stadium is on the National Historical Registry. I asked my wife how many bricks or façades have to be removed before a place becomes historically unregistered? They call this the "New Yankee Stadium," but there is nothing Yankee Stadium about it. I couldn't picture Mantle in this place; couldn't connect a memory to anything. Except for having my son along, the afternoon was a bust.

The next morning I got up early and walked up to 59th Street where it becomes Central Park South. Mantle had a restaurant here called Mickey Mantle's. It was closed at that time of day. Peering into a window, I saw that it was nothing more than a glorified bar and grill. Moreover, it reminded me of Mantle's alcoholism, and that diminished the man. I had run out of places to experience Mantle's aura.

Then I remembered Felix Pinella. Felix is a doorman for one of those posh apartment-condo complexes over on Lexington Avenue. I met Felix on a trip to Europe a number of years ago. He had worn a Yankee cap—the old kind from the 1950's, which molded itself to the skull without the high bossing so common on today's caps. He had given me his address, and I still had it in my wallet. I looked him up, and we renewed our friendship.

Felix was a regular at Yankee home games in the 1950's and early 1960's. I asked him what explained Mantle's charisma. Felix thought about it for a minute; then he reeled off a bill of particulars on the Mick. There was the wonderful alliteration of his name, his boyish good looks, his compact, muscular body, but most of all his demonstrations of explosive power from either side of the plate, violent jolts that made him the greatest switch-hitter the game has ever known. Felix brought it all into focus for me: Mantle was beautiful and terrifying at the same time. That was the source of his allure for me and everybody else. I finally had my answer.

Shortly after Mantle's death in August 1995, I went up to my attic in Asheville. After some considerable searching, I found an old Tampa Nuggets cigar box. Inside was the stadium program from August 11, 1958. I found the scorecard I had faithfully noted throughout the game. I learned that on that hot August afternoon in New York City, Mickey Charles Mantle did what he did better than anyone before him to play that beautiful game I once knew as baseball: He struck out twice in three official at bats. .

School
Days

This book would be incomplete without some recounting of John's and my early education and the teachers at Davidson Elementary School. Margaret Adams was our first grade teacher—we called her "Miss Margaret." She was a short, bespectacled white-haired woman in her mid-sixties, gracious and kindly, a well-respected teacher in the town since before World War I. Gladys Barnhardt, wife of our father's cousin Robert, who drove the green Studebaker and brought me to justice for tossing books out the classroom window (see Chapter 3), was our second-grade teacher. Our third-grade teacher, Jean Mattison, simply couldn't control John and me, or anybody else for that matter, and she spent much of her time doling out public spankings at the front of the room. My fourth grade experience is remembered primarily for the time I ran down Sarah Jetton, our teacher and umpire, at home plate and fractured her clavicle. In the fifth grade I paid more attention to my studies than previously, primarily because I had such great affection for our teacher, Elizabeth Davidson, a close friend of Aunt Louise.

In the sixth grade, under Gladys Cashion, I paid much less attention to schoolwork and endured on a regular basis after-school "detention halls" for my recalcitrance. Despite my less than stellar classroom performance, the school chose me for the Safety Patrol. This made my head swell, and I thought I could use the position to impress the girls.

The job of the Safety Patrol was to assist children across School Street at the crosswalks located at the northern and southern ends of the school property, to prevent any traffic on School Street from entering the drop-off zone while a bus was unloading, and to raise the American flag in the morning and lower and fold it properly in the afternoon. We ran the patrol in morning and afternoon shifts. Doug Cantrell and I formed one of the two teams.

Everything went without incident until the spring term, when one afternoon a bus made its turn onto School Street and uphill toward the drop-off zone, where I was on duty. At exactly the same time, a funeral procession, led by the Cathy Hoyle Funeral Home hearse, approached the drop-off zone from the opposite direction, heading toward the Mimosa Cemetery. Sizing up the situation, I moved to the center of the street and held out my stop sign to the hearse, even though the bus was still nowhere near the zone. The funeral procession came to a dead standstill as I waited for the bus to move into the zone. The hearse driver rolled down his window and said he would have my badge, such as it was, for impeding a funeral procession. That really unnerved me—I was afraid the school principal would fire me right then and there from the Safety Patrol. Instead, he praised me for standing my ground, even though I had misjudged the situation. That didn't stop tongues wagging in the town, however, about that "damn fool boy stopping a funeral."

In the seventh grade I showed some improvement in my schoolwork in the vise grip of "Miss Winnie" Potts, a lovable, if somewhat histrionic, teacher who used to shout at the entire class, "Have you lost your minds?" Once John reduced her to tears with his ineptitude in math—dumfounded by Miss Winnie's theatrics (she was wracked with grief over a C she had given him), all he could say was, "Please don't cry, Miss Potts."

During the summer before my eighth grade year, the global situation deteriorated dramatically. In August 1961, the Soviets began sealing off West Berlin. It looked as though our worst fears could actually become a fiery reality.

Since the late 1950's the government had done all it could do to prepare America for an all-out nuclear attack. These preparations were collectively known as Civil Defense. At school we routinely had Civil Defense drills. The town installed a new, louder fire alarm in front of the old Blake House on Main Street. During those drills at Davidson Elementary, school alarm bells alerted us to the possibility of incoming missiles. We were told to crawl under our desks or tables and cover out heads. When the all-clear bell rang, the teachers marched us out onto the upper playground, where, in the event of the real thing, if time allowed, our parents would pick us up and take us to the town shelter.

For years the basement of Johnson Gymnasium served as the shelter for the town of Davidson and Davidson College. Shelves filled with Civil Defense survival supplies filled virtually every inch of unused space. I would estimate that at that time the town and gown population totaled approximately 3,000 people. Even through my college years, 1966-1970, the college faithfully maintained the facility. We never actually believed that we would have to use it.

Nuclear preparedness for some families meant home bomb shelters. I am aware of only one such shelter having been built in Davidson. Winston Reid's father was particularly anxious about the whole thing and with good reason. We were well aware of the dangers of a proximity blast and its attendant radioactive fallout. Parents were even becoming concerned about radioactive strontium accumulating in cow milk from all the aboveground nuclear testing.

I visited the Reid shelter once. It was an underground, prefabricated affair well stocked for a siege. I suppose that those who built such shelters were the primordial American survivalists. There was just one small problem with the shelters.

I asked Winston what they planned to use for air. He described the air filtration system. We later learned that no system could filter out the radioactivity. The shelter would give protection from blast effects, but no matter how deep you dug it or how thick you made the walls, in the end the contaminated air could get you. You would also have to contend with panicky neighbors coming to call at the door of your little hole in the ground. We had yet to hear the term "nuclear winter."

All of this worried me tremendously. I begged Dad, to no avail, to build a shelter for us in the basement of our home. In the 1950's a Nike missile plant had opened in Charlotte. Those missiles had nuclear capability and made Charlotte at least a secondary, if not primary, nuclear target. Dad was adamant that a bomb shelter was a useless contraption, and he wasn't going to shell out a penny for such tom-foolery. Not persuaded, I began to pilfer canned goods from the kitchen pantry and after a time had a goodly stash hidden away for us in the basement.

In that prevailing atmosphere of fear and concern, we began to prepare for the school year, 1961-62. At the time Dad was far more concerned about our lackadaisical school performance than the pros-pect of a nuclear blast. One evening in late August, reacting to some-thing we had said, Dad worked himself into a lather and gave us his "elevator to success not running" speech. He had run out of patience. The following week we started the eighth grade. It was a turning point.

For the 1961-62 academic year the county board of education combined the eighth grades at the Davidson and Cornelius elemen-tary schools and then sorted the students into "regular" and "gifted" classes, both of which were housed on the same floor at the Davidson School. An out-of-towner, Miriam Elam, arrived to teach the gifted class. Another new teacher, Baxter Jones, was assigned to float be-tween the regular and gifted classes, teaching the slower students sci-ence and the advanced class algebra and science. John, Nancy With-ers, and I were among the unlucky students who were assigned to the slower class. Being labeled "regular" was not a confidence builder.

Lucille Trivette from Mooresville, the mill town seven miles north of Davidson, was the new regular eighth-grade teacher at the Davidson School. Her first husband had died, and she had recently married a Mooresville dentist. My first impression of her was "Looks mean, but will be a pushover." I was wrong—very wrong. I should have taken a hint from her eyes—she could chew you up and spit you out with those eyes.

On the first day of class, knowing my history as an underachiever, she took me aside and said something that would affect me for the rest of my life—and something I would never forget: "I don't care what you have or have not done before. What I do care about is what you do for me!" There was academic salvation of a sorts and forgiveness for past failings. From that day forward I became an overachiever.

It was not just to please her. There was something about Mrs. Trivette that made me want to learn—it went well beyond her stern disciplinarian approach. She had an uncanny ability to make just about any subject interesting. What she did with North Carolina history was nothing short of amazing.

There is, in my opinion, nothing potentially duller than N.C. state history. I base these comments on having suffered through that subject with my son, Jim, in his eighth grade year. Somehow, Mrs. Trivette made all of it, even John Locke and the Lord Proprietors, relevant and enjoyable. She also stressed to us the importance of good reading—John and I discovered, to our great delight, Edgar Allen Poe, Victor Hugo, and Arthur Conan Doyle in the small library she kept in the back of the classroom. She frequently had us write book reports, which she graded as much on the quality of the book itself as the written presentation. Under her tutelage I began to develop a genuine love of reading.

Baxter Colin Jones, from Sylva, in the mountains of western North Carolina, who arrived with a trove of moonshiner tales, also had a hand in teaching us. He was a hard-edged fellow who had fought in the Korean War and took no flak from any student. He was also flamboyant and a bit eccentric—he drove a souped-up black and white Ford Fairlane (it had a Chrysler V-8 in it), and with his slicked-black hair, he looked like the rock and roll idol in *Bye, Bye Birdie*. Most important, he was a fine teacher. Deciding that the regular eighth grade was as capable as the so-called gifted class, Mr. Jones introduced us to algebra at a time when the subject was not included in the county's regular eighth-grade course of study. And he was hard. I recall failing at least one test—I couldn't quite get those trains to meet at the station at the same time. At all events, in combination, BC Jones and Lucille Trivette bolstered my confidence and took the sting off the insult of being labeled "regular."

As an aside, I would note that Mrs. Trivette's regulars regularly stomped Mrs. Elam's gifted class on the playing fields of the Davidson

School—football, kickball, softball, and whatever. We sarcastically dubbed Mrs. Elam "Commander May Lay"—the vocalization of Elam spelled backwards. Her charges were "Elam's All Stars." This was a fierce competition, and Mrs. Trivette seemed to relish it. It played out in Commander May Lay's classroom one day as Mrs. Trivette, after careful preparations, sent John and me over to teach the All Stars about the Soviet Union (John enthralled the class with his presentation on the Politbureau).

Mrs. Trivette wanted to prepare us well for high school. She gave rigorous semester exams in every subject. When the final grades were in, and the school year ended in late May of 1962, Nancy Withers and I had straight A's for the year. My parents were astonished. Mrs. Templeton, one of the superintendents from the county office, had driven up from Charlotte two years before and pronounced our class incorrigible. Now she called us "luminaries," which was probably stretching it, but Mrs. Trivette had indeed worked a miracle.

As part of our final exam in state history that year, she asked us to do a project on North Carolina. I chose to make a scrapbook filled with vignettes on each of the state's one hundred counties. I worked on it for weeks. Hoke Lumber Company cut up some scrap pieces of pine board that I used for the binding. Mr. McKissick gave me some rawhide strands to tie it all together. I painted the state flag on the front cover. Mrs. Trivette was delighted with it and gave me an A. I recall that I was among the few students who fared well on that project. I was mighty proud of my effort. I still have that scrapbook stored away in my attic as a tangible memory of the most defining year of my life.

Four years later I graduated as the valedictorian of the North Mecklenburg High School class of 1966. Nancy Withers was the salutatorian. John, who caught "senioritis" in the spring term, finished ninth.

We didn't see Mrs. Trivette much after that eighth grade year. John and I last spoke with her at a five-and-ten store in Mooresville when we were seniors in college. She flashed those eyes, but instead of the impassioned, stern glance, which was so familiar from bygone years, she had tears in them, and I knew that she was proud of us.

Scarcely a day passes that I don't think of her. Lucille Trivette was the hardest teacher I ever had—and she forced a 180-degree turn in my attitude toward books and learning. She was, quite simply, my finest teacher.

Wahoo

In late August 1962, Margaret Banks invited John and me to a get-acquainted party at her plantation home near Huntersville. That night I met several teens who would be in my junior high school class at Alexander Junior High that coming school year. I also met Bill Hough, a rising sophomore at North Mecklenburg High School. Ginger and Bill's sister, Zoe Ann, were classmates and good friends. That night Bill and I struck up a lasting friendship. I learned from him that his mother, Ruth Hough, would be my ninth grade English teacher.

By October of 1962, with Mrs. Hough's help, I had integrated myself into the academic and social circles of my new school. She was a wonderful teacher, and I looked forward to her class every day. Things were really going well for me—world events were the last thing on my mind now. But the Cold War was about to go hot as America confronted the Missiles of October.

We didn't know anything about what was happening in Cuba until President Kennedy addressed the nation on television on October 22. Kennedy told us that the Russians were deploying nuclear warheads on the island. He showed us aerial photographs of some of the Russian ships transporting missiles to Cuba and the installations, which were already in operation. The Russian missiles would be poised to take out every major city on the East Coast.

I recall that this was really a frightening time for my friends and me. During the crisis Judy Norman, who sat across from me, cried through each English class. She was afraid that her brother, Ronnie, would be drafted. The rest of us were more concerned about being vaporized or dusted off permanently by radioactive fallout.

Kennedy's Secretary of State, Dean Rusk, was a Davidson College graduate. Dad felt confident that Rusk would find a diplomatic solution to the crisis, but I had some serious doubts. When Kennedy gave the Russians an ultimatum in the form of a naval blockade, the entire mess almost reached critical mass. It looked like we were goners.

When the Russian ships turned around, I believe the entire country collectively exhaled long and hard. There were still some problems left to work out, but, for practical purposes, the crisis had passed. The future looked a little brighter.

The remainder of that school year passed peacefully. By springtime the world situation had resumed some semblance of stability, and I finished out the year attending to the ordinary crises of adolescent development. The following fall I entered North Mecklenburg High, where Mrs. Hough's husband was the principal.

North Mecklenburg was eleven miles from Davidson, located less than a half mile down Highway 115 from Alexander Junior High, and the postal address was Huntersville. North was one of four comprehensive high schools Mecklenburg County had built during a frenzy of city-county consolidation in the early 1950's. William A. Hough was the principal during the years John and I attended North: 1963-1966. He was immensely popular with students.

Behind his back everybody affectionately called Mr. Hough "W.A." and "Wahoo." He was one of the kindest, most thoroughly decent men I have ever met. He was also one of the most empathetic, fair, and supportive teachers anyone from my neck of the woods could remember. I count the privilege of having had his good counsel for three years among the great blessings of my life.

Mr. Hough was first and foremost a Christian gentleman. He was thoroughly Baptist and a graduate of Wake Forest University, to boot. Wake never had a greater fan. We always rooted for the Demon Deacons during those years simply because we wanted the school to win for Mr. Hough's sake. W.A.'s Christian enthusiasm was contagious. In the years before school prayer was finally outlawed (in North Carolina schools it outlasted the 1962 constitutional ban for at least a decade), he made certain that we had daily devotions at the school. One of the students would read scripture from the Bible, and a prayer always followed the reading. Morning devotion was the only time W.A. openly expressed his faith. The rest of the time he simply lived it.

Wahoo had a good sense of humor, although it could occasionally lead him into uncharted territory. That became apparent during and after the infamous Sandra Umburger incident. Miss Umburger was the school's vivacious young librarian. One spring morning at the annual awards day presentations, Mr. Hough announced, "The Teacher of the Year Award goes to Miss Sandra Hamburger." The laughter started in the back of the gymnasium and worked itself forward until the entire place was rocking. After a couple of minutes, things had died down sufficiently for W.A. to continue to dig his hole. Blushing, he said, "Well, she looks good enough to eat." The gym thundered with laughter and wild applause. Miss Umburger made a hasty retreat back to her seat. W.A. stood up there on the stage with a puzzled look on his face. I don't think he ever got it.

I had some memorable friends at North. One of them was Gene Holton, whose defining moment came in his effort to outwit Cop Cook, the constable in Huntersville. Officer Cook took great delight in setting up speed traps and was notorious for keeping the town coffers filled with revenues received from catching speeders. He was relentless. Holton said that as one of his responsibilities he helped run the small licensing station for the Department of Motor Vehicles (DMV). The station's reputation for failing first-time applicants was so horrendous that no one from the high school dared go there for a license. Most of my classmates went to the U.S. Highway 29 DMV in north Charlotte, where virtually no one failed the first time.

Holton declared that things were going to change. Shortly after his sixteenth birthday he let it be known that he was going to take the driver's exam in Huntersville and become the first high school student in recent memory to pass it there. We wished him well that day when he set off to get his license. The next morning when I saw him in the hall, I asked him how things had gone with the exam. He looked dejected and somewhat bruised-up. He said that things were going well until he got to a stop sign, which he failed to see. He ran the sign and was T-boned by a truck on the passenger side. The inspector wound up in the hospital. I said, "I guess you didn't get your license?" He replied, "I don't know—I haven't heard yet."

Another memorable character from those years is Monroe Caldwell. Monroe was the quintessential greaser of the early 1960's. He was a good natured fellow and would have been better looking, I think, were it not for his black hair which was perpetually slicked down by mountains of Brylcreem. He and I took several classes together. Monroe took pride in his occasional F's, claiming "F" stood for "fun." That was generally how he approached things. He really was a likable guy.

One night during our junior year he and some others were milling around in the parking lot at Shoney's, a restaurant on the Plaza in Charlotte, when a car roared by. We learned that Monroe yelled something at the driver. The car backed up, and a man with a handgun got out and shot Monroe dead on the spot. Mr. Hough, who had tried to be a father figure to Monroe, was shaken by his death—he was near tears when he announced it over the P.A. system. Monroe was the first of my peers to die. We all took it pretty hard.

Perhaps the most memorable people from those years, however, were the teachers. Mr. Hough had assembled a top-notch teaching staff. Many of them used their tenures at North as stepping-stones to distinguished college teaching careers.

Eleanor Rigney taught world history and debating. I was in her advanced history class during my sophomore year. A truly intellectual person, she had the unique ability to make history come alive. For every event described in the text, she presented supportive material that enlivened it and made it stick in memory. I remember that we read, among other things, a brief history of the ancient Near East. One afternoon the discussion moved into the cedars of Lebanon— we spent thirty minutes discussing building materials in ancient Israel.

I suppose it was appropriate that I happened to be in Miss Rigney's history classroom on a fateful autumn day of my sophomore year. November 22, 1963, was a splendid Indian summer day in the North Carolina Piedmont; the temperature was in the sixties, and the sky was cloudless. None of us knew that President Kennedy had gone to Dallas to bind up some party wounds, and had we known, we wouldn't have cared.

The day had gone quite uneventfully. I finished lunch around 1 p.m. and cut up some in the next class. The bell rang at 2 p.m., and I went to Miss Rigney's world history class. Nothing was awry—at least not until Mr. Rafferty came in as we were getting settled in for our last class of the day. He was wearing a short-sleeve shirt and red tie. He quietly walked into the room and spoke with Miss Rigney. She exclaimed, "What? No!" I was in the first seat by the door. She looked straight at me and said, "Kennedy's been shot!" I said to her, "You're kidding. They don't shoot Presidents in America anymore."

Mr. Hough came over the intercom with an announcement, "This is something you will all want to hear." The front office turned CBS radio's affiliate station WBT in Charlotte onto the system. I remember Walter Cronkite's solemn words, "Shots were fired at the President's motorcade. The President was wounded, perhaps fatally." (Kennedy was shot at 12:30 p.m. CST.) A few minutes later Cronkite, his voice choking, announced, "President Kennedy died at 1 p.m. Dallas time," or words to that effect. In her seat in the back of the room, Charlene Wilson was sobbing uncontrollably. Mr. Hough called off school early. All activities were cancelled for the remainder of the day. The afternoon was warm and bright. I remember riding the bus back to Davidson. All along the way flags were being lowered to half-staff.

Early that night John and I huddled around the television and watched the broadcast from Andrews Air Force Base in Maryland. We watched as Air Force One landed, and people removed the President's casket from the plane. His brother Bobby was holding Jackie Kennedy's hand—she had blood all over her. President Johnson gave a brief speech asking for our help and God's. Next, the television announcer read Walt Whitman's "O Captain, My Captain." That's all I can remember from that day.

On Saturday, November 23, we awoke to a heavy rain that would last throughout the day and into the night. It remains an appropriate metaphor for the sorrow we all felt. We adored Kennedy. He was young and brilliant and seemed to stand for everything that was right in America. We admired the way he had stood up to the Russians during the Cuban Missile Crisis of 1962. We really believed that the torch had been passed to a new generation of Americans—our generation. Now he and all he stood for were gone. It was worth crying over. America would never be quite the same. We know that now, and I believe we knew it then.

The next day was a beautiful, warm, Indian summer Sunday. My family went to church. Mr. Harper prayed for the country. Everyone did. We got home from church around noon and turned on Aunt Louise's television set just in time to watch Jack Ruby shoot Lee Harvey Oswald in the basement of the central Dallas police station. It was the first live-televised murder in history. We saw it all.

That afternoon we watched as the President's body was taken from the White House to the Capitol Rotunda. I was very impressed by the sailor who followed the casket with the Presidential flag. No one in the procession seemed to miss a step, although William Manchester in his book *The Death of a President* writes that the bearers nearly dropped the casket. I remember a military band playing the "Navy Hymn."

President Johnson declared Monday, November 25, a national day of mourning. For reasons, which still elude me, the basketball staff at North called us to announce that we were having a mandatory junior varsity basketball practice that afternoon. "Mandatory" meant we would have to have a pressing excuse to miss the practice. An unexcused cut would mean possible dismissal from the team, and we would not be allowed to participate in any other sport if that happened. I thought the death of a President was pressing enough, but the staff apparently thought differently. This was particularly unusual because some of the coaches taught U.S. and world history. Consequently, John and I had to catch filmed highlights of JFK's funeral on the news that night.

William Manchester wrote that what we witnessed that weekend was the greatest single outpouring of collective grief in American history. We did not understand that then—only later. We did not know then what we now know about Kennedy—the womanizing and all. Even that knowledge in no way diminishes the memory of how we felt *then*. It would probably be a much different world today had he lived. We all felt cheated by his death.

On Tuesday, November 26, we returned to Miss Rigney's history class to begin where we had left off. I liked her so much that I did my utmost to do well. Van Lear Logan, my neighbor from Davidson, was a senior and certainly the most knowledgeable student in the class. I learned a lot from her. I did well enough to rank second in the history class—until the final exam that year.

Rumor had it that Miss Rigney always used the New York Regent's Exams as the format for her finals. I bought a review book and began going through it. Aunt Louise taught U.S. history at East Mecklenburg High School, just east of Charlotte. She had a copy of the world history text we used, including a copy of the test questions. I used the test questions as practice questions for the exam. I felt uncomfortable going into the final. Rigney was going to murder us with those New York questions.

What I saw on the exam was straight out of the book that my aunt had loaned me. I sailed through the test and made a hundred. I suppose I should have felt bad about it at the time, but I reasoned that I hadn't done anything technically wrong. My aunt told me to let it lie; I had used the resources available to me and had done it honestly. Still, I have this inkling of guilt about it even to this day.

The following year, in late 1964, Miss Rigney organized a debate team and invited me to try out. I made the team after doing well in the trials. She teamed me up with Bill Hough, W.A.'s son, to take the negative side in the debates. The national topic that year dealt with the development of an international organization to regulate the proliferation of nuclear weapons. Bill and I spent days in the Davidson College library coming up with a foolproof strategy. With Miss Rigney's assistance we developed an argument that centered on national sovereignty. We argued that no nation would willingly relinquish its sovereignty to any international organization outside of gunpoint. We traced the history of national sovereignty all the way back to ancient Egyptian and Hebraic boundary laws; we even quoted from the *Book of Leviticus* in the *Bible*.

In our preliminary rounds Bill and I smothered our opposition. Our affirmative team had a more formidable task. They won their preliminary debates but their wins were not as impressive as ours. They clearly had the more difficult position. When we learned that we had qualified for the state regional debates, I was confident Bill and I could hold our own; I was concerned for our teammates, however.

The regional debates were held in Shelby, North Carolina, in the winter of 1965. Bill and I easily won our debates that day. Our affirmative side made a surprisingly strong showing and won all of theirs. Unfortunately, when officials tallied all the scores, our total team score fell two points behind the winner. Bill and I were particularly disappointed because we thought we had a shot at the state title. Anyway, we all felt good about our effort and the fact that we had done so well in the inaugural year of debating at North.

The following year, Miss Rigney declined to coach debating again. Bill Hough had graduated, so my brother and I formed the negative end of the debate squad. That year, because of all sorts of other commitments, we decided not to try for the state competition. Instead, we chose to go to a statewide invitational debate held at Davidson College. The team picked to win the state competition that year was Reynolds High School in Winston-Salem.

The topic was "Resolved, the United States Government Should Arbitrate Disputes between Labor and Management." John and I recast the sovereignty arguments and backed our points with some sound research on constitutional law. We manhandled the Myers Park (Charlotte) team. That was surprising since everyone thought that they were the second best team in the state.

That afternoon we made it into the final round with the Reynolds affirmative team. The opening speech was by a girl who restricted the topic to government-mandated arbitration of labor-management disputes *only* in time of declared war. Changing the topic in this manner was a flagrant violation of the rules. John and I repeatedly asked for a disqualification ruling, which was not forthcoming. Improvising wildly, we somehow did well enough to lose by only two points.

I later learned why we lost from a Davidson student. The girl wore our judge's fraternity pin; he was a college junior, and she was a high school senior. They were later married. It was a bitter lesson in *Realpolitik.*

Another memorable event from my North years indirectly involved my sophomore English teacher, Margaret Smith. In the spring of 1964 the English department brought in a student teacher, Miss Horton, who was the first runner-up in one of the Miss North Carolina pageants. She was drop-dead gorgeous!

We were studying William Shakespeare's *Julius Caesar.* Miss Horton had taken over the teaching duties from Miss Smith that morning. She had each of us stand before the class and recite Mark Anthony's funeral oration. Fred Nelson's was the most entertaining. Miss Horton was seated on a table in the back of the room with her lovely limbs crossed. She moved to change position as Fred boomed out Mark Anthony's "Friends, Romans, countrymen, lend me your [pause] LEGS!" For one brief, shining moment every male eye in the class was riveted on the back of the room. Miss Horton blushingly smiled and said, "Thank you."

Another memorable teacher was Jean Holtzclaw. A vivacious and energetic teacher, she was in her twenties when she taught me French during my junior and senior years. Jean took her classes Christmas caroling every year. We always went to Davidson, where we would hit some of the faculty homes on Main Street, sing *Un Flambeau, Jeannette Isabella* at every stop, and then cap it off at the college president's home. We were awful. I suppose we more resembled loutish drunks babbling off-key than the graceful nineteenth century carolers we were supposed to emulate.

In 1964-65 Jean was the advisor for the high school's National Honor Society, of which John and I were members. In the spring of that year North Mecklenburg hosted the North Carolina state convention at the Golden Eagle Motel in Charlotte. Jean spent much of the year getting the event organized. She even got Stan Brookshire, the mayor of Charlotte, to put in an appearance. Unlucky me, I got to meet His Honor; I introduced myself first and put out my hand to shake his. The mayor handed me a lit cigarette, and I got burned. It was a bizarre moment. I don't recall that Brookshire said anything at all to me; I do remember that he didn't apologize—and my memory of the incident still rankles.

At all events, I left North in 1966 for the broader world. In time I would forget much of my French, displacing it with the language of medicine and the German I studied in college and improved upon during my two-year Army stay in Germany. But I would not forget Jean Holtzclaw.

Another memorable character from my high school days was Mack Haynes. He is far better remembered as the head football coach rather than as a history and physical education (P.E.) teacher, charades that fronted his real job as coach. He was a stubby fellow with a remarkable sense of humor.

During my sophomore year at North, Mack was my P.E. teacher. He tended to favor his star junior varsity (J.V.) football players by always putting them out of harm's way. I remember how he used to make sure that all of his players were on the same team when we played touch football. That way they wouldn't be butting into each other and risking injury. That didn't bode well for the rest of us. This almost got Fred Nelson killed.

Poor Fred was the quarterback for our P.E. team one hot morning in the early fall of 1963. Walter Shaw was a tackle on the J.V. squad. He blitzed Fred and slammed him to the ground, breaking Fred's arm. Poor Fred walked around in a daze, babbling, "Mr. Haynes, I broke my arm!" We carted him off to the school nurse's office and refused to play any more under Mack's rules. Fortunately, he arranged the teams more fairly after that.

I had my moments with Mack. In the winter of 1964 we were into basketball. I was chosen to jump center against my cousin Mike Kelly. Mack tossed up the jump ball, and when I hit the floor coming down, I saw Mack in a most peculiar, contorted position on the gym floor. He was moaning, "Puckett! Puckett! Damn Puckett!" Somehow in going up for the ball, I had nailed his gonads with one of my feet. It must have been a perfect hit, because it took him two days to get over it.

Mack put North on the state football map my senior year in high school. Davidson contributed its fair share of players. Buddy Caldwell was the quarterback, and Jim Mc Ever was an All-State halfback.

Mike Kelly from Cornelius was a stellar tight end. I remember that the team started out ranked second in the state. They were really good, and the games were great fun to watch.

John and I and our circle of friends seldom took dates to the games. George Watkins drove us to most of them in his father's Mercedes, which gave us some sense of class. After each game hundreds of North students assembled at the Shoney's restaurant on the Plaza—the same Shoney's where Monroe Caldwell was shot. We had a rollicking good time.

The major competition was, as always, Myers Park High School in Charlotte. Myers Park was a very affluent school located right next door to the Charlotte Country Club. The school always fielded superb athletic teams. They were perennial state champions or contenders in most sports, beneficiaries of an enthusiastic and wealthy booster club. In that 1965 season the Myers Park football team boasted no less than three All-South players. One was a fullback expatriate from Greenwood, South Carolina. I heard that the Myers Park Booster Club had actually recruited him and bought a house for him, his teen bride, and their baby. Another was their quarterback, Neb Hayden. The team also had a superb African American tailback named Jimmy Kilpatrick. Harris Woodside was an All-State wide receiver. And there was Louis Jewell, an eccentric sprinter on the track team who caught passes in the fall. I would get to know Jewell the following spring in track. He always talked about himself in the third person and called himself, "The Jewell." He had a great sense of humor, and we became friends.

Myers Park's privilege was a sore subject for Wahoo. He complained that Myers Park was getting an enormously disproportionate amount of money from the county. The county superintendent's son went to Myers Park. By the time the North-Myers Park game rolled around, there was plenty of ill will on our side. The Myers Park crowds thought we were country bumpkins, which was particularly offensive to those of us who believed we were above that sort of thing.

The night of the game, September 25, 1965, I was dating my friend Mary Whitton, who happened to be a student at Myers Park and a member of their marching band. She somehow got herself excused and sat on the North side with me at the game, which was played in the Myers Park Stadium. The place was packed. It was a balmy, clear evening and the game was played under lights. Both teams were undefeated. It was advertised as the biggest game ever played in Mecklenburg County. My former next-door neighbor, Shaw Smith, who played defensive safety in that game, estimates that the crowd was thirty thousand. I believe that is an accurate appraisal.

On the first play from scrimmage North was on its own twenty-yard line. Buddy Caldwell took the snap and handed off to Mike Ray, one of the halfbacks. Ray, a former junior high quarterback, threw the old halfback bomb, which was one of the finest passes I've ever seen. Mike Kelly at tight end had gotten past the Myers Park secondary; he caught the ball, and easily outran the defenders to the end zone. The Myers Park crowd stood stone silent. No one had scored on the Mustangs that early in anybody's memory. On the other side of the field the crowd went wild.

Then the unbelievable happened. I can still see it in slow motion. Kelly has just emerged from the end zone. An official is dropping a white flag near the line of scrimmage. He rules "Holding." I can't believe it. The play is long over, and the ref drops a flag. It was home cooking at its worst. Mack nearly went crazy. It took about ten minutes before the game resumed.

The North players really got mad. They started to gang-tackle the Myers Park ball carriers. I remember vividly how one of the Mustang backs, after taking a demolishing hit, yelled, "Don't hurt my legs!" That only added fuel to the fire.

All of that wasn't enough. Myers Park receivers were catching passes on short hops and being credited with receptions. The refs were unbelievable. We later heard that the Myers Park Booster Club had bought them off. It was a night of dreadful frustration. Myers Park led 13-6, when in the waning moments North scored to make it 13-12. Rather than go for a two-point conversion and a possible victory, Coach Haynes decided to kick for the single extra point. He figured a tie would give North a share of the state championship (a statewide poll of sportswriters designated the state champion in that era). It proved to be a bad gamble: the North kicker couldn't convert the extra point, and that was the end of it. Myers Park finished the season undefeated and tied with Durham High for the state title. North ranked third behind them. It was a wound that never healed.

It is remarkable that two of the North Mecklenburg players, my cousin Mike Kelly and Larry Hefner, went on to play in the National Football League. Several other players including Jim McEver and Walter Shaw were named to the All-State team that year. Shaw Smith is today a professor at Davidson College. Our quarterback, Buddy Caldwell, played baseball at the University of South Carolina under Coach Bobby Richardson (of Yankee fame) and later played Double-A ball in the minors. Buddy married Mike Kelly's sister, Judy. I suppose that sort of makes him family.

I didn't follow North football after that year. I last saw Mack Haynes at a reception at our church in Concord in the late 1980's. He looked like the Mack of old, only a little heavier. We reminisced about the 1965 football team. He said that if that ref hadn't dropped the flag after Mike Kelly's reception, North would have walked all over Myers Park. We'll never know. I learned that Mack died a few years ago. I still can't get that basketball mishap/groin kick out of my mind. I thought I had killed him.

There is one other very memorable teacher from that group recruited by Mr. Hough. She was my father's sister, Louise Puckett. Louise was born two years after my dad in 1908. She graduated from the Cornelius town high school and received her B.A. at the Women's College in Greensboro—now the University of North Carolina at Greensboro. And she did masters work at the University of North Carolina, Chapel Hill. Louise became a schoolteacher in the early 1930's and taught high school history at the Cornelius School until the 1950's, when four new consolidated high schools were created in Mecklenburg County and merged into the Charlotte city school system. She taught at East Mecklenburg High School for ten years and came to North in 1964.

Louise was the most unselfish person I've ever met. She devoted herself to her friends and family. She never married, although she once told me she had almost accepted a proposal. She was always a member of my immediate family, and she's a part of many of my favorite early childhood memories.

Until I was six Louise lived in Cornelius with her father, Lonnie Puckett ("Papa"). My grandmother, Molly Washam Puckett ("Miss Molly"), had a stroke in the mid 1940's and was virtually unresponsive thereafter. Louise helped Papa care for her at home. She came home from school twice every day to feed Miss Molly through a stomach tube. In all the years that Louise looked after her mother, her patient never developed a bedsore. Louise was always proud of that. After Miss Molly's death, Papa slowly descended into what was then diagnosed as dementia—probably what we now know as Alzheimer's disease.

After Papa died in 1954, Louise took a job with the history department at East Mecklenburg High School. She lived in a teacherage in Matthews, North Carolina, outside of Charlotte. Often on weekends she came home to Davidson, where she maintained an apartment in our home, the Blake House on Main Street, which my father rented from the college. We were always delighted to see Louise on those weekends and looked forward excitedly to her arrival.

One of my favorite memories of "Aunt Ease," as we called her when we were small children, was cooking breakfast with her in her upstairs apartment. I loved making French toast. It was the only thing I could cook and then eat. She gave me free range of her kitchen. I loved Louise with all my heart—she was our extended family. Mom didn't mind at all. She and Louise were always the closest of friends.

Louise spent as much time with my family as possible. When my parents built our new house on the corner of Lorimer Road and College Drive in 1956, she paid to build a wing of the house as an apartment, which she would call her own for over thirty years. She brought to the house a sense of peace and gentleness that I still blissfully remember. She was very artistic, and she surrounded herself with paintings, some of which were her own. She rotated books in and out of her small library, which was a perpetual source of fascination for John and me.

I remember how much I missed Louise when the family went to Williamstown, Massachusetts, for the summer of 1958. She was off at summer school that year, and only late in the summer was she able to spend some time with us. She flew into Troy, New York, and I remember picking her up on a rainy afternoon and driving into the

Berkshires. John and I were very excited. We felt that we had so many interesting things to show her. Louise gladly soaked it all up. She really enjoyed our company, as we did hers.

In time Louise grew weary of the weekend trips to Davidson and began searching for a new job closer to home. W.A. Hough was looking for a new U.S. history teacher, and he offered her a position with the school district's approval. It was the best thing that could have happened to me.

Louise accepted the job at North and began teaching there in the fall of 1964. She was delighted to be finally at home. She moved permanently into her apartment at our house. This guaranteed John and me a ride to school each morning and freed us up from the tedium of the Love Bird Express. Louise became so popular that the entire neighborhood would show up looking for a lift. Almost forty years later some of the old gang still talk about riding to North with Louise.

Louise was a marvelous teacher. She hit the high spots hard. Eleanor Rigney had planted in me a love for history, and Louise nurtured it admirably. She had us do projects and papers on select topics in U.S. history. I remember writing a term paper on Warren Harding and the Tea Pot Dome Scandal, which was the greatest presidential scandal prior to Watergate. In later years I told her that the paper had given me a humorous basis for comparison with President Clinton and his shenanigans. Warren Harding was just about the worst President in American history. Still, the people loved him.

When Dad died in 1972, Louise became my mother's constant companion and closest confidant. Mom developed insulin-dependent diabetes and suffered a mild heart attack. Over the years she gradually began to lose her cognitive faculties. Louise tried to manage her at home but really couldn't handle the situation. Mom's personality change made it difficult for Margaret and me to keep her at our house in Concord, where I practiced medicine at the time. We eventually had to place her in a local nursing home.

Mom died on June 3, 1985. It was late in the evening and before going home from the hospital that day, I stopped by for a short visit at the nursing home. Mom was unresponsive. A short time later the home called to say she had passed and to ask if I would fill out the death certificate. I went there and sadly completed that task. Two days later we had a memorial service for her at the college church. Charlie Raynal, the minister, read Mom's favorite poem, Tennyson's "Crossing the Bar," and he noted rightly that Virginia Puckett had been a loving and devoted mother.

Louise lived in our home at 105 College Drive until The Pines, a beautiful retirement home, opened in Davidson. My parents' wills had arranged for Louise to sell the house and use the money for her new home and continued retirement. Louise was one of the charter members at The Pines. My sister, Ginger, came down from Roanoke Rapids and helped her move into her new apartment. I had the pleasure of clearing out the attic and the bookshelves of what we had called for over thirty years "the new house." Happily, Louise seemed content at The Pines, and she had a wide array of both old and new friends there.

Over the years I enjoyed sharing my love of history with Louise. I would often tell her all about what I was reading. We shared a common bond in that interest. I watched her as she aged and knew that some day we would have to give her up. I just hoped that when the time came, she wouldn't suffer.

In February 1997, Louise had a heart attack and died two days later. She was spared the indignities of extreme old age. She had her health and a superb quality of life right up to the end. She gave my family, her students, and her friends eighty-nine gracious years.

Ginger immediately arrived from Roanoke Rapids to handle the funeral arrangements. John was in Magdeburg, Germany, teaching on a Fulbright scholarship at the university there. He somehow managed to arrange a flight out of Berlin. We received a call from Mr. Hough, who told us how much he valued the friendship our families had shared over the years.

My teachers from that era retired years ago, and many have died. Mr. Hough remained a vibrant link to some of the best years of my life until his own death just recently. In an era before Advanced Placement and honors programs were widely available (there were none at North), John and I encountered at North Mecklenburg a core of teachers who were highly qualified in their disciplines and heavily invested in their profession—teachers who prepared us well in every way for the liberal arts curriculum we would have to negotiate at

Davidson College. North in the mid-1960's was no rural hick high school. I count myself blessed to have passed that way and to have come of age in that place.

Wild
Bill

When our baseball days were done, someone appraised the Puckett twins' physiques and declared, "Why, you're natural born runners!" At that time I gave the matter no thought. I was still smarting from an earlier, unfavorable appraisal of my body by my friend Will Brown: "Why you're the most pathetic example of a human specimen I've ever seen." Fortunately, that kind of derision would soon pass.

Sterling Martin, a star runner at the college, watched John, then a ninth grader, run a 440-yard dash in the fall of 1962. John turned in a 59.0 second quarter, running in tennis shoes and trouncing Eddie Beam, who had cockily challenged him to a race. Not bad for a kid with absolutely no prior training. Sterling was ecstatic and encouraged both of us to go out for track in the spring of our ninth-grade year, in 1963.

John and I both planned to run in the spring, but first we wanted to play on the basketball team. Lewis Walker, a math teacher at Alexander Junior High School, was our coach. He was a fine teacher and a prince of a fellow. Unfortunately, we didn't have a gym. The county had planned to complete a new gymnasium by the beginning of the 1962-63 school year, but because of construction delays, the facility would not be available until late the following spring.

In that fall of 1962, the county relegated us to an ancient gym at the Huntersville Elementary School. The place was tiny. In fact, it looked like the gym in the movie *Hoosiers*, only more cramped. A regulation floor was its only merit. The south goal rose from the stands, and the north end had only about an eight-foot clearance from the back wall. It was a lethal place for lay-up attempts, the thin safety padding offering little protection. The stands were on the east side. The west wall was only about five feet from the court. A small fireplace on the west side was meant to provide heat for the gym, a relic dating from the 1920's. In the end, however, that pathetic little gym would make us a team.

The season ran from November through February. When the cold weather came, the gym became like something surreal out of *Dr. Zhivago*. I remember one afternoon when the outdoor temperature hovered around five degrees, with wind chills below zero, and there we were bundled up for practice. The building had no central heating. No one dared build a fire for fear of burning down the place. We were too cold to do anything but lay-ups and complain about the lousy accommodations.

I remember two games from that season. Both were with Spaugh Junior High from west Charlotte, the best team in the county. They beat—and humiliated—us by twenty-six points on their home court. Several weeks later the Spaugh team came calling at the Huntersville gym. I remember that when they came in, we were already warming up. We heard at first some snickers, then outright laughter. They were making fun of our gym! That really set us off. Despite its pathetic appearance and apparent dangers, we had grown very fond of our little arena. Jim Mc Ever said, "Well, you heard 'em. You know what to do."

Spaugh was never in the game. We were steamed up—three or four of us would eventually foul out. We must have stolen the ball ten times for easy lay-ups. Everything we put up went in, and the Spaugh team wasn't able to put anything together. They hadn't run into anything that season like our juggernaut —it was easily our best effort of the season. In the end we won by twenty-six points. It could have been a lot worse if Coach Walker hadn't substituted. When the Spaugh players left the gym for their bus, some of them were crying. One of our players remarked disdainfully, "You shouldn't have made fun of our gym. We're kinda partial to it." For that one moment we were glad the new gym hadn't been completed.

In the late winter of 1963 John and I went out for the track team at Alexander. A P.E. teacher named Joe "Mac" Mcginnis was the coach. On the first day of practice he had us all race a 440-yard dash. I couldn't even make it around the track. John flashed by in 58.0 seconds and whipped us all.

Mac got us into shape, and we had a good team. Jim McEver ran the 100-yard dash in 10.2 seconds, which was great for a ninth grade white male in those years. I ran on the 880 and mile-relay teams. John was our 440-yard dash runner.

The first meet of the season was held on a cold March day against Eastway Junior High on the North Mecklenburg High School track. John won the 440 in around 56.0 seconds. I ran the relays, which we easily won. After the meet, as we were leaving the track, Mac introduced me to Mr. William Cochran, the track and cross-country coach at North Mecklenburg. One of the team members joked, "You know they call him 'Wild Bill.'" I didn't have a clue what he was talking about.

Countywide meets highlighted the season. The first was held at East Mecklenburg High School. Jim McEver met his match there with a runner named Jamie Erwin, from Alexander Graham Bell Junior High. They tied at 10.2 seconds in the 100. John won the 440 in 54.4 seconds, just beating out a McClintock Junior High runner. We both ran in several races that afternoon. Our team placed second in the 880-yard relay and second in the mile-relay when a fellow from McClintock named Bruce Cunningham (a future Morehead Scholar) beat me at the tape. After the meet a judge disqualified John for running in too many races. Mr. Mcginnis pointed out to him that there was a twin afoot.

The second county meet was at Myers Park. I remember John blasting out of the blocks in the 440-yard dash. Coming into the third turn he was way ahead of everyone, on a sub-50 second pace. Diane Neil, a friend of ours from Huntersville, was watching. She cried,

"Look at him go! They'll never catch him!" Joe McGinnis remarked, "Either he's got something I don't know about, or he's going to die pretty soon." When I looked at my stopwatch, I said, "He'll never hold it." John didn't. It was one of those tragic finishes—flailing arms, slow-motion agony, and a body crying for a ventilator. John finished fifth and out of the medals.

That night I anchored both our 880-yard and mile-relay teams each to a second-place finish. That was my best effort to date. I recall I ran the final leg on the mile relay in 53.0 seconds. That was a good time for a ninth grader in those years.

The following autumn of 1963 we were at North Mecklenburg High School as tenth graders. John and I opted to play junior varsity basketball (J.V.) rather than run on Mr. William Cochran's cross-country team. That turned out to be a mistake.

Mr. Joe White was the J.V. basketball coach. John and I had managed to make his team and were among the original starting five as forwards. We had a potentially good team. Things looked bright for us, having come off an 8-2 season in the ninth grade.

The season started out smoothly enough for the J.V. team. We easily won our first three games. John and I were starters. As we were twins and generally facing man-to-man defenses, inevitably someone would confuse things and leave one of us wide open under the basket for an easy lay-up. Then disaster struck.

The varsity squad was losing and groping for new talent. Mike Kelly, our center, got the call to the varsity. Then Doug Robinson, a future All-County player, decided to take over the J.V. team, and he started gunning and never passing off. Doug ran up some big numbers, but we were on a losing streak. Then Coach Everett Pigg, the varsity coach, called Doug up, and the varsity now had two sophomore starters.

Lacking a big man and any inside muscle, we began losing at a frenetic pace with spreads as high as thirty to forty-five points. One afternoon after practice Mr. White called a team conference and told us that his wife thought we were the worst team he had ever coached. In all fairness, I think he was doing his best, but he didn't have much to work with. Regardless, we were demoralized and wanted to quit the team, but Mr. Hough encouraged us to tough it out.

It was the winter of our discontent. After that baleful season ended, John and I vowed to give up high school basketball altogether and that spring seek our fortunes with track and Coach William Cochran.

After the basketball season ended, the car pools from Davidson dried up. None of us owned a car in those days. When John and I ran cross-country and track at North, we had to hitch rides to Davidson after practice. Getting to Huntersville was never a problem, and we always stopped at Neil's Drugstore for an orange drink or soda pop.

Joe Neil was the Huntersville pharmacist. He had two daughters, Diane and Sally, who were our contemporaries. Both were lovely girls. We were good friends, and John and I visited at the Neils' house often during our years at North. Diane was the only girl to ever slap me. It all had to do with my divulging a particularly good poker hand she held.

Mr. Neil had endured bilateral lower extremity amputations because of peripheral vascular disease. That didn't seem to phase his spirits; he bore his physical infirmities with quiet grace and dignity. Mr. Neil was always smiling, and he had only good things to say about life and people. He died prematurely a year or two after I graduated from North. After she graduated from UNC-Chapel Hill, Diane married, moved into the house across the street from her mother, and started a long and distinguished teaching career at North Mecklenburg.

I visited in the Neil home shortly after completing my oncology fellowship at Wake Forest University School of Medicine in 1981. I was driving to Columbia, South Carolina, where I had accepted a faculty position at the University of South Carolina School of Medicine. I was puffed up with pride and confidence when I stopped in Huntersville to visit with Mrs. Neil, Diane, and her sister Sally. They probably thought I had become overbearing and conceited. I felt badly about it afterwards.

At any rate, after spending some time at Neil's Drug after track or cross-country practice, it was anybody's guess how John and I would get home from there. We thumbed down some memorable drivers. One of them was Jerry Byers from Cornelius. I think Jerry had a death wish. He took great delight in passing cars on blind hills outside Huntersville in his Ford Thunderbird. After one particularly terrifying near miss, we refused to ride with him again.

Over time we got to know many of the folks in the northern part of the county by our presence on the road. One woman in particular regularly gave us lifts. She drove a black 1953 Ford sedan and always had her small child seated next to her on the front seat passenger's side. One afternoon on Highway 115 it was obvious she was having a bad day. She hit ninety miles per hour on a straight stretch out of Caldwell Station heading into Cornelius. I asked her to please slow down. She sharply replied, "I don't care what happens to anyone in this car except my baby (unbelted in the suicide seat)!"

In February 1964 we joined the track team. Mr. Cochran, a Christian and a WWII veteran, was a pleasant enough fellow although a little eccentric. We began to understand why the older boys called him "Wild Bill." An industrial arts ("shop") teacher at North, he also taught an unauthorized course in sex education on the side.

I remember the first day of track practice. Wild Bill gathered us on the infield down by the jumping pits and proceeded to lecture us on the virtues of chastity. After that, not a day passed without a lecture of some kind on the topic, usually ending in the refrain: "Gentlemen, keep the dilly-whacker in your pants, and you'll be all right." I never knew exactly whom he was addressing. After all, this was 1964 in the Bible Belt, and most of us wouldn't have dared do what he was talking about. I, for one, didn't have the moral aptitude for it. Most of the girls I knew had long since drawn their boundaries.

Sandwiched somewhere in there we got some practice in. To get things started, Brother John usually had to say in a long, slow drawl, "Mr. Cochran, the sun is slowly setting in the west," and that would finally get us to the business at hand. Our sophomore year John and I ran the 220-yard dash, the 440-yard dash, and the mile-relay. Jim McEver was our 100-yard dash specialist. Doug Bostic, a senior, also ran the 440. Wayne Cline, a senior, who would win a track scholarship to N.C. State, was our half-miler.

One afternoon WBTV in Charlotte sent a reporter up to do a story on the team. I remember that they filmed John, Doug, Wayne and me standing around in our white and blue track suits together.

That was the first time we had ever received any media attention. It sure beat the heck out of J.V. basketball.

In those days North had a bus for the high school's athletic teams; it was a rundown affair, painted blue and affectionately known as the Blue Goose. Its counterpart at Alexander Junior High was the Blue Bastard. Mr. Cochran's 1957 gold Chrysler Imperial station wagon was crowned the Golden Goose. Wild Bill sometimes drove with his knee, which was always really scary. It usually signaled that he was about to say or do something really off the wall. He was driving with his knee the day he shot up the car.

In the spring of 1964 North received an invitation to participate in the Duke-Durham Relays at Duke University. Teams from all over the Southeast competed. Five or six of us drove over to the meet with Wild Bill in the Golden Goose. Somewhere outside of Greensboro, Bob Harry from Mallard Creek started mouthing off in the backseat. Mr. Cochran told him to clam it, but Harry was just getting wound up—he really had a big mouth. Wild Bill turned over the controls to his left knee and angrily pointed his finger at Harry. Bob just wouldn't shut up. Wild Bill suddenly pulled out his starter's gun from the glove compartment and fired it into the floorboard. That got Bob's and everybody else's attention in a hurry.

A few seconds later we learned about Wild Bill's brakes. In all the excitement we passed the only rest stop between Greensboro and Durham. Wild Bill had to take a leak—and he smashed the brakes. Those brakes must have been made in some other part of the universe. They made a surreal, horrible screeching noise. Here came this car full of yelling boys, the front seat wafted by smoke, and brakes howling like the Baskervilles. Then Wild Bill did the unthinkable: He threw the car into reverse and backed up the interstate into the rest stop!

The afternoon in Durham was terribly hot with temperatures in the nineties. There were no shaded areas, so we sweated it out waiting for our races. We didn't even get a time in the mile-relay, but the meet directors gave us a nice key chain memento, which I still proudly possess.

After we'd showered and eaten at one of the Duke dinning halls, Mr. Cochran took us over to the Duke Gardens just as night was falling. Then Bob Harry started up all over again. Bob had chanced upon a couple plugged into each other in the bushes. His eyes bulging, he yelled, "Mr. Cochran, Mr. Cochran, get over here quick!" We all hurried over to the spot. Well, there it was in all its glory—my first primal scene. Caught in *flagrante delicto*, the boy and girl were naked as blue jays, and they uncoupled and grabbed at their clothes in a hurry. I think the episode thoroughly vexed Mr. Cochran—it was a flagrant violation of his favorite maxim. This isn't kind to say, but it was the highlight of our season.

The following autumn of 1964 John and I, as juniors, joined the cross-country team. Mr. Cochran had carved out a two-mile course through the woods and around the school's athletic fields. Our first meet was at Garinger High School, against Garinger and Harding High. We won handily, and John and I finished 1-2. In the following meets John did quite well, usually placing first individually.

The Western 4A Conference meet was held at Revolution Park in Charlotte and was won by Mike Smith from Myers Park. John placed third, and I was twelfth. The team was third overall, the best showing ever for a North team in conference cross-country competition.

The next meet was a statewide affair at Wake Forest, with some teams coming from Virginia. John and I took off and were leading the pack at the end of 1.25 miles. At that point in the race both of us started to burn out. John made it in ahead of me by a full minute, placing fifth overall. I was completely *kaputt*—I don't even remember crossing the finish line. Somehow I got across, in twenty-ninth place, and promptly passed out. I came to and was lying on the track when one of the officials came over and told a Wake student, "Put him over there on top of his brother." I can't ever remember feeling so sick or weak. It took me days to get over it.

The next week was the state meet at Chapel Hill. I vowed not to pull any rabbit stunts again—I wouldn't go for the lead. In the state meet John finished fifth, I was twenty-ninth, and the team finished sixth. John made the All-State team. It was the best a North running team had done in the school's fourteen-year history.

In the spring of 1965 we hit the cinders again. In our opening track meet with Mooresville, John ran the 440-yard dash in 50.6

seconds and I was second in 52.0 seconds. John continued to improve. I got the flu and never completely recovered to make much of the season. *The Charlotte Observer* ran an article on us, replete with a photo, which was cornily titled "Puckett Twins Leave Track Foes Seeing Double." The article said that John was the better runner, but I was a little stronger academically.

For reasons that still elude me, John and I began bringing lemons to the track meets. We would sit in the infield and suck on the horribly sour fruit. Other teams must have thought it gave us some mystic powers; soon practically everyone at those meets was sucking lemons.

The best 440-yard runner in the county was Jeff Prather from West Mecklenburg High. He and John ran neck and neck throughout the season, Prather always winning by one-tenth of a second. They both qualified for the 440 in the state meet that May. I went with John, Doug McElroy, and Mr. Cochran to Raleigh for the meet. That night John got a bum deal from the authority that ran the meet.

Until it ended the practice in 1966, the North Carolina High School Athletic Association (NCHSAA) took advantage of a quirk in the configuration of the N.C. State track to jack down the times in the 220, 440, and 880. On the far side of the stadium an eight-lane track started at the head of a tunnel and merged with the regular 440-yard oval at a point just after the first turn—creating a 220-yard straightaway on the backside. By starting races at the tunnel, NCHSAA eliminated the first turn in the race, virtually guaranteeing a faster race. The resulting times, however inflated, were reported nationally.

On the night in question the 440 was run out of the tunnel—without a staggered start. John, who unfortunately was in lane eight, had to cross seven lanes to reach the break point. He finished fourth with a 50.4 second time—for what amounted to a 450-yard run (which converts to 49.6 seconds for the legal distance). Jeff Prather was first in 49.2 seconds. After the race Jeff, a really nice guy, told us he had been offered a full track scholarship at N.C. State based on his performance that night. We were happy for him because he, from a family of limited means, might otherwise have not been able to afford college.

Before leaving the spring of 1965, I want to mention a minor social disaster that Wild Bill set in motion. It was our great misfortune that Mr. Cochran decided to schedule the North Mecklenburg Invitational Track Meet the same Friday afternoon of the 1965 Junior-Senior Prom. That he didn't schedule it that Thursday was baffling to us. A word about the North Invitational: Mr. Cochran was very selective in his choice of teams—he invited only teams he knew we could beat. State track powerhouse Myers Park was never invited to the North Invitational.

On this particular afternoon, the sun sank in the west and darkness descended as we lined up for the mile-relay, the final event of the day. Wild Bill's meet was running one to two hours in arrears—it was now 7:30. Somehow he had let the thing slow down to a snail's pace. John and I were painfully mindful that the prom was scheduled to start at the National Guard Amory in Charlotte at 8, and there we were stuck in the cinders on the North track. Mom went to the gym and called our dates to let them know we would be a little late. She cautioned John that his date, Diane Neil, was "mildly distressed."

The meet finally ended and we hustled back to Davidson, showered, scrambled into our rented white dinner jackets and black ties, grabbed a quick bite to eat, and headed out of town on Highway 115 in the Puckett family's '65 white Malibu coup (I was driving). It was now 9:15. We stopped first in Huntersville to pick up Diane. To say she was not pleased is extravagant understatement. Then we drove to the Derita community in north Charlotte to pick up my date, Julie Eatman. It was 10:30 by the time we finally arrived at the National Guard Armory at the old Douglas Municipal Airport, which was on the far west side of the city. Many of our friends were already leaving the building to do whatever kids did on prom night in those years. The prom was scheduled to end at 11:00. We barely had enough time to get our prom photos taken. The band was shutting down, the refreshments were exhausted, and the chaperones were leaving. Julie took the debacle pretty much in stride. Not so Diane, who was apoplectic. Indeed when John called her twenty-five years later to get the address of a former North High student who lived in Holland, Diane was still angry about it.

With the track season and that unfortunate prom behind us, we entered the summer of 1965 with jobs at the Davidson College Library and a heavy running schedule. Before going to work each morning we would run six miles on the college cross-country course and follow that up with another eight miles that evening or night. Mom received calls from concerned neighbors notifying her that her sons were gallivanting naked through the town. At all events, we were in very good shape by the time the cross-country season started.

I remember the first day of cross-country practice my senior year. Mr. Cochran asked us to sit down by the track and asked, "How would you boys like to win the state championship?" I didn't know what to say. At that time I didn't think we had a chance because Myers Park reputedly had the most powerful team in state history. Mr. Cochran believed if we stayed healthy, we might have a shot. It all depended on how good the Mustangs really were.

They were very good. They had superb runners in Larry Forrester and Phil Wilson, both of whom would later run at Duke University. The Myers Park booster club brought in an exchange student from Norway who just happened to be one of the best cross-country runners in Scandinavia. They also had a lot of depth. We would learn early in the season just how good they were. They had chosen us as their inaugural (cannon fodder) meet.

The better teams chose teams they knew they could beat for the early meets. These were warm-up meets for the tougher competition to come. Myers Park knew we would be competitive that season, but not at their level. The county sports pundits thought we didn't have a chicken's chance at Holly Farms. That was before Thursday, September 23, 1965.

With a tractor mower and machete, Mr. Cochran had labored mightily that summer to expand the course into a 2.5-mile jaunt through fields and woods. It was longer and rougher than any we had run before. He knew that would keep us in top shape.

We began that season with a new course and a more competitive team. Five of us formed the squad for scoring purposes: Doug McElroy, Wayne Ritterscamp, Joe Abernathy, and two Pucketts.

On the morning of September 23, I arrived at school with a migraine headache. I had thrown up several times, and it was doubtful I could run. I explained my situation to Mr. Cochran, who told me that if I didn't run, we wouldn't have a chance. At 3:30 p.m. I dragged myself to the starting line. When the gun went off, I realized that I was actually very relaxed. The headache had abated somewhat, and my strength was returning. All things considered, I ran very well. John won handily. Myers Park finished 2-3 and then we swept the remaining slots, winning 27-38 (low score wins in cross-country). I think we were just as stunned as Myers Park. Mr. Cochran was ecstatic. It was the first time that any team in Mecklenburg County had beaten Myers Park in cross-country, and this was supposed to be their school's best team ever. All the other coaches in the county called it a fluke. We would have three more meets with them to prove or disprove that argument.

The next meet was again at North. This time Charlotte Catholic and West Mecklenburg participated. West had a runner named David McCall, who had finished ninth in the state the preceding season. Charlotte Catholic had Carl Hubey, who was supposed to be the finest Catholic high school cross-country runner in the nation. We had the dubious pleasure of meeting his father.

When we walked out onto the course that afternoon, Mr. Hubey came up to John and me and shoved a stopwatch in our faces. He said, "See this time. This is my son's winning time last week at Harding, where he broke the course record."

Mr. Cochran, the meet director, lined us up on the North track at the start, and the younger Hubey positioned himself right beside John. When the gun went off, John and Hubey jumped out in front. Mr. Hubey positioned himself by our father on the sidelines. Much of the race was run out of the spectators' view. A few hundred yards past the two mile point, two runners in white jerseys and blue shorts emerged from the woods in the distance. My father said, "I wonder if they're my sons?" The senior Hubey remarked, "That's my boy in front. He'll win." Back in the pack I saw what happened shortly thereafter, and it was startling.

John and Hubey were running neck and neck when they hit the final 220-yard straightaway for the finish. John exploded in a finishing sprint down the track and beat Hubey solidly by eight seconds. Hubey was so astonished he all but walked in. That was my inspiration, and I beat McCall for third place. Afterwards, Mr. Hubey told John, "You won today because my son has a cold." Dad told us not to pay any attention to him.

The next competition was a countywide meet at Freedom Park in Charlotte. Myers Park and Catholic were among the teams competing. I remember that it was a cloudy early October day. I didn't feel right when the gun went off. The race entailed two laps around the entire length of the park. John won, but the rest of us made a sorry showing, and our team finished second behind Myers Park. Mr. Cochran was upset. He said we had blown the opportunity to become the first undefeated team in any sport in the history of North Mecklenburg. I suppose Mr. Hubey was more upset. He attributed his son's defeat this time to some vitamin pills he had taken that morning.

We still had time to redeem ourselves. The Western 4A Conference meet was held the following week at Harding High School. John won again, setting a course record. We have a picture of him crossing the finish line with Dad standing there clapping, a cigarette in hand, looking out in the distance for his other son. I beat a Myers Park runner out for tenth place just at the finish line. When the scores were tallied, we had won by one point. It was North's first ever conference title in cross-country. Mr. Cochran was beside himself with joy.

The following week was the Wake Forest Invitational. John had to see a specialist in Charlotte about blood in his urine, a condition he learned was endemic to many long-distance runners. The doctor gave him a green light to run after a week's rest. Mr. Cochran decided to rest all of us that week in preparation for the state championship the following week at Chapel Hill. In our absence Myers Park easily won at Wake.

As we prepared for the state meet, things almost unraveled. Wayne Ritterscamp, our number four runner, came up lame, and it was doubtful that he could run in the state meet. He courageously decided to give it the old Gipper try—just to give the team a chance. He could hardly walk by the weekend. Mr. Cochran was sick about it. The trainer taped him up the night before, and we hoped for the best. We also got a scare when John stupidly accepted a challenge from one of the football players to go head to head in a 50-yard dash. John won and strained his right hamstring. That was Thursday afternoon, two days before the meet; he would arrive in Chapel Hill with an ace bandage on his leg.

The following Saturday, November 5, 1965, most of the larger high schools in the state sent teams to compete in the state championship meet at Finley Golf Course on the campus of the University of North Carolina. We left early for Chapel Hill, but not early enough. Mr. Cochran had reverted again to Wild Bill.

The meet was slated to begin at 11 a.m. Mr. Cochran's plan was to arrive at Finley around 10:30 a.m. to get us warmed up for the race. Mom and Aunt Louise would be our cheering section. Dad had to teach a Saturday class at the college and couldn't come.

At 10:30 a.m. sharp we drove onto the University of North Carolina golf course and were horrified to see everyone lined up about to begin the race. Wild Bill's schedule was thirty minutes off. The race had a 10:30 start time. We didn't even have a lane assignment! For some reason, which can only be explained by Divine Providence, the team that drew lane one had withdrawn, and the officials told us to take that lane. We were set for the start. The officials gave us only a few minutes to warm up.

It was a glorious autumn morning. The foliage had peaked a week or two earlier, but the colors were still quite lovely. The air was crisp, and the dew was still on the golf course that served as the race venue. The gun went off, and we sprinted out for position. John, Kenny Helms from East Mecklenburg, and Phil Wilson ran abreast in the lead. Things were pretty stiff for me until the half-mile mark where a runner from Asheville High School started shoving and cursing me for no apparent reason. He bumped into me, lost his balance, and went sprawling into a ditch. I remember him screaming obscenities, which quickly faded in my rear. At the mile point John was in front, followed closely by Helms. Coming around for the second mile I saw some Chapel Hill kids hanging out of trees yelling for their team. I came up the last hill for the finish line. Whatever John had been involved in was well over by now. Some Chapel Hill runners were breathing down my neck. Mr. Cochran started yelling at me from the area around the finish line, and I poured on what little I had left. They never caught me.

I found John after the race. He had won the individual title and had completed the 2.2-mile course in 10 minutes 13.3 seconds, breaking the state record by over ten seconds. Our friend Kenny Helms from East Mecklenburg was second. We didn't know at that point how the team had fared in the overall scoring. I figured we wouldn't even be in the scoring because there was no way Ritterscamp could have made it.

I didn't see Wayne, so I assumed he was still somewhere out on the course. I started down the fairway to find him, but stopped short when I saw him sitting under a nearby oak tree nursing his leg. He was grinning. I asked how he had done. He smiled and exclaimed, "I finished sixteenth!" I couldn't believe it. Wayne wouldn't walk without crutches for the next two weeks.

Doug McElroy ran up to me and said he'd finished ninth. Shortly after that the race officials announced that North had won the state title. Here is how we achieved our ninety points low score compared to Myers Park's second place ninety-seven points: 1-Puckett, 9-McElroy, 16-Ritterscamp, 30-Puckett, and 34-Abernathy. Mr. Cochran was right. We had won our state championship, and only one team had beaten us that season. John finished out the season undefeated. We were only the second North Mecklenburg athletic team to ever achieve a state title to that date. I learned later that Mr. Cochran went back the following weekend to West Virginia, where he had grown up, to show the team trophy to his friends and relatives.

We received an invitation to the national cross-country championship meet in Tennessee but declined. We believed that we should quit while we were ahead. We had pulled off an upset and would be pressing our luck. Or was it an upset? Looking back, I think we were the better team. We had beaten Myers Park three times out of four.

The moment of victory is fleeting, and we had to move on to the track season. John and I worked out on the college track through the winter months in 1966. Davidson had Alan Turner, the Southern Conference's top sprinter, who helped us with the workouts. We geared our winter training for the 440-yard dash.

Coach Heath Whittle, at the college, suggested that I try the 880-yard run; Mr. Cochran also thought it was a good idea. Joe Abernathy and I would run the 880 and John the 440. That would spread us out a bit.

We were invited to a statewide indoor invitational meet at Chapel Hill in February. For a reason I've long since forgotten, Mr. Cochran could not accompany us on that trip. He registered us for the meet, which would take place at UNC, and he gave us the day and time and his blessing. Wayne Ritterscamp's mother, a professional opera singer, agreed to drive and serve as the team's adult sponsor. Five of us and Mrs. Ritterscamp made the 140-mile trip to Chapel Hill, which gave us a nice respite from having to attend school on a Friday. When we arrived at the Carolina campus, we went straight to the indoor track at the old Tin Can, which was next door to Woolen Gymnasium. What to our wondering eyes did appear? No track meet—nary a team in sight, just a handful of joggers and some guys shooting hoops in the inner court of the banked wooden track. We wandered next door to Woolen Gym and the office of Joe Hilton, the head track coach at UNC. Coach Hilton told us that Wild Bill had given us the wrong date. Back at North, Wild Bill, perplexed and profusely apologetic, explained that he had mistakenly given us the previous year's date. I'll put this in quick perspective—Wild Bill's boner was a very far cry from the magnitude of what happened to Eddie Hart, America's top sprinter and the gold medal favorite at the 1972 Munich Olympics: Hart's coach gave him the wrong starting time for his qualifying heat, and he was disqualified from the competition, no medal, nothing. Suffice it to say, we didn't compete in the state indoor meet that year, and we were henceforth very much on our guard about relying on Wild Bill to be in the right place at the right time.

In March 1966 we had time trials at North. Mr. Cochran decided to race John against me in the 880 just to give me some competition. John beat me with a time of two minutes flat. He was hardly winded. In the opening meets I easily won the 880, but my times were not good—usually 2.02 or 2.04. Regardless, I was winning.

John was having problems. He won all of his early 440 races handily beating others considered among the best in the state, but he couldn't get his time under 50 seconds. He had simply over-trained. To give him a change of pace, Mr. Cochran decided to let him run in the 880 when we met the Davidson College freshmen track team up at Davidson. There were only three of us in the race. Heath Whittle, the Davidson coach, was the starter. John took the lead immediately. He finished well ahead of me with a sprint to the finish, leaving me in second place. The winning time was 1:56.2 which tied the state record at that time. I came in around two minutes flat. When John's time was printed in *The Charlotte Observer* the next day, no one would have believed it had Coach Whittle not been officiating at the meet.

Unfortunately John wasn't able to capitalize on his newfound prowess in the 880. He developed a calcium deposit in his left thigh, and on recovering from that, he developed tendonitis in an Achilles tendon. He had to sit out an entire month before the Queen City Relays at Myers Park.

We had no depth on the team, but we did have four good runners who could possibly put together a respectable two-mile relay team (4 X 880). We decided to stack the event and go for a state record. The day of the race John had to have an abscessing tooth repaired. Because he was ailing that evening and hadn't run for a month, we let him be the leadoff runner. He miraculously gave us a good lead with an opening time of less than two minutes, again hardly breathing. By the time I got the baton for the anchor leg, we were already a lap ahead of some of the teams. On the bell lap I almost ran over some runners making their exchanges. I finished the race in a sprint. We won convincingly and broke both the Queen City and state two-mile relay marks—records that stood for fifteen years.

The following week we participated in the Western 4A meet at East Mecklenburg. John won the 880 and I finished a disappointing fourth. Ahead of me were a sophomore from Garinger named Tom Gibbons and our own Joe Abernathy. It occurred to me that if I didn't get my act together, I might not qualify for the state meet.

Doug McElroy got himself boxed-in during the mile run. Coming down the home stretch he stumbled into the three leading runners and knocked them down like bowling pins, disqualifying him in the process. He laughed about it later and remarked, "Well, I took those Myers Park guys down with me."

In that conference meet I ran anchor on the mile-relay. We didn't have a chance to place, but we ran it for the sake of competing. Frank Simmons, an African-American teammate (North had fully integrated that year) couldn't connect with me on the anchor leg. We missed the baton pass, and I overran the exchange zone. Frank just laughed and threw the baton to me, yelling, "Catch, Puckett!" I finished the race as well as I could but knew we were disqualified.

The last week of the regular season was the regional qualifying meet for the state finals, held at Myers Park on a rain-soaked cinder track. We knew we had the four best 880 runners in the state in our region, and three of us were on the same team. Only three runners would make it to Raleigh. The race was never in doubt as to the winner—John led the pack through a quagmire of mud and cinders to the tape. The remaining qualifying positions weren't decided until the finish line where Gibbons beat me by a step, and I beat Joe Abernathy by a step. I was going to the state meet. While I felt sorry for Joe, he would have his chance the following year.

The state high school track meet was in Raleigh on a Friday night in mid-May 1966. I had developed an upper respiratory infection the day before the meet and felt terrible. To make matters worse, a front had brought rainy weather, and the cinder track at N.C. State was a mess. We arrived on the campus at mid-afternoon; it had stopped raining, but the track was still under water.

We had an early dinner at one of the university cafeterias. As we left the dining hall, we noticed that a cat was trying to get into a bird's nest high up in a tree. A flock of birds was attacking the cat. It was really funny, and the moment sticks in my memory. A crowd of perhaps one hundred students was cheering the avian effort. All that excitement didn't help me feel any better, however.

By the time the meet started, the track had drained off its sheen of water. The final of the 880, however, would be run in the latter part of the meet when the soaked track had taken a beating from the earlier races. In the 880 there were nine runners. We would run the first 440 yards in staggered lanes and then break for the pole for the second lap. This year the 220 straightaway gimmick of previous years was out—this was a fully legitimate 880, with four turns on the oval. John drew lane 1, and I was in lane 4. When the announcer introduced the runners, he had to catch himself. He said, "That's right, Puckett, North Mecklenburg, lane 1 and Puckett, North Mecklenburg, lane 4. Same family I suppose."

The starter raised his gun. I felt awful. I floated out with the blast. It went so quickly—and I could hardly breathe. At the end of the very fast first lap I was dead last. I said to myself, "Finish this thing and don't finish last." On the straightaway of the bell lap I caught the pack.

John pulled out in front and took off, mud spewing in his wake. I tried to catch up but couldn't break out of fourth place. That would be a credible finish, so I accepted it.

John won in 1:57, a slow time in absolute terms, but relative to the awful condition of the track, not a bad time at all. Tom Gibbons of Garinger High placed second; I was fourth with a time of 2:00. A track official told us later that had the track been in good condition, our times would have been four or five seconds faster. I was simply glad to have finished. I got a medal for my efforts—a tiny little bronze piece engraved "880-yard dash" on the back. It was no Olympic medal, but I was proud to have it.

Doug McElroy finished third in the mile. The scoring gave us eight total team points, which surprisingly tied us for fourth place in the state. The following year the school annual would mention the 1966 track season, and my finish was a footnote. I've always believed I could have taken second place that night if I had been healthy.

That was the last time we ran for Mr. Cochran. Late that night, on the way home near Siler City, we stopped for some burgers. Nearly missing his turn into the restaurant, Wild Bill hit the Golden Goose's brakes, which sounded like wailing banshees. Everybody in the joint dived for cover. When he finally dropped us off in Davidson around 3 a.m., he thanked us for the three good seasons that we'd given him. We thanked him for all the good times. I suppose Mr. Cochran went back to West Virginia to celebrate one last time with his folks and friends.

I only saw Mr. Cochran infrequently after that year. His later teams never quite enjoyed the success we achieved. Mr. Cochran had his days in the sun in the 1965-66 campaigns, and we had ours. I'll always be grateful to him for that.

I participated in track and cross-country as a student at Davidson College. During the three years of my NCAA eligibility, the college awarded me five athletic letters. Yet I never came close to the level I had reached as a high school runner. Davidson was, and remains, a rigorous academic institution, and my academic life put severe restrictions on the time I could dedicate to training. But there was another reason as well. My heart just wasn't in it anymore. I could never recapture what I had felt on that rutted cinder track and beaten up cross-country course several miles south of Huntersville, in the woods of northern Mecklenburg County.

In November 2000, after a hiatus of thirty-five years, North finally won its second state championship in cross-country. North's All-American runner, Stephen Haas, was the individual winner. In an article comparing the 1965 and 2000 teams, *The Charlotte Observer* featured a retrospective article on John, including a photo of him crossing the finish line on Finley Golf Course in Chapel Hill. The piece included a picture of our old team juxtaposed with a photo of the 2000 team. Ours is a formal pose, and theirs is very relaxed and informal. To honor the 1965 team, the 2000 team wore replicas of our 1965 jerseys at the state meet with "65" emblazoned on the Mercury shoe emblem. I consider that quite an honor.

I miss those days—the camaraderie, the thrill of friendly competition, the Indian summer afternoons and those seemingly endless lectures on the virtues of abstinence, and the Golden Goose and her screaming brakes. Most of all I miss Wild Bill.

Someone recently told me that Mr. Cochran died a few years back. That person said that they buried him in a peaceful place among family and friends in the rolling hills of his beautiful native West Virginia. I suppose that's almost Heaven.

The Midnight Ride
of
Bobby Lee Honeycutt

The Southern Railroad line leading up from Charlotte strung the towns of northern Mecklenburg County like pearls on a necklace. In my early years passenger trains pulled by steam locomotives still plied the rails of Piedmont North Carolina. I remember on warm summer nights the sound of the *10 O'clock Special* lumbering through town. The tracks ran along a ridge behind the volunteer fire department, no more than 150 yards from our house on Main Street. Our windows were always open, the smell of DDT laced the air, and the mournful wail of the whistle still runs down the line of my memory.

I remember as a small child going with my dad to the Spencer Shops near Salisbury, North Carolina, a large switchyard and repair facility—real locomotives in real shops with real roundhouses. I remember seeing the huge hoists that lifted large steam engines to the ceiling of the shop and listening to Dad talk with some of the workers and engineers. Later the Spencer Shops moved to a new switchyard a few miles east of the town. In time the old shops decayed, but the state has resurrected the site as the North Carolina Transportation Museum.

One of my most pleasant memories of the railroad in Davidson comes from the late autumn of 1952. President-Elect Eisenhower was coming to town—rather, he was passing through town on the train. The elementary school emptied, and the entire town and college turned out at the train depot to welcome him. I had heard my folks talk a lot about Ike, and here was this great man coming in person. As the train came slowly down the track, Ike came into view standing on a platform at the end of the last passenger car (there was no caboose). There he stands forever in my memory, clothed in a smart gray suit, smiling and waving.

Another memory is the burning of the Southern Cottonseed Oil complex in Davidson. The rail line crossed over N.C. 115 near the plant and ran right behind it, heading north through Davidson. The railroad supplied the plant with raw materials, the end products of which were cottonseed and highly flammable cottonseed oil. One summer night in the early 1950's all of that went up in smoke. A fire broke out in the complex, and within minutes Davidson had a roaring conflagration on its hands. We were at Papa and Aunt Louise's house in Cornelius when the sirens went off. The whole sky was lit up, and I can still see the flames high above the trees just down the road. We walked to the railroad overpass and sat down by the tracks. Soon a sizable crowd assembled.

Fire departments from four counties responded. Someone commented that the railroad would have to be notified immediately since it was obvious that the tracks would be impassable for days and service shut down on all trains headed north out of Charlotte. Another bystander remarked that the *10 O'clock Special* would be coming in another hour and might not get the message. Fortunately, the train was rerouted at the last minute. It was the only time in my memory that a train didn't run at night.

The fire burned for over four days—the largest conflagration in my memories of Davidson. It was a chemical fire and didn't respond well to water. As a result the entire complex was leveled. The huge concrete foundation block would stand as a pathetic decaying memorial to the site up until a few years ago when it was razed for a new building.

For all the nostalgia it evoked, the railway was generally a dangerous place. The Parker boys up on Main Street played chicken with the trains. This was a game where one of the boys would stand on the track in the face of an onrushing locomotive and see how close he could get to the train before leaping to safety. It was a frightening spectacle. I was terrified when this happened and refused to play in this potentially lethal game. The Southern Railroad finally put an end to this with a call to the mayor. He promptly alerted the parents, who were thoroughly shaken by the news.

With the demise of this rite of adolescent passage, the emphasis shifted to the tall water tower that loomed over the old college cemetery on North Main, which abutted the rail line. The new rite of passage became a climb to the top of the tower. This afforded a grand view of the town, and on clear days you could see the Blue Ridge Mountains to the west and the skyline of Charlotte to the south. My one and only time at the top is best described as the most harrowing event of my life. Once again, the parents got wind of the scheme, and another testosterone challenge passed into history.

In the years of my youth the danger of the railroad was attributable to a particularly lethal blend of androgen-driven teens and a startling lack of gated crossings on the rail line through northern Mecklenburg County. Yet all the gated crossings in the world could not have prevented what happened to Marilyn Cook's prized cow.

The Cooks had a farm adjoining our small farm off U.S. 21 just south of Cornelius. Marilyn Cook, who attended North High with me, had a prizewinning cow, Elizabeth, which was the joy and glory of her life. One ill-fated summer night, Elizabeth wandered off and somehow worked her way over to the railroad tracks just outside of Cornelius. Along came the *10 O'clock Special*. The collision literally disintegrated the poor cow into countless crimson pieces. The only recognizable parts were bits of hoof and the tail. Marilyn was devastated when she finally figured out that the cow killed on the local rail line was hers. But cows were not the only creatures to suffer injury or death on the tracks.

One winter night in 1965 John and I were visiting the Bridger girls, Donna and Ann, at their home at the Mt. Zion Methodist Church manse in Cornelius. Their father was the minister at Mt. Zion, and both the manse and church complex stood by the railroad track, which ran parallel to Highway 115 though Cornelius. That night Marianne Kerns and her brother Tommy, from Huntersville, had joined the party, which broke up shortly before 10 p.m. The Kerns siblings drove out toward the railroad track where there was no gated crossing; the road crossed the track on a diagonal, which made it difficult to see the train before reaching the crossing. We had forgotten about the train, which was usually late anyway. That night, however, it came through at just about 10 sharp. Marianne and Tommy must have had their car radio playing—they didn't hear the train. Standing in the Bridgers' front yard, we saw the dire situation unfolding; all we could do was run after the car screaming and hollering. Marianne and Tommy didn't hear us. I really thought they were goners. Fortunately they got to the crossing just ahead of the train, which missed them by slightest of margins.

Folks began to complain to the Southern Railroad. Something had to be done. Unfortunately, it seemed it would take a fatal accident to get the railroad to adopt a safer crossing policy. That almost happened that same winter of 1965 when a faculty family was returning to Davidson from a college basketball game in Charlotte. It was a cold and foggy night. Coming off Highway 21, they drove up Griffith Street to the unprotected rail crossing near the college campus on Main Street. There were no warning lights. The unsuspecting father ran the car into the side of a slow moving *10 O'clock Special*. Fortunately no one was injured. But worse was yet to come.

One of the most popular girls at North High lived in Davidson. Her brothers were among our best friends. Their mother, a single parent, worked in Charlotte and was in a car pool that went into the city every weekday. Returning home from work one afternoon in the spring of 1965, the car in which their mother was riding crossed over the railroad tracks at an unmarked, ungated crossing at Caldwell Station, an unincorporated village between Huntersville and Cornelius. One of the afternoon trains slammed into the car, killing our friends' mother instantly. The northern end of the county was stunned and angered. That's when Bobby Lee Honeycutt snapped.

The story came to me second-hand. I learned that the perpetrator was Bobby Lee Honeycutt, a boy from the northern end of the county whom I didn't know. His real name may actually be shrouded in the mists of myth and legend. Regardless, the appellation is well chosen. Honeycutt is a good Mecklenburg County name. Bobby Lee? Well, more than a few Southern stockcar drivers bear the name of the beloved general of the Late Unpleasantness.

Bobby Lee was the quintessential 1960's era hot-rodder. He drove a souped-up late model Ford and boasted that he could hit 120 miles per hour out on U.S. 21. He took special delight in roaring through Huntersville and outrunning Cop Cook. Bobby Lee took the death of his friends' mother hard. This and other incidents, which he felt were due to the negligence of the railroad, outraged him, and he decided to issue a protest.

Bobby Lee's protest took the form of a vehicular dexterity never before witnessed in northern Mecklenburg County. He let it be known that he was going to screw up a train as it wended its way north from Charlotte to Davidson. When I later learned about his incredible deed, it brought to mind the song "Leadfoot." It was about a speed-crazed teen (with a heavy foot), who, with his pedal to the metal, raced a train to a rail crossing with disastrous results.

Honeycutt's plan was to play chicken with a train at every rail-road crossing along N.C. 115 from the Charlotte train station on Tryon Street to the Griffith Street crossing in Davidson, a distance of roughly twenty-two miles. Bobby Lee would cross the tracks a split second ahead of the train and then roar on to the next crossing. There would be about a dozen crossings to negotiate. Bobby Lee had carefully marked his prey. It was the *10 O'Clock Special.*

That fateful night the *Special* pulled out at around 11 p.m., running very late. This meant that the engineer would try to make up for lost time, a factor that did not bode well for Bobby Lee. The midnight rider got things rolling at the crossings in Charlotte, to the engineer's surprise and chagrin. As the city gave way to the northern Mecklenburg countryside, Bobby Lee raced his car up Highway 115 running parallel with the train; by this time the engineer had probably reckoned he had a lunatic on his hands. It was the same scenario at every crossing—car hurtling across the tracks, an onrushing train wildly blasting its whistle, and at the last second before impact, Bobby Lee's Ford coming out on the other side unscathed and racing furiously on to the next crossing.

And so it went. On through the night rode Bobby Lee Honeycutt. On through the night roared his message of defiance. His mad game continued up to the Griffith Street crossing in Davidson, where Bobby Lee idled his car a hundred feet or so from the tracks. The engineer must have thought the gambit was over when he approached the crossing with no car in sight. Suddenly, from out of nowhere, Honeycutt gunned the car across the tracks, completely unraveling the infuriated engineer, who hit the brakes hard and sat on his whistle with the train at a standstill. Local lore would call it the loudest and longest railroad noise in the history of Davidson. Bobby Lee Honeycutt had ridden from obscurity into local legend.

Shortly after that incident, gated crossings began to spring up in northern Mecklenburg County, and the number of accidents and near accidents dropped dramatically. Still, the Griffith Street crossing would remain the only gated crossing in Davidson.

In 1969 one of my classmates at Davidson College put the Griffith Street crossing in the news. He was a rail buff who had virtually every Southern Railroad schedule memorized and hopped trains on the weekends for the love of the rails—generally riding in boxcars. On the centennial of the Golden Spike ceremony at Promontory, Utah, he and several other students somehow briefly rewired the crossing on Griffith Street. They formed a human train and chugged up the tracks. As they passed the crossing, the lights started flashing and down came the gates.

The Southern Railway tracks are still where they were during my childhood. The trains that plied them have all moved into the recesses of my memory. In my mind I still hear the clatter of a train on a warm summer night as it rolls through the town issuing a mournful whistle. I hear the coupling and uncoupling of boxcars along the sidings of the town's textile and asbestos mills. I see crazy, exuberant kids dashing into and out of the path of onrushing disaster along the ridgeline behind North Main. But above all I see a daring teenager, a leadfoot vigilante, in a dangerous race to the crossing. All and all, I think I have a most singular view of American railroading.

Lefty

and

Homer

During my years in Davidson, the college supported a student body of approximately one thousand young men. The college placed a great deal of emphasis on physical training. Physical education was a mandatory, albeit non-credit, course for freshmen. Approximately forty percent of the student body participated in intercollegiate athletics, and most male sports were represented.

Davidson College athletics had its ups and downs in the twentieth century. In the early part of century the college was competitive with just about every college and university in the state; teams from the school regularly did well against the likes of Duke, UNC, and N.C. State. In the 1950's, when most of the larger schools were developing athletic scholarship programs, little Davidson relied on its excellent academic program to draw potential athletes. The teams generally weren't very good, but the young men who participated were legitimate scholar-athletes. For example, my father took great pride in the football team of 1958. Eleven members of that squad went to medical school following their senior year. In the early 1960's the athletic department, in order to remain competitive in NCAA Division I sports, began giving scholarships in basketball and football.

Thus began the glory years of Davidson athletics—which would last for a decade.

The football and basketball scholarships brought in athletes who often participated in more than one sport, sometimes at the same time. All-American basketball player and later NBA star Dick Snyder '66, while pitching in a baseball game against Furman, between innings walked up the hill to the track where Davidson was competing with the Citadel, changed into tennis shoes, and won the broad jump in his baseball uniform.

With the scholarship program came a generation of high-powered coaches who knew how to win in big-time college athletics. Traditionally Davidson students had played for love of the sport. In the 1960's the whole attitude at the college changed. Everybody was fed up with losing all the time. Win fever seized the campus and the town. Calibrated to a high level of intensity and expectation, the basketball and football programs would bring us some of our highest and lowest moments. Two coaches stand out from that era, Charles G. "Lefty" Driesell and Homer Smith of basketball and football fame, respectively.

Lefty Driesell

The basketball teams at Davidson played in Johnson Gymnasium, which was built in 1948. Johnson Gym was a cramped facility with rollout bleachers that held approximately three thousand fans. A full house could raise a good head of steam—the noise could be deafening. Prior to 1960, that rarely happened; in fact, the school was lucky to draw a crowd of four to five hundred to watch the Wildcats tangle with such powerhouses as Elon and Presbyterian.

During these games we kids often played courtside and in areas under the bleachers. A favorite game was pitching popcorn boxes or cola cups at a portable basket on the side of one of the bleachers. No one seemed to care. Of course, the team lost a lot.

In previous decades there had been some high points. Dean Rusk, President Kennedy's Secretary of State, was a basketball player at Davidson in the early 1930's. That was back before that other Dean (if anyone from Carolina can remember that far back), when

Davidson regularly beat UNC and N.C. State. Hobby Cobb in the 1940's and Dave Hollingsworth in the 1950's were probably All-American caliber players, but they didn't get any publicity. Semi (I don't know where his other half got to) Metz led the NCAA in free throw percentage one year (not that his feat drew much attention). Unfortunately, Davidson with its no scholarship approach was a perennial loser, the "misnamed Wildcats," according to *Sports Illustrated.* All of that was before Lefty (BL).

The last BL coach was Dr. Tom Scott, who had been head basketball coach at UNC before coming to Davidson in the mid-1950's. He was also the athletic director and golf coach. Golf and tennis were the only perennially successful Davidson sports. Tom Scott's basketball teams were mediocre, but again, he had no scholarship athletes to work with. That all changed in 1960.

Dr. Grier Martin was president of the college at that time, and he and Dr. Scott decided, to the great delight of the alumni, to recruit a topflight basketball coach. Since no one from the college ranks would consider the position at such a small institution, Grier and Tom searched the Southeastern high schools for capable applicants. That's when they found Lefty.

Lefty Driesell, a successful twenty-seven-year-old coach at Newport News High in Virginia, where his teams had a fifty-seven game winning streak, accepted the job at Davidson. The college allowed him only eleven scholarships. At Davidson, which had virtually no recruiting budget, Lefty recruited out of the back of his Chevy station wagon, using it as both office and bedroom on the road. The first player he coaxed into coming to Davidson was Terry Holland from Clinton, North Carolina. Terry would eventually succeed Lefty as head coach at Davidson; he would later become head basketball coach at the University of Virginia, then athletic director at Davidson, and finally athletic director at UVA.

I attended the first game Driesell coached at Davidson. Wake Forest was in town. They were ranked third in NCAA Division I and would finish in the Final Four that year. Davidson was ranked last in the Southern Conference. To this day no one really understands why Wake scheduled Davidson—it was such an enormous mismatch. Wake had big Len Chapell, a consensus All-American center, along with Billy Packer (later the TV guru of NCAA basketball) and Norman Sneed (of Washington Red Skins quarterbacking fame) at guard and forward, respectively.

Most people, I expect, came to watch Chapell dunk the lights out at Johnson Gym. I wouldn't have missed it for anything. I now remember it as one of the grandest things I've ever seen. Bill Jarman, Jim Nuckolls, D.G. Martin, Jr. (the president's son), Joe Markee, and Danny Carrell were the Davidson starters. Wake had the lead early but couldn't keep it. Late in the second half it was mind-bogglingly apparent that Davidson was actually in control of the game. When the sweat was finally wiped from the floor, Davidson had won it 65-59. The moon turned blue. Jim Nuckolls danced at mid-court. Quite simply, the place went berserk.

After the game I ran over to the Teen Canteen and announced that Davidson had stuck it to Wake. My friends laughed and asked me to tell them the real score. When the Davidson fight song (a feisty rendition of the alma mater hymn) blared out over the loud speakers in the dome of Chambers Building, they became believers, and that place also went berserk. We all were literally dancing in the streets. Wake Forest never lived it down. Score one for the high church Presbyterians.

The athletes that comprised that team were typical of Davidson teams of the era in terms of their intellectual abilities. Jarman, Nuckolls, and Markee became doctors. D.G. Martin became a prominent attorney. Danny Carrell won a Rhodes Scholarship.

The Wake game was clearly the high watermark of Lefty's first season. Unbelievably, Davidson lost to Elon in the next game and then dropped more games in a row than I care to remember, finishing 9-14 for the year.

Lefty was distracted for most of that season. His heart was in Washington, D.C., where he was recruiting a blue chip high school player named Fred Hetzel, an All-American, who at six-foot-nine was the tallest player anyone around Davidson had ever seen. Driesell somehow talked Fred into attending Davidson on scholarship. Lefty also signed a prospect from Ohio who had the unlikely name of Don Davidson—he would play forward. Next in line was an ambidextrous guard named Barry Teague, and another guard named Charlie Marcon.

These four freshmen would be the nucleus of the miracle years to come.

In 1962 Lefty's starters included seniors Jarman, Holland, and sophomores Hetzel, Teague, and Davidson. Their first big game was at Duke, where the nationally second-ranked Blue Devils under Coach Vic Bubas won by the relatively narrow margin of nine points. The Davidson team even got an ovation from the otherwise obstreperous crowd as they left the floor.

Davidson played Duke again at the Charlotte Coliseum in early December of that year. Art Heyman, a Jewish guard from New York and three-time NCAA Player of the Year, led the Duke team. All-American Jeff Mullins was the other guard. Two redwood pines, Jay Buckley and Hack Tyson, and another Blue Devil, lost to my memory, rounded out the Blue Devil squad.

Duke jumped off to a quick 6-0 lead. Jarman began a Davidson run with a corner swish. Hetzel got cranked up, and by halftime it was Davidson by fifteen. Duke closed the lead late in the game. In fact, the Blue Devils had a chance to take the lead, but Heyman blew a breakaway lay-up by dropping it off the front of the rim (these were the days before slam dunks, and college basketball in the South was still a mostly segregated game). Davidson held a one-point lead with five seconds left at 70-69. Heyman was setting up for the final shot when he wound up missing the ball. Teague stole it from him and was immediately fouled. A picture from the college annual of that year sums it all up: Teague is shown firing up the second of his free throws over the lonesome pines of Duke with the score 71-69. The second shot made it 72-69. (This was years before the three-point shot was allowed.) As Duke gamely in-bounded the ball, a mournful cry arose from high in the rafters—"Poooor Dooook." It was the grandest basketball victory in the history of the college. The place went nuts. The headline of *The Charlotte Observer* the following day read, "Hetzel's 27 Rockets Davidson over Duke." The *Observer* called it "the biggest upset in these parts since the mountaineers shot Major Ferguson off the top of Kings Mountain," or something like that. A newspaper in Tokyo, Japan, ran a sports page headline that read "David (son) slays Goliath."

Driesell was instantly elevated to god-like status. But it didn't last long. Little Davidson's next game was at Cincinnati against the undefeated top-ranked team in the nation. The Cats lost by a whopping twenty-five to a clearly superior team, including Tony Gates, George Wilson, and Ron Bonham among others. Cincinnati was loaded with fine black players. That was still four years away for Davidson.

Driesell was a big fellow at about six-foot-six. And he had a hot temper. I particularly remember his white towel. Lefty would keep it wrapped around his neck, and at an irritating moment he would slam it on the floor, on the nearest player, or most often on poor Joe Hunt, the assistant coach. He is best remembered, however, for his "Lefty Stomp." He would leap to his feet, scream at the refs or players, and then stomp his left foot on the court as hard as he could.

Davidson went on to lose to All-American Rod Thorne and the West Virginia Mountaineers in the finals of the Southern Conference tournament that spring of 1963. Hetzel, as a sophomore, was named honorable mention All-America and was designated Player of the Year in the Southern Conference. Things looked promising for 1963-64 with the return of the junior group and the advent of Dick Snyder.

Snyder was from Canton, Ohio. An All-American football and basketball player, he was heavily recruited, especially by Ohio State. He chose Davidson and was arguably the finest all-round athlete to ever attend the college. Some sportswriters predicted that little Davidson would make the top ten rankings that year.

One game that stands out in my memory from that year was against sixth-ranked Ohio State. Davidson went up to play them on their home court in Columbus, where the fast-breaking Buckeyes had a fifty-game winning streak. We watched it on television. The Wildcats routed them. Snyder added insult to injury by putting in a half-court bomb-swish at the halftime buzzer. Davidson went on to win by twenty-three points. The following Tuesday both major wire polls ranked the team in the top ten in the country.

Davidson played Duke that season at Cameron Indoor Stadium in Durham. It was such a highly publicized game that the college installed huge closed circuit television screens at the Charlotte Coliseum and at Johnston Gym to accommodate the interest. Duke won a close game. Thinking the boisterous crowd and the refs had stolen the game, Lefty demanded a rematch away from the Duke campus. Then he threw a barb at Duke's head coach, Vic Bubas: "If he doesn't come to my place next year, he's yellow." Lefty proceeded to kick in the door of the visitors' dressing room at Cameron Indoor Stadium in what was described as his nastiest tirade to date. This behavior was all the more unexpected since Lefty was a Duke graduate and a former teammate of Vic Bubas.

As good as this Davidson team was, it still couldn't win the big one, even the little big one that was the final of the Southern Conference Tournament, which in that era was the gateway to the NCAA Tournament qualifying round. Davidson played an also-ran VMI team on an unfortunate night in February 1964. To the abject horror of Lefty and the Wildcat loyal, VMI kept it tight. Unbelievably, VMI held a one-point lead with three seconds left in the game. Davidson put the ball in play under its own basket. Guard Barry Teague lofted a twelve-foot jumper. The ball rimmed, and rimmed, and rimmed. I can still see it frozen in time. It rimmed out, and VMI won.

1964-65 looked to be the best season yet. Incredibly, *Sports Illustrated* ranked tiny Davidson #1 in the nation in its preseason poll and had even had a picture of Fred Hetzel on its cover, along with Bill Bradley of Princeton and Cazzie Russell of Michigan. C.W. Stacks presciently called it the "kiss of death." In those years teams ranked first by *S.I.* rarely made it to the Final Four.

C.W. hit it right on the mark. Davidson lost its first away game to Jack Ramsey's St. Joseph Hawks in the Palestra in Philadelphia. That loss was followed by a long winning streak that lasted until the West Virginia game in the Morgantown Barn. Davidson had a one-point lead with three seconds left in that game. West Virginia in-bounded at its end of the court; a Mountaineer heaved a Hail Mary throw from the mid-court line by the scorer's table. The ball drifted up toward the rafters and sailed down toward the basket. Hetzel was about halfway between the basket and the foul line. He halfheartedly jumped up and caught the ball. To everyone's astonishment the ref called goaltending on the play and awarded the basket and the game to West Virginia. Driesell was beside himself with disbelief and rage, stomping his leg like Rumpelstiltskin.

They must have played the game films over a hundred times. In the end Lefty had to suck it up, and the team went on to finish the regular season without another loss.

About this time WBTV in Charlotte began experimenting with videotaping sports events. One night at Johnson Gym the station broadcast a game and showed the first-ever video replays of a sporting event. The technology was such that they could only do reruns of foul shots. I'm not certain what the glitch was, but like the Wright brothers, they were off the ground.

The most memorable thing about that unlikely season for me was the Charlotte Invitational Tournament over Christmas 1964 at the Charlotte Coliseum. Princeton was invited. They had Bill Bradley, who well before his Oxford, NBA, and Senate days, was touted as the best college basketball player ever (with the possible exception of Oscar Robertson). The athletic department at the college asked John and me to be the ball boys. Somebody thought it would be novel to have one of a pair of identical twins at each end of the court.

For two nights we sat mesmerized as Bradley put on the best hoops show we had ever seen. Bradley had a strange good luck ritual that only a ball boy would have noticed. After each pre-game and halftime warmup, he would make sure that his ball was the last ball to be put into the ball bag. He was very amicable with John and me and talked with us during the warm-ups—and he made sure his ball was on top of the bag.

As usual, the season all came down to the Southern Conference Tournament. Winning this year seemed simple enough since there was virtually no competition in the field for mighty Davidson. Sadly, astoundingly, history repeated itself. Davidson fell to West Virginia in the finals. Hetzel, Davidson, Teague, and Marcon were history. We were sick about it. Poor Lefty.

1965-66 was a rebuilding year. Lefty had a good freshmen class with two high school All-Americans. This was supposed to be Dick Snyder's year. 1966 was the Chinese Year of the Horse. The students called Snyder "Super Horse." Following a letdown in the second half of the season, however, he would only make second team All-America in both major polls.

Lefty was a little scarce on players that year. He barely scraped up ten on the team. Lefty even had his manager, senior Jim Hyder, suit up to have enough players for the pre-game warm-ups. The West Virginia game in Charlotte was particularly memorable that year. Davidson routed Bucky Waters' Mountaineers. In the last minute of the game Lefty sent in Hyder to give him the chance to play in a major college game.

With three seconds remaining, the ball was in-bounded to a solitary Davidson player standing at half-court. At first he acted like he didn't know what to do with it, but then he turned and heaved the ball toward the basket. It was a splendid two-handed, high-arc set shot that almost stripped the nets. To add to West Virginia's agony, the Davidson manager had scored the last basket.

The team went on to win the Southern Conference Tournament that year. Syracuse, led by Dave Bing, defeated the Cats in the opening round of the NCAA Tournament, but Lefty had proved that he at least could win a little big one. Better times were to come.

I entered Davidson College as a student in the autumn of 1966. The incoming freshman basketball players made up one of the best freshmen teams in the country. At center was a six-foot-seven high school All-American from New York City named Mike Maloy, an African American athlete who had acquired the unusual skill of dunking two basketballs one after the other in the same leap. Jerry Kroll from Texas and Doug Cook from New Jersey were the forwards. Fox Demoisey and Randy Jones (my nursery school assailant) were the starting guards. These were scholar-athletes who were expected to perform both in class and on the court. They went 15-0 as a frosh class.

My sophomore year at Davidson saw the team nationally ranked and something to behold. Still, nothing could compare to John Wooden's powerful UCLA team with Lew Alcindor (the future Kareem Abdul-Jabbar). The best any other team could expect to do was fall flat on its face in the national finals against UCLA.

We all ducked reality and actually thought our boys might have a shot at it. This team was clearly the best ever at Davidson. Maloy had sensational moves. The NCAA had outlawed dunking by the time of his arrival—because Alcindor was wreaking too much havoc with that shot. Mike did everything but dunk. He could almost touch the top of the backboard and was the best leaper I had ever seen. It was about that time that Lefty's sideline antics came under heavy fire.

The boys were up at West Virginia and were winning handily by seventeen points. The West Virginia fans behind the Wildcat bench began some weird chanting, howling, mercilessly baiting the coach and his team. The Davidson lead dwindled. Witnesses said that as Davidson's advantage dwindled, Lefty turned, and made an unfortunate gesture toward the crowd. A lot of controversy about it ensued. Coach Driesell always caused lots of conversation.

The team easily won the conference title in 1968 and qualified for the NCAA Eastern Regional. They got into the semifinal game with Columbia. Davidson had a one point lead with virtually no time on the clock. A Columbia player had a one-and-one situation at the line. Driesell called time out to let him think about it. This sparked a controversy about Lefty's game conduct and ethics. Nobody would think anything of it these days. Those days, they did. Anyway, the Columbia guy missed the free throw, and Davidson advanced to the finals against the North Carolina Tar Heels, Larry Miller, and Dean Smith.

Doug Cook, the big Davidson forward, had a hip injury and couldn't play. *The Charlotte Observer* described it as a game that would be long remembered along Tobacco Road. In a closely fought contest, UNC won 70-66. They, of course, got to play Big Lew and UCLA in the next round and were defeated soundly. (Rusty Clark, the big center for Carolina, would be a friend of mine in medical school. He told me that he wished Davidson had won and spared the Tar Heels their embarrassing defeat).

The following season, 1968-69, saw the Davidson team's high national ranking and great sport in ripping apart the competition. Along for the ride, we had a great time. Tiny Johnson Gym became a gate to hell for opposing teams. The Charlotte Coliseum with 11,666 seats wasn't much better. We were really riding high.

The high point of the season came in the NCAA Eastern Regional Finals in March of that year. Davidson again faced UNC, and this time their All-American was Charlie Scott. An African American,

Scott had signed with Davidson in 1996 and had been slated to begin classes in the fall of that year, but he never got there.

Scott was on the Davidson campus during the summer of 1966. The story goes that he wandered over to the Coffee Cup restaurant on Depot Street, where he encountered a vestige of Jim Crow. The Coffee Cup worked around the 1964 Civil Rights Act by seating blacks and whites at separate tables once they were inside the restaurant. Scott saw through this overt segregation and decided he would play his college ball in a more cosmopolitan milieu. He withdrew his application and to Lefty's horror, signed with Dean Smith, who was building a perennial national power at Chapel Hill.

The 1969 Eastern Regional final game was extremely close. It was Scott, the Tar Heel All-American, versus Maloy, the Davidson All-American. This year Doug Cook was in good health, and the teams were evenly matched. Carolina was up by one at the half, 47-46. The game seesawed back and forth down the stretch and was tied at 85-85 with 1:05 remaining. Then one of our guys committed an offensive foul, turning the ball over to the Heels and the red-hot Scott, who had scored eleven of Carolina's last sixteen points. I could almost hear Charlie shouting, "Remember the Coffee Cup!" when he hit the winning jumper at the buzzer.

1969-1970 was a lackluster season at best. The team made it into the Eastern Regionals but lost to St. Bonaventure and big Bob Lanier. After the season Lefty announced that he was leaving Davidson to become the head basketball coach at the University of Maryland. The alumni bought him a big red Thunderbird in a pitiful attempt to coax him into staying. It didn't work. He moved on, taking that fancy car with him. Terry Holland replaced him as coach at Davidson.

Lefty remained at Maryland until the Len Bias cocaine scandal. He left us with some good memories. It's fair to say he did accomplish a great deal at an academically tough school with a student body of only one thousand. I have since wondered what it would have been like if Lefty had stayed. I had actually grown fond of him.

I last saw him in 1972 before a Maryland game on the University of North Carolina campus. We spoke on the steps of Carmichael Auditorium. I asked him how Dean Smith had let him get away with violating NCAA restrictions on entertaining recruits off campus (Lefty took them to Charlotte). He smiled and said, "I had more on Dean Smith than he had on me."

Lefty built Maryland into a national basketball power. His greatest team was the one that challenged N.C. State in three overtimes in the ACC final in 1973, what some sports pundits call the greatest college game ever played. Maryland lost, and N.C. State went on to upset the Bill Walton Gang from UCLA and win the national title.

A number of years ago the Cats moved out of Johnson Gym into the Baker athletic complex, which was erected on the site of the old baseball field. I attended the last game in Johnson Gym. The announcer reminded everyone about the glory days. It was a lackluster game, certainly nothing for future generations of grads to reminisce over. I also attended the first game in the new facility. It wasn't the same. There were no bleachers to wander under, no side goals for shooting hoops with cola cups and popcorn boxes, and no deafening din to fire up the team.

Homer Smith

Davidson College was never a football powerhouse. Its teams perennially stood at the bottom of the Southern Conference. The college had only limited scholarships, so almost every player was a walk-on. It was not unheard of to have coaches roaming the dormitories looking for any and all willing to be thrown into the Gipper meat-grinder.

The tiny stadium at Richardson Field was erected in the 1920's. Consisting of east and west stands built of concrete, it housed a football field and outdoor cinder track. The entire complex seated approximately 8000 fans, but to the best of my knowledge was never filled until the arrival of Coach Homer Smith. During Homer's fourth game, the stadium was packed with fans and sportswriters who watched an unbeaten, untied Wildcat team fall to a William and Mary juggernaut that ran roughshod over the hapless Red and Black.

Davidson football was generally a relatively gentle and simplistic affair. An ambulance sitting at one of the gates was there as a reminder that on rare occasions somebody got roughed up. When that happened, it was usually a Davidson player on the stretcher.

The home games were played on Saturday afternoons. The college was beautiful in the autumn. People were always remarking on the vast number of oak and maple trees and how resplendent they made the campus look in that season. We wiled away those autumn Saturdays of our youth at Richardson Field.

A student at the college could park himself at the college library, leave his books on a study table, and five minutes before kickoff amble over to the stadium. If he chose, he could relax in the end zone farthest from the action. In those years it was usually the opponent's end zone because the Davidson team rarely got the ball into scoring position.

Because we were faculty kids, we had free admission. We usually had our own games going either on the sidelines or occasionally in the opponent's end zone. This infuriated some of the older alumni, who felt that we were degrading the team. We didn't have to do that—the other teams were more than well equipped for the job. We really preferred to be on the field.

Our open admission seats were always on the east side of the stadium looking straight into the afternoon sun. The college claimed there were just enough seats on the Davidson side to accommodate students, faculty, and alumni. This put us right behind the opposing team's bench and right in the heart of their supporters. I remember once joining the Presbyterian College cheerleaders and rallying the opposition's supporters. That really ticked Dad off.

When we were ten years old, the Lions Club, which ran the stadium concession booths, let us sell food and soft drinks in the stands. I usually wound up with peanuts and popcorn. The popcorn came packaged in small megaphones, which the crowd used to stir up a little noise. We worked on consignment, and on a good Saturday we could take home seven or eight dollars, which was a lot of money for kids back then.

William Dole, Sr., was the football coach up until the early 1960's. He was a good, decent man who lived just up the street from us on Lorimer Road. Coach Dole taught his squads to play for the love of the game and to accept defeat (which came often) with grace and dignity.

The college never fired coaches for not winning. Had it done so, there would have been few or no coaches. Every student had the opportunity to participate in one or more sports if he chose to do so. As mentioned earlier, nearly forty percent of the student body was involved in NCAA Division I sports. The coaches were there to teach fundamentals and teamwork. Winning was nice, but it was not the ultimate objective. Academics at Davidson were far and away the college's top priority.

One game from the Dole years stands out in my memory—it was a game none of us attended because they played it in Blacksburg, Virginia, against Virginia Polytechnic Institute (VPI). VPI was a perpetual football power and was ranked in the top twenty in 1960. Somehow they fitted little Davidson into their schedule.

Davidson, as usual, was in the dungeon of the Southern Conference. The sportswriters expected a massacre of Custer proportions at VPI. One commented that the results would be "doleful." Another ruminated that this could be worse than the beating Georgia Tech once gave poor Cumberland, 220-0—clearly the most lopsided football game ever played.

That beautiful November afternoon we were playing on the college outdoor basketball courts. Sometime around 4 p.m., as the shadows lengthened, we heard the Davidson fight song blaring out from the loudspeakers high atop Chambers Building. We thought that perhaps the cross-country or soccer team had won. They always played the fight song when a Davidson team won anything. We knew it couldn't be the football team, which was in a Waring blender in Blacksburg.

Suddenly, David Lloyd came running down to the courts screaming, "Davidson won! Davidson won!" The campus erupted—horns blaring, students yelling—the football team had implausibly, miraculously defeated VPI 9-7. The moon turned blue.

The team members proudly brought the game ball back with them. The bronzed ball still stands in the college trophy collection—dedicated to young men who played the game for the pure joy of it.

To digress slightly from the subject of Davidson College football, it should be noted that in the fall seasons of the 1950's and early 60's the college leased Richardson Field on Friday nights to local high school teams for their football games. Bill Kimbrough, the son of John

T. Kimbrough, a legendary Davidson mathematics professor, and John Woods' next-door neighbor on Lorimer Road, often did the play-by-play work at Davidson's rendition of "Friday Night Lights." We attended those high school games more to imbibe Bill's hilarious antics than to watch what was happening on the field. When the home team screwed up, Bill would bark into the microphone, "Whose fault is it? Is it the fans?" In unison the crowd howled "No!" "Is it the team's fault?" A little bit louder now, the crowd roared "No!" "Is it the coach's fault?" A thousand voices raged, "Yes!" Bill's commentary was definitely original. Whenever a ref threw a flag, Bill called it "There's a rag on the play!" A bone-crunching tackle merited "Wow! That smarted!" Bill lived a few doors down from Coach Dole, which may explain how he got his gig.

When Coach Dole retired, Homer Smith came to the college as the new head football coach. The fortunes of Davidson football were about to change. The alumni were clamoring for football glory, and Homer vowed to give it to them.

Homer was a "cerebral" coach who related well to Davidson athletes—he had a BA degree from Princeton and an MBA from Stanford. And he had a knack for fielding good teams. Davidson started to have winning seasons. Smith was particularly good at tapping the local pool of academically talented high school footballers. He signed an exceptional student named Jimmy Poole, who was in my sister's class at North Mecklenburg. Poole was instrumental in establishing Davidson as a Southern Conference contender.

By my senior year at Davidson, Smith had put together the best team in the college's history. In 1966 he had brought in my cousin Mike Kelly, an All-State and All-South player at tight end. He also recruited a top quarterback named Gordon Slade. In 1969 the team went 8-2 for the season, winning the Southern Conference title with Gordon Slade shining as one of the nation's leading passers. Surprisingly, the Tangerine Bowl committee in Orlando, Florida, issued an invitation for Davidson to play nineteenth ranked Toledo in late December. Who would have ever believed Davidson would have a post-season in football?

The game was played in the Tangerine Bowl at Orlando, Florida. This was the pre-Disney city—Walt Disney World was still on the drawing board. Grif Bowen, one of our best friends at Davidson, drove John and me down for the game. We stopped to spend a rainy night in Savannah, Georgia. The next day we visited Leland Park, the current college librarian, and his family in Orlando. We stayed at the home of our old Montreat friend, Wilson Greene, who lived in Winter Park.

The game was a hoot. Half the town showed up, and half of them were blitzed. My former pastor Curtis Harper was there lending order to the spectacle. Feeling no pain whatsoever, Bill Kimbrough and Bub Cashion sat right behind us. Toledo had Davidson down 42-7 at the half. Homer Smith looked down and out. I don't know what he told Kelly, Slade et al. at halftime, but a different Davidson team showed up on the field for the second half.

The team took off like a rocket. Davidson scored one TD after another against what suddenly had become a vulnerable Toledo squad. When the dust had finally settled, Toledo held on for a 56-42 win. It was a great game.

After that Homer lost interest in Davidson football. We learned that like Lefty he was leaving for a "better" job. In Homer's case it was to be head football coach at the College of the Pacific. His last head-coaching job would be at West Point. It turned out, however, that head coaching wasn't his forte—Homer would make a name for himself as an offensive coordinator at powerhouses like UCLA, Alabama, and Arizona. In 1990 he was named *The Sporting News* Offensive Coach of the Year. Along the way he coached in a dozen bowl games, including four Rose Bowls.

Lefty and Homer gave our little college a decade's worth of excitement. They were flamboyant characters who left an indelible imprint on my memory and the town's. That their paths crossed in the same small place was our great fortune.

Profiles
of a
College

I had the unique fortune of growing up in a small college town and attending that college as a student. I knew most of the staff and professors at the college long before coming under their tutelage. The following people and my memories associated with them are not given in any particular order of importance—they simply appear in the order I recalled them as I write this book.

Chalmers Gaston Davidson

Dr. Chalmers Davidson, a history professor with his Ph.D. from Harvard University, was Director of the Library (all honored him with this title) at Davidson College. He and his wife, Alice, had three children one of whom, their daughter Alice, was my contemporary. The Davidson family lived out Concord Road in a house called Hurricane Hill. The derivation of the name is unclear since the only hurricane ever to hit Davidson was Hurricane Hugo in 1989.

Dr. Davidson was proudly aware of his Davidson family roots, descended from Major John Davidson, who was probably related to General William Lee Davidson for whom Davidson College is named.

Dr. Davidson was a bastion for an unapologetic champion of the South. He could often be seen walking the campus in a white suit and sometimes wearing a Panama hat. Rumor had it that he had turned his Phi Beta Kappa pin into a tie clasp. A master of Southern gentility and a paragon of the Code of Gentlemanly Conduct, he was a brilliant man who held a Ph.D. in American history from Harvard University. He was a regional author, and I particularly enjoyed his book *Piedmont Partisan*, a biography of William Lee Davidson.

In the summers during our high school years, Dr. Davidson employed John and me in the acquisitions section of the library, where we worked in a basement room for seventy-five cents an hour under the general supervision of the library staff: Carrie Britain, Della Shore, and Joy McEver. John and I prepared books for the library shelves, always in the following sequence for each book: First we would paste a college information sticker on the inside cover and include a donation sticker if the book was a gift to the college. Next we stamped *Davidson College Library* at the top of page thirty-nine. Then we affixed the book's Dewey Decimal System number on the binding. Finally, we painted the hard cover book jacket with a preservative lacquer. It was a tedious yet good job because we got to pick our own hours of employment. Occasionally we got to work the front desk at the library, which paid us a dollar an hour with far less work. In fact the only times I had to work hard at all at the desk were the sporadic occasions when Dr. Alan Brinkley would appear with his little red wagon to return or tote out scores of books. The deskwork on each book had to be done entirely by hand.

During my years as a student at Davidson, Dr. Davidson taught a hodgepodge course on American cultural history from the Civil War to the 1950's. I enrolled in his class in the autumn of 1969. Students called it "Cocktail History." On the first day of class, news circulated that a certain Davidson student, Mr. Hanes (not his actual name), had impregnated a girl from Queens College in Charlotte and had eloped with her the night before. He obviously was cutting the class. Dr. Davidson began that first lecture with these words: "Gentlemen, there are but three reasons for cutting my class. They are in order: birth, death, and copulation. Mr. Hanes is excused."

The course covered just about anything and everything "cultural," that is to say, art, religion, movies, sports, newspapers and a variety of other subjects from the Civil War forward. We even wrote letters (and occasionally received replies) to movie stars of the Silent Era. Dr. Davidson always gave us prepared lecture notes to which we added volumes as he rattled off one fact after another. The course had a peculiarly Southern slant.

Dr. Davidson's tests were difficult. I remember vividly the day he handed out an original studio program from the premier of *Gone with the Wind*, which he must have attended in Atlanta in 1939. He had highlighted for us one page with pictures of the major characters in the film. He asked us to name the characters and the actors and actresses who played them. I was the only one in the class who knew that Alicia Rhett from Charleston played India Wilkes.

God knows I tried hard in his class. The best I could do, however, was B+ work. I remember that he called me into his office one morning and told me I needed to work harder. He said that I was *"A"* potential and added, "Do it for your mother." Hard as I tried I never got the A.

During my college years we called those students who did nothing else but study "Nerds." Others of us were "Flies." Flies studied hard but participated in other college activities. There was even a Fly of the Year Award, given annually and satirically to the Davidson student who studied the hardest but got the least out of it. In 1968 John Lawrence Puckett received the coveted accolade. A picture of the award ceremony was supposed to appear in the college newspaper, *The Davidsonian.*

I was standing in the foyer of the library when the photographer arrived. John was nowhere to be found. The photographer remarked, "That's OK. I'll just take a shot of the empty front desk of the library and make the cut line read, 'John Puckett, Fly of the Year.' He was studying and didn't have time to show up for the award." Actually, John did in time redeem himself and in the end made Phi Beta Kappa. He, too, could wear his pin as a tie clasp, which he never did—only Chalmers Davidson could have gotten away with that. John is currently a professor and associate dean at the University of Pennsylvania.

Dr. Davidson was instrumental in one of the grandest social events in town history—an event that I regrettably didn't attend even though I had an invitation. I will pass on the description that made the rounds in the town.

Alice Davidson, Chalmers' daughter, was engaged to a Northern gentleman recently graduated from The Citadel. For the wedding ceremony the groomsmen were arrayed in Confederate dress gray and Union dress blue—all carried sabers. The bridesmaids wore hoop skirts. The gala was replete with orchestra and refreshments, which included liberal libations. While the libations flowed freely, the orchestra played Civil War tunes from both North and South. The story goes that Dr. Davidson gave careful instructions to the bandmaster. "When you play 'Yankee Doodle,' you must follow with 'Bonnie Blue Flag.' When you play 'The Battle Hymn of the Republic,' you must play 'Dixie.' If you play 'Marching through Georgia,' I'll fire you."

Dr. Davidson retired to become the college archivist. He and Mrs. Davidson moved to his lovely ancestral plantation home called Beaver Dam on N.C. 73, just east of town. I wrote to him in 1991 and thanked him for being my mentor and friend. I reiterated some of the trivia he had taught me to show him that I really did get something from his teaching. I apologized for not getting the A.

Dr. Davidson sent me an eloquent reply. It was a kind and flattering letter, and so typical of his old Southern courtesy. I keep it among my own most valued papers. Dr. Davidson wrote it at Beaver Dam on July 6, 1991

Dear James,

Yours is the kind of letter that warms the cockles of an old professor's heart (whatever valves cockles may be). I will certainly put it with my most valued papers—to be disposed of by Leland Park after my demise.

Any busy doctor who would take time to write a letter like that—after all the grades are in—is a man with a caring heart, the ideal physician. Your patients are amongst the fortunate of today's world.

I regret that your brilliant father did not live to know your
success. He, too, was a caring person and one of the
leaders in making Davidson a uniquely good college. I see
evidences of his unique influence here and in many alumni.
My sincere best wishes to you and yours.

Affectionately yours,

Chalmers Davidson

Nelson Mebane

Dr. Nelson Mebane taught physics and applied mathematics at
the college and retired to take on a part time job as campus surveyor.
He and Mrs. Mebane lived near us in a house fronting Woodland
Road. We probably would have never gotten to know the Mebanes
well had it not been for their grandchildren, Tom and Cissy Bell, who
came up from Columbia, South Carolina, to visit their grandparents
every summer.

I remember Tom as one of the most gregarious people I've ever
met. He was a blonde-hair youth who had a devilish smile and a hoarse
laugh that would send John and me into convulsions. Girls adored
Tom, and he never missed an opportunity to let us know that or to
give us advice about the art of love. Tom was also a vigorous competitor and he had a knack for getting all of us into trouble. On the
other hand, his lovely sister was quite reserved and stayed out of the
limelight.

My earliest memory of Tom was in the summer of 1953 when
my family went to Pawley's Island on the South Carolina coast. Tom,
who was visiting the Mebanes at the time, needed a ride to Conway,
near Myrtle Beach, to visit his paternal grandparents. The Mebanes
arranged with Mom and Dad to drop Tom off in Conway. I remember the picnic we had that day on the Pee Dee River. The day was
hot, and the picnic area was sandy, which only made the heat worse.
We cut up terribly all afternoon, and our parents were much relieved
to see the "incorrigible Bell boy" delivered to his relatives.

John, Tom, and I were inseparable during summers in the late 1950's and early 1960's. We played baseball in the back sandlot and ping-pong in the Shaw Smiths' backyard. Tom was a lefty with a big slam. Our favorite game, however, was croquet. The Mebanes had the only workable set in the neighborhood. The games were highly competitive, and the winner was usually offered first pick of a variety of Mrs. Mebane's confections.

Mrs. Mebane was well known in town for her fine candies. She made the best golden-brown taffy I've ever tasted. Every summer she would invite all the children in the neighborhood over to her back-yard to pull and eat the delicious stuff. Because of this we called her "Taffy."

Dr. Mebane occasionally employed me to help with his survey-ing in the summers. That was always a treat because he let me operate his push-button- drive 1957 Dodge De Soto. I remember long sum-mer evenings out in the briars and brambles hauling the pole while Dr. Mebane shouted directions. I remember doing surveying for the lower tennis courts at the college. Dr. Mebane always rewarded me with a spin around the campus—letting me push the transmission buttons.

When I was a medical student at the University of North Caro-lina, I saw Cissy Bell on occasion. She was an undergraduate student there and as lovely as ever. I asked her once what had become of Tom. She gently told me that he had contracted rheumatic fever as a child—something no one, not even Tom, had ever mentioned to either John or me. Tom had mitral stenosis, and he died during a mitral valve repair operation.

I can still see Tom and his fierce left uppercut ping-pong swing. And I can still hear his raucously hoarse laughter pealing throughout the neighborhood. He is still there in my memory, on a warm summer night coaching John and me how to kiss Pattie Newell and Becky Caldwell. I can still see us all covered in hot golden-brown taffy.

Charles Lloyd

Mr. Charles Lloyd came to Davidson in the mid-1950's. The Lloyds had five children, of whom David and Jimmy were my contemporaries. Shortly after moving to Davidson, the Lloyds lost their youngest child, Robert, to leukemia. They settled in an old wood frame house on a property at the end of North Main Street. Located at a far distance from the street in a copse of trees, the house brought to mind Norman Bates' home in the Hitchcock film *Psycho*. Starting our third-grade year, John and I went there often to play.

Mr. Lloyd soon gained a reputation among students and faculty as an expert in just about every field imaginable. Dad said that Mr. Lloyd could either speak or read in thirteen languages. While I was a student at Davidson, I often spoke with him in German. He told me he had learned his German during his Army days in Austria at the close of World War II. At Davidson he was officially called Mr. Lloyd; he didn't have a Ph.D. When the college asked him to complete his doctorate, he supposedly replied, "In what?" He was eminently qualified in a number of fields, including English, German, Latin, mathematics, and who knows what else. In deference to his vast knowledge, most town folks and students called him "Dr. Lloyd."

One of his favorite pastimes was reading the funnies in the daily papers. He became so knowledgeable on the subject that he was scheduled to be on the *$64,000 Question* T.V. quiz show. Unfortunately that was right in the midst of the quiz show scandals of the late 1950's. The networks cancelled all of their quiz shows, and Mr. Lloyd never got to appear.

In 1958 Davidson fielded a team to appear on General Electric's *College Bowl* quiz show. Davidson made a miserable showing and bowed out after the first session. It was not until 1969 that the college received an invitation to try again. This time the faculty chose Mr. Lloyd to coach the team. After tryouts he selected four students and one alternate to represent the school. We remembered the massacre of '58 and held out little hope for this team. We vastly underestimated Mr. Lloyd.

Mr. Lloyd asked the student body to send in questions. The team seemed to be able to answer most of them. (I sent in the question: "Where is the Island of His?" That stumped them—it's an old name for a part of the human heart.) Renaissance man Mr. Lloyd came up with his own questions from the myriad fields of his expertise. Most important, he taught the Davidson team to sit on the buzzer.

Davidson appeared in New York on the *College Bowl* in the spring of 1969. The team annihilated the competition in a tour de force rarely seen on that program. Robert Bryan from La Grange, Georgia, was a one-man show. He frequently answered questions before host Allan Ludden had finished asking them. He even answered one question in Latin! Robert was an also-ran academically at Davidson, ranking somewhere down in the middle of the class. However, he was far smarter than that. His genius for this sort of trivia contests led Davidson through five victorious Sundays. The network retired them after the last win. The program directors said that Robert Bryan was one of the top five contestants in the long history of *College Bowl*, and the team gave all the credit to Mr. Lloyd.

Hundreds of congratulatory letters poured in. One elderly gentleman, a VPI graduate, wrote viperous letters after each victory. He lambasted the college and the team—especially Robert Bryan's thick Southern drawl. Each week we gathered around the Union bulletin board to check out the weekly harangue from this obviously deranged man. After the final victory the college sent out a form letter thanking the public for its support. Mr. Lloyd made certain that this particularly onerous individual received a special note that read something like: "Due to the high volume of letters received, we cannot individually answer each one. We are grateful for the kindness and support which you have shown to both the College Bowl team and Davidson College."

Sometime after that the show went off the air. After a ten-year hiatus, PBS revived the *College Bowl* in 1979 as an international competition. Mr. Lloyd was once again in the coach's box. This time he fielded a spectacular team that routed Harvard 405-110 en route to winning the national competition. Not bad for a bunch of country bumpkins. From there the team went to England for the international finals against one of the Oxford colleges. The score was tied right down to the last question. Then the host queried, "Who was Jean Armand du Plessis?" The Davidson squad froze. One of the Brits answered, "Cardinal Richelieu." Anyway it was a grand season, and the alums were mighty proud.

Henry T. Lilly

Dr. Henry T. Lilly taught English at Davidson, and his wife, Grace, worked as a learning specialist for the college. They lived in a fine Tudor house on Concord Road at the eastern end of town.

Grace Lilly taught John and me in Sunday school. I fondly remember her classes at DCPC during our seventh and eighth grade years. Mrs. Lilly taught straight from the *Bible* and placed particular emphasis on the great stories of the *Old Testament.* I remember one session in which she spent forty-five minutes struggling to push Joshua and the Hebrews across the Jordan at Gilgal.

Henry Lilly is best remembered as a highly literate, humorous, and kindly man who was highly popular with the students. He could also take a joke. He had a ritual of always entering the classroom by giving the door a hard push. Next he would go to the window and pull the shade down a little. Then he would go to the speaker's podium on the small stage, and, regardless of its position, push it forward. One bright Saturday autumn morning on Homecoming Weekend in the late 1950's, his students decided they had no interest whatsoever in being cooped up in Professor Lilly's classroom with their dates waiting outside. They took the door off its hinges, loosened up the shade, and positioned the podium at the edge of the stage. Dr. Lilly pushed open the door, which promptly crashed to the floor. Next he sauntered across the flattened door to the window and pulled the shade off the wall. Then he walked onto the stage and pushed the podium into the wildly cheering audience. Finally, he proclaimed, "Class dismissed!"

On another occasion Dr. Lilly came to class with a large bandage on the back of his head. His students inquired as to the etiology of the injury. Dr. Lilly answered that the ceiling plaster in his bedroom had crashed on top of his head. "It certainly could have been much worse," Dr. Lilly ruminated. "Had I been in a different position, my wife would have taken it right in the face!"

Daniel Rhodes

Dr. Daniel Rhodes and his wife, Ethel, moved to Davidson in 1960. Dan Rhodes, a Davidson graduate, taught in the religion department at the college. He was the spitting image of Abraham Lincoln—the resemblance was uncanny. Dan and Ethel had four children—Elaine, Truscott, Robin, and Noel. They lived a block up the street from us in a white frame house on the corner of Lorimer and Woodland. Truscott and Robin ("Toothie") became familiar faces on our end of the block.

In the early 1960's our neighborhood gang played football in a vacant lot on Lorimer Road, just above the College Drive intersection. It wasn't much of a field, measuring only about fifty by twenty yards. John and I would get the word out in the neighborhood when a big game was on. Ten or twelve kids usually showed up. Bruce Parker would quarterback one team and Judy Sailstad the other. Randomly picked captains would then choose up sides. Occasionally, Jim McEver showed up and insisted on playing. We made a point not to invite Jim since he was so big and pugilistic. Truscott was the only one of us who was big enough to take on Jim. We had a rule that Jim and Truscott always had to be on opposite sides.

Our Rhodes-Sailstad football era petered out when we started junior high school. Judy Sailstad grew into young womanhood, and in that pre-feminist era her mother forbade her to continue playing roughshod with the boys. Without Judy we had a hard time putting a good game together. We just didn't have anyone of her caliber to replace her at quarterback. By the time Truscott's brother, Robin, who was four years our junior, was old enough to play that position (he would be the starting quarterback at North in the late 1960's), the tiny field had gone to seed.

During my junior year at North, Truscott, Ann Bridger, and Shaw Smith formed a singing trio named The Prophets, and they were really quite good. Truscott and Shaw played guitar and Ann did vocals. They performed folk songs and played at all sorts of high school shows, dances and talent contests. Truscott was part of the group that crammed into Aunt Louise's Buick every morning for the drive down Highway 21, the "fast way" to North Mecklenburg.

Truscott was highly popular at North Mecklenburg and was elected 1967 student council president at the high school. He cut an impressive figure—tall, dignified, poised, articulate. He was immensely likable. After his graduation he attended Furman University in

Greenville, South Carolina, I don't know for how long. Along the way something in Truscott's life went badly awry. Mom told me that he got into drugs. I never knew the full story, and I'm just as glad I didn't.

I was a medical student at Chapel Hill in the early 1970's when I received a letter from Mom telling me, "We buried Truscott Rhodes today." She wrote that Truscott had walked out in front of a truck on the interstate outside Atlanta. At the funeral Will Terry said that Truscott had at last found peace with himself. His death devastated the Rhodes family and the entire community. After that I never knew what to say to Dan or Ethel—Truscott was an unspoken sadness. I don't believe that any of us who knew and loved Truscott ever completely recovered from his death. He was so bright and held so much promise. He was the first of my Davidson childhood friends to die.

Arthur Gwynn Griffin

When I first knew them, the Griffins lived on North Main Street across the street from the Parkers. Gwynn and his wife, Christa, had four sons; their youngest son, Morris, was the only Griffin boy I had any contact with in my childhood—and he was six years older than John and I. Of course, the age difference didn't stop Morris, then a ninth grader, from being our accomplice in the chemistry experiment that blew up our room. (Morris would receive a Morehead Scholarship at UNC-Chapel Hill and go on to become a prominent Durham dentist.)

Like the Pucketts, the Griffins built a new house in the residential development that replaced Johnsie Shelton's horse pasture in the mid-1950's; it was a split-level red-brick house located directly across the street from us on Lorimer Road. In the late 1950's and 1960's the Griffins rented out their basement to students who wanted to live off campus. This brought us into contact with a motley assortment of college boys. I fondly recall playing Frisbee out in Lorimer Road with some of those students.

Mr. Griffin taught economics at the college. He was partially paralyzed by a benign spinal tumor and walked with a cane. Mrs. Griffin taught mathematics at North Mecklenburg High School. Both continued to teach long after their sons had left home.

Mr. Griffin and Dad were very close friends. From April through October, they could be seen evenings seated in lawn chairs in the Griffins' front yard. John and I often pulled up a chair just to listen in—the conversation was usually very interesting.

I regret that I never took economics in college. I understand that Mr. Griffin was a marvelous teacher. When I married Margaret, we went to him for advice on how to budget our finances. He was a big help.

Gwynn Griffin was one of the kindest, gentlest Christian men I have known. After he passed on, Mrs. Griffin, Mom, and Aunt Louise became inseparable friends. Mrs. Griffin was well into her nineties, living at The Pines, when I last saw her in 1997.

I miss those gatherings in Mr. Griffin's yard. There was a sense of neighborliness then that I have never encountered anywhere else. When Mr. Griffin died, I wrote Mrs. Griffin to tell her I believed there was small part of Heaven where two aging men had retired to lawn chairs to while away a never-ending summer evening.

John Gallent

The students called John R. Cunningham, the president of Davidson College in the 1940's and 1950's, "Slick John the Divine." DCPC was named "The Cathedral of Slick John the Divine." The church still bears that name in the memories of those who lived in Davidson or attended the college in those years.

Dr. Cunningham's antithesis in nickname only was Dr. John Gallent, who taught in the chemistry department at Davidson. A delightful person, Dr. Gallent happened to be one of the most disorganized human beings I have ever met. His office resembled an academic Pop Copeland's. Campus scuttlebutt had it that ungraded exam papers dating back at least twenty years lay under the mountains of paper that littered the entire room. According to one apocryphal story, Dr. Gallent would throw his students' essay exams down the staircase in the Martin Chemistry Building and make up his grade curve based on the distance each traveled. Dr. Gallent was known on campus as "Slick John the Bastard."

I remember John Gallent as a neighbor and friend. In the years before the college built the Dana Science Building, his office was located just down from Dad's in the old Martin Building. During my years as a student of chemistry at Davidson, I frequently stopped by to speak with him. Despite his nickname, Dr. Gallent was highly popular on campus.

Mrs. Gallent ran the only kindergarten in town. It became a rite of passage for local children to attend. I looked forward to the day I, too, would get to go, but Mom had other ideas. Mrs. Gallent's kindergarten was privately operated, hence tuition-charging. Mom was a certified teacher, and to save the cost of sending two children to Mrs. Gallent, she decided to home school John and me during the 1953-54 school year. She bought a large portable blackboard and tutored us for several hours each day. I have only fleeting memories of that year. John and I wanted to be with our playmates, who seemed to be having a grand time at Mrs. Gallent's school. I do know that I didn't learn to read until the next year in Miss Margaret Adams' first grade classroom.

George Arthur Buttrick

George Arthur Buttrick was the famous pastor of the Collegiate Presbyterian Church in New York City and also the editor of the twenty or more volumes of the massive *Interpreter's Bible*. This great theologian came to Davidson College in his eighty-fifth year to teach a course in theological expository writing. I eagerly enrolled in his class in the spring of 1970. My first impression of the man called to mind a last autumnal leaf clinging to a broken bough in a whipping wind. He was small, frail, and supported by a cane. Yet Dr. Buttrick was sharp as a tack and filled with the Holy Spirit. And he was a marvelous teacher.

"Sacred Art", as we called him, knew just about everything theological. He waxed eloquently and passionately on such difficult subjects as human suffering and free will. We read his books and wrestled with the abstract points of his arguments. Word got out around campus about his riveting lectures, and curious students, including Brother John, showed up to see what all the excitement was about. Twice weekly Dr. Buttrick played to a full house in the Dome Room of Chambers Building.

I once asked Dr. Buttrick to define the difference between subjectivity and objectivity. He told me, "Envision a space ship carrying two astronauts. The objective man spends all of his time observing and categorizing every nuance of the ship, and when he has completed that, he begins all over and reclassifies it. The subjective man, on the other hand, has stuck his head through a port hole and is peering out at the cosmos!"

Ernest Patterson

Dr. Ernest Patterson came to Davidson in the late 1950's to teach economics. His only son, Ernie, became a good friend of ours. Dr. Patterson would have probably lived out a quiet tenure at Davidson had it not been for the Vietnam War.

As things heated up in Vietnam, we began to hear more student discussion on the issue. Most of the college and town supported the Federal Government's position in Southeast Asia. After all, the United States Government had led the nation through the Great Depression and World War II. Now it was leading the world against Communism. We naively believed that America could do no wrong.

In 1966 some of the students became more vocal on the war. Dr. Patterson passionately felt that the war was wrong. He organized what became known as the "Peace Vigil." This involved a cadre of students willing to rotate through morning, noon, and night shifts throughout the academic year. There were usually six or seven of them at one time, all holding lighted white candles, standing out in front of the college church.

Initially most of the other students derided them for their alleged anti-Americanism and after a time paid them little attention. Dr. Patterson became infamously known as "Red Ernie" for his participation. At the time I thought of him and his group as an idiosyncrasy that was woodenheaded but harmless.

The Peace Vigil endured for several years and was gaining more support as the 1960's drew to a close. It took my summer in ROTC basic training at Ft. Bragg to show me that there were some gapping holes in American foreign policy. Up to that time I had found it hard to accept what many were now saying on campus. By then it was apparent that Vietnam was a moral fiasco of gargantuan proportions.

In 1970 Richard Nixon ordered the bombing of Cambodia. I think that was the last straw for most of us. Perhaps I'm wrong, but I don't recall that Dr. Patterson ever gave a public speech against the war. He didn't need to—the very fact of his presence, come rain or shine, out in front of the church spoke volumes. I have never seen a more moving or powerful antiwar statement.

In early 1970 many Davidson students in ROTC who had signed military service contracts asked to be allowed to withdraw from the program. Colonel Virgil Foster, the department head, stuck his head on the block to help these students quietly exit the program and take their chances on getting a low enough lottery number to avoid the draft. I had this option but decided to plan for my military service, which would follow my four-year deferment to attend medical school. I thought the war was wrong but not the obligation of military service itself. In my patriotic soul I still thought of that as a citizen's duty.

A number of years later I met with Dr. Patterson as he lay on his deathbed. I told him I had come to realize that he had always been right about the Vietnam War. I apologized for any derisive remarks I may have made about him or the Peace Vigil. Finally I told him that had the rest of the country taken his stand early on, things would have worked out far differently.

My lasting memory of "Red Ernie" is of a man wearing a gray overcoat with matching fur hat, standing in a snowy twilight, and lifting a candle to enlighten a nation that was fading into the darkness of a totally senseless and unjustified war.

James Fredericksen

Affectionately known as "Freddy," Dr. James Fredericksen, a tall, gangly gentleman, came to Davidson in the late 1950's to teach in the chemistry department. I didn't get to know Freddy personally until I enrolled in his basic chemistry course as a freshman. His class was the beginning of my premedical education at Davidson.

I can only describe Freddy's classes as entertaining and enlightening. He obviously loved teaching. His lectures were punctuated by the history of chemistry and anecdotes about his years at the University of Virginia. We learned all about the idiosyncrasies of that noble institution, including the Secret Seven—seven men elected by their predecessors and known but to God, dedicated to helping those in distress. Freddy explained that a needy person could leave a written request at the foot of Thomas Jefferson's statue in the Rotunda, and if the Seven deemed it worthy, they would lend a helping hand.

Dr. Ralph Gable complemented Freddy's classes with his Friday afternoon labs. Normally labs could be tedious and boring, but I actually looked forward to Dr. Gable's since he made them so interesting. He was full of enthusiasm and roamed the lab looking for students needing help.

The lab was in the basement of the Martin Chemistry Laboratory. The bases of the windows on the western side of the lab were flush with the ground outside the windows. I remembered how as a child I enjoyed rummaging the area around those windows looking for discarded but still usable chemistry ware.

After every Friday session my freshman year I stayed behind to look for any discarded items, and if they met my standards (based on my third grade experiences), I carefully laid them out on the ground in the hope that some child might begin his or her own learning of chemistry. If the items were gone by the following week, I set out more. If they remained, then I simply turned them into the stock room for disposal. I suppose Dr. Gable knew what I was doing, but he never mentioned it.

During my junior year, 1968-69, I studied organic chemistry under Dr. Fredericksen. It was one of the most interesting courses I had in college and provided the basis for my studies in biochemistry, pharmacology, and physiology during my med school years. His tests were hard, consisting entirely of synthesis-type problems. We had to use fraternity "spots" (former exams collected by the brothers) to get some idea about how each test might run. Of course, the problems were always different since there were innumerable possibilities.

Grif Bowen, whose father, Sumter Bowen, had been in my Dad's class of 1927, was my lab partner for the year. We had been good friends since our freshman year. Grif was brilliant. He graduated second in the Class of 1970 and attended medical school at UNC on a Morehead Scholarship. Grif was a perfectionist, and that is a prerequisite for a good chemist. We worked well together and generally made A's. Dr. Fredericksen's office adjoined the lab, and he was always available to help us or just to pass the time in conversation.

I remember that on one occasion two of our classmates, David Troxler and John Passmore, decided to pull a practical joke on the rest of the lab section. They told us that Freddy wanted everyone to add a compound to speed up a reaction we had been putting together each afternoon for three days. Grif and I sensed a scam. We asked the professor what he thought about it. He replied, "Go tell them that this is a great idea, but don't any of the rest of you try it." Our buddies struck at the bait and lost three days of work.

During my senior year the college asked me to consider applying for a Watson (IBM) Scholarship for a year of study in Europe. Since my Dad was so ill at the time, I went to Dr. Fredericksen for advice. He asked me about my plans beyond medical school. I explained that I owed the Army two years through my ROTC obligation. He told me that accepting the Watson Scholarship would mean delaying my medical education, perhaps losing my momentum, and at best putting me three years behind civilian medical practice instead of two. In his judgment, delay was not a good strategy. I took his advice and have no regrets about having made that choice.

For me James Fredricksen typified the Davidson professor of that era: One who was dedicated to the development of both mind and character. I have locked much of what he taught me about chemistry in some garret room of my brain, and I have yet to find the key. Yet I'll always remember the man himself—a genial scholar who loved teaching and always had time for his students.

William Hight

My first semester at Davidson was going well until exam time, when I hit the proverbial wall. I had no clue how to study for three-hour exams in six subjects. I asked around for help, and someone recommended that I see Dr. Hight in the education department.

I liked Dr. Hight from the moment I met him. He reminded me both of a wise owl and of Trevor Howard, who played Captain Bligh in the film *Mutiny on the Bounty*. He asked me to take a seat in his office, and as we talked about my classes, he began to outline a study schedule for me. He said that success in Davidson's semester examinations depended on keeping up with and reviewing the subject material throughout the entire semester—cramming wouldn't work. I assured him I had done that. The challenge now was to figure out how I might maximize my use of the three-day reading period before the tests. Using examples, Dr. Hight began by telling me how *not* to study.

First was his story of a premed student who needed an A on his final exam in organic chemistry to beef up his chances of getting into medical school. The student had studied diligently and plowed his way through the course material, from dusk to dawn, night after night, on a steady intake of amphetamines. On the afternoon of the exam his mind was in overdrive. The professor collected the papers and later reported a tale of woe to the dean of students. What that poor student had accomplished in three hours was to write his entire exam on one side of a single sheet of paper, continuously writing over and over on the same page, creating a black wall of lead, and then signing the pledge that he had not cheated.

Next was a student who had to make an A on an English final in order to pull his grade point average up enough to graduate. That student pulled three all-nighters in a row. On exam day he was nowhere to be seen. He had slept through the exam.

Finally, there was a freshman who had not joined a fraternity. In fact the entire system had turned him down. It was probably for the best since he was a poor student. Despite his rejection he still had the gumption to go around the fraternity court asking for spots for a history exam, hoping to get all the questions down before the test. What he got from the prankish brothers of one frat were bogus tests filled with incorrect answers. He didn't return the following semester. The moral of that study was not to rely on spots.

Having made his points, Dr. Hight proceeded to help me block out a workable schedule that included liberal doses of study complemented by plenty of running and sleep. I took his lessons to heart and made A's on most of my finals that first semester. I used his study system all the way through medical school and my postgraduate medical education.

That spring of my freshman year I had a story of my own for Dr. Hight. I had just joined the Alpha Tau Omega (ATO) fraternity. The brothers gave the pledges special assignments. They assigned me to see that one certain brother graduated. This particular brother nicknamed "Fox", whose true name I never learned, was in jeopardy of flunking out at the end of his junior year. For three years he had spent most of his out-of-class time playing "Third Lucky Caller Has a Chance to Win" on one of the Charlotte radio stations. He never won. He only came into contention twice in those years and failed to answer the question on both occasions. The brothers told me if he failed his history exam, he would be out—too many F's on the transcript. Fox had a fundamental problem in addition to his wayward approach to studying. His biological clock was about three hours behind the rest of us. In a system that regularly held 8 a.m. classes, Fox didn't fare well. He had reached the maximum number of unexcused cuts and was hovering between a D and an F in his history course. The brothers stressed to me how important it was to see that Fox got to that final exam on time and in a lucid state. I assured them I would do my best.

I certainly did my best for my 8 a.m. final in calculus on the same morning of Fox's 8 a.m. exam. Midway through the test I realized I had forgotten something, but I couldn't quite put a finger on it. When I took a bathroom break, I ran into one of my fraternity brothers, who asked me about Fox's exam. I gulped and told him that Fox had slept well. To my horror I learned later that he had slept through the exam; in fact, we never saw him again. Surprisingly no one said anything about it to me. I guess the other brothers had already given up on him.

I saw Dr. Hight years later shortly before he died. I thanked him for helping me organize my time at Davidson and told him that I was still using his system. He seemed pleased. We talked about the screwups of students past, especially the exam oddballs, and we both got a good laugh out of that. I never had him for a course, but I carry his lessons with me to this day.

Tony Abbott

As the first semester of my freshman year at Davidson College geared up, we began to write papers and have "reviews" (Davidson's euphemism for a hard-ass test) in all of our courses. The first grade I received at Davidson was a C+ on a paper assignment in Dr. Tony Abbott's English class. I had grown up in Davidson and knew how hard college would be. I was ecstatic over that first grade. I had passed!

Dr. Abbott, who held a doctorate from Princeton, was one of the finest teachers I have ever known. I believe that one characteristic of a great teacher is the ability to unveil and develop latent talents that students never knew they possessed.

I held out little hope for creative writing and had already accepted what would certainly be a C or C+ in the course. Still, I resolved to do better. William Faulkner said that we always write best when we draw from our own experiences. That's what I did to write perhaps the best paper of my life.

I was certainly not one of those geniuses who could start and finish a paper the night before it was due and come up with an A. My plodding efforts generally took two to three weeks. For Dr. Abbott's class, I chose to write about the grave-robbing business that involved the old North Carolina Medical College in Davidson around the turn of the twentieth century. My father had told me tales about this all my life. I decided to put some of them into writing.

Gone With The Wind was one of my favorite novels. I learned that Margaret Mitchell had written much of her story on location. If she wanted to describe a Georgia red clay road, she would find one and write about it. I decided to take the same approach in my paper. As I explain in Chapter 5, during my years growing up in Davidson, the North Carolina Medical College no longer existed, but the original building was still there and it was divided into apartments for faculty families. I had spent a lot of time in that old building as a child. I returned to the place and described what I saw in detail for my paper. My wanderings also carried me up to the old black cemetery at the northern end of the campus, which had been the target of the grave-robbing expeditions that involved the medical students.

Dr. Abbott gave me an A and a lot of praise for the paper. In fact, he read it aloud in class. At the end of the academic year, that paper joined several others in a college publication called *Inklings*, which was a compilation of the best works from all the freshman English classes. I was tickled pink.

For the next paper Dr. Abbott asked us to develop a composition around a metaphor. I was a history buff and knew a lot about the D-Day invasion of June 6, 1944. Much of what happened that day revolved around the weather—one of the worst Channel storms of the century preceded the Normandy invasion. Using a fictitious Catholic priest who was a member of the French Underground as my primary character, I developed a metaphor of the Channel storm and the torrent of invasion that befell the Norman coast that day. When Dr. Abbott returned the papers, I found that he had written on mine, "I had to read this several times before I caught your meaning. A very sophisticated piece of writing." He gave me an A.

I was on a roll. The next creative paper dealt with any topic we wanted to choose. I created a short story around the Battle of Cowan's Ford in Mecklenburg County on February 1, 1781. My primary character was a partisan in the Mecklenburg militia who was captured by Cornwallis' troops during the battle. I traced the prisoner's travails through the Battle of Guilford Courthouse and his imprisonment on a British ship at Yorktown. Dr. Abbott liked it, and I continued my winning streak.

I was really enjoying writing. Then the bottom almost fell out. I tried to compare life in a small town (Davidson) to life in the city (Charlotte). I had no problem with small town life. The problem was that I had no knowledge of what growing up in a city was like. Dr. Abbott caught it immediately and "flagged" the work (Davidson jargon for an F).

I proceeded to drive more nails into my literary coffin. My first semester term paper was on Grand Field Marshal Michel Ney, whose story is described in Chapter 2. I spent weeks researching the topic. The library had a great deal of material on the man. Dr. Abbott told me that if the paper was worthy, he might consider asking the college to publish it. When Dr. Abbott returned the paper, he noted that I had made thirty-six spelling errors including the title page, which read "The

Duel Identity of Peter Stuart Ney." I couldn't even get the title right! Needless to say, the paper never reached a publisher. I never could spell well—which I hope is not too obvious here.

We did a lot of things in the class other than write creative pieces and term papers. Dr. Abbott introduced us to a world of short stories, poetry, essays, and books. I distinctly remember so much of what he taught us. I could not have had a finer teacher.

For the final term paper of the year, I chose to write, "The Life of Mark Twain Reflected in His Writings." This was a subject my brother had attacked in high school. I decided to go for it in considerable depth. I worked really hard on that one. Dr. Abbott gave me an A and the comment, "This is the finest term paper I have ever read." I'm certain that he has since seen hundreds of papers more worthy than mine, but I still cherish the compliment.

I wrote a short poem as an addendum to the paper. It was trite and could well have ruined the piece. Since it is one of the very few poems I have ever written and is highly unlikely to be published elsewhere, I will repeat it here.

The World Mark Twain Left Behind

One thousand miles he rambles
Before he turns that bend.
One thousand miles, one hundred years
Recall a time when
Lightening split the darkness, and
Volleys of thunder rolled.
A raft carried to midstream,
An American idyll gone,
A boy and slave in the night.

One thousand miles he rambles.
One thousand miles, one hundred years
Bring pleasure to my mind,
To see my friends Tom and Huck
And the world Mark Twain left behind.

Dr. Abbott taught me a great deal, and I am grateful for that. I hope that this book in no way reflects ill upon his teaching. I would want him to know that I have spent the past thirty years writing only medical papers, which can be unimaginably dull.

Charles Parker

Charles Parker taught physical education and was the wrestling coach at Davidson College. He, his wife, Blanche, and their children, Glenda, Janice, Charles ("Buzz"), and Bruce lived up on North Main Street until the mid-1950's when they moved to their new home on Dogwood Lane. Of the Parker children only Bruce was my contemporary, and we went all the way through grades 1-12 together.

As a small child I didn't know Bruce very well. We were in the same Sunday school classes and attended the same birthday parties and outings at the college, but these were just passing acquaintances. That all changed on the first day of my first grade year at Davidson Elementary. Miss Margaret Adams was our teacher. She had taught generations of first graders in Davidson. I don't think anything quite prepared her for us.

That morning when I walked into the class, a commotion was going on in the third row of desks. The whole class was jockeying for a seat near Bruce Parker. Sensing that I was missing something, I threw myself into the melee. After a round of pushing and shoving, I found myself two seats ahead of Bruce. To this day I have no idea what triggered the frenzy. Years later "Miss Margaret" told me our behavior that day had completely baffled her.

John and I became frequent after-school visitors at the Parker home on Main Street. The railroad tracks ran directly behind the house. We delighted in putting pennies on the tracks and retrieving the flattened remnants after a freight train passed. Bruce's older brother, Buzz, and Morris Griffin, who lived across the street, showed us how to play chicken with the train. Buzz almost bought the farm on one occasion. Our parents raised the roof when they got wind of this behavior, and that was the end of it.

When the Parkers moved into their new home, John and I practically moved right in with them. The whole neighborhood of kids showed up during my seventh and eighth grade years to hang out at the Parkers, reviving our passion for touch football, played in the nearby vacant lot almost every afternoon. Even without blocking, these games were rough, and the injuries were frequent, especially if Jim McEver showed up. After Bruce shattered a kneecap, the mothers prohibited us from playing football again. We simply moved our sport across the street and took up slam-dunk basketball on Vic Blackwell's short goal with equally injurious results.

The elder Parkers endowed their sons with a strong work ethic. Both boys had paper routes. Buzz and Bruce could be found at Cashion's Gulf every morning at 5:30 assembling their *Charlotte Observer* copies for bicycle delivery. They worked throughout the year regardless of the weather. I always admired them for that.

Bruce was an outstanding student at North Mecklenburg High School and was a star on the tennis team. After graduation he attended Southwestern University in Memphis, Tennessee. Bruce had a strong interest in chemistry and worked during the summer months at the Reeves Company in Cornelius, manufacturing foam rubber products. Bruce later parlayed that interest into a new method for making orthopedic splints and within a few short years built his company into the world's largest of its kind. Several years ago I saw an article in *The Charlotte Observer* on Bruce. He had sold his business for millions. He said it wasn't right to keep all that money, so he started a foundation in his parents' memory. That was vintage Bruce. No one deserved success more than he.

During my years as a Davidson student, physical education was mandatory for freshmen. The college espoused that a strong body should complement a strong mind. Before the start of classes, freshmen at Davidson had to take an athletic proficiency test, which included various exercises such as kicking footballs, throwing softballs, and running the 100-yard dash. I suppose they did this to separate the stronger physical forms from the less endowed to prevent loss of life and limb in the P.E. classes.

One member of our class was the classic ninety-eight pound weakling. He kicked the football over his head, fell flat on his face in the 100, and knocked himself out by throwing the softball into the back of his head—a feat that actually took a considerable amount of dexterity. John and I fared much better. I remember doing the hundred in 10.9 seconds in tennis shoes from a standup start. John ran a 10.5 hundred and threw the softball 259 feet, a heave that surprised the coaches.

Physical education was a non-credit course. You still had to have a semester of it to graduate. I cut P.E. classes as much as possible since I already had six academic courses and was running cross-country in the afternoon. John and I pleaded with Coach Parker and Terry Holland, the assistant basketball coach, for a reprieve for P.E., noting that we were already engaged in a competitive sport. Never one to let somebody off the hook without a quid pro quo, Coach Parker agreed to waive us on the condition that "I get to see those two boys wrestle each other." He thought that might be fun to watch.

Coach Parker was a Greco-Roman wrestling expert. The only wrestling I knew was *Live Championship Wrestling* hosted by "Big Bill" Ward on WBTV at Charlotte's Radio Center. This show was a predecessor of today's wild free-for-alls on Turner Broadcasting. Growing up, John and I had great fun watching it. In the sixth grade we staged wrestling bouts in our bedroom almost nightly. I would be the Great Bolo or Billy Two Rivers and John played Danny "the Claw" McShay or Bobby Weaver. Bolo wore a hideous, tight facemask and allegedly had a steel plate underneath, which covered his forehead and allowed him to knock his victims senseless with head butts. Billy Two Rivers was known for his Mohawk hairdo and his Popeye spinach routine. Invariably Billy would be taking a vicious pounding, and when he was all but out for the count, he would miraculously rise from the mat, go into a ferocious war dance, and clobber his now terrified opponent with his infamous "Tomahawk Chop." Danny McShay had a dreaded claw hold, which John never got down pat—it just tickled like hell. Weaver had the sleeper hold, but we never could get it to work. Somewhere in there was an atomic drop where the heavy wrestler picked up his hapless opponent and dropped him backwards onto his knee. Ouch! This was the primordial pile driver, which nearly did in comedian Andy Kaufman years later.

One of us would assume the Big Bill Ward role and introduce the wrestlers. Next, we pulled our beds together to create a mat and began doing all those fancy moves we had seen on TV. Occasionally a bout would get out of hand and lead to a fist fight. When the dining room ceiling plaster started coming down in chunks, Mom called the whole thing off. Good thing. In time we would probably have killed each other.

Coach Parker billed the P.E. wrestling event as *Puckett versus Puckett.* It was *Live Championship Wrestling* all over again. At the signal John and I leaped all over each other, clawing up the mat and writhing to a draw, much to Coach Parker's amusement. Laughing, he remarked sarcastically, "I like your technique." The following day the physical education department at Davidson College released John and me from the program. The official reason that entered our transcripts was a comment that read something like, "Excused with passing grade because of participation in intercollegiate athletics." We received course credit and could not have been more pleased.

Coach Parker was highly successful at Davidson, both on and off the mat. Gruff and genial at the same time, he was a popular figure among students and town folk alike. In 1959-60 he served as a member of the U.S. Olympic Wrestling Committee. Judging from Bruce's exuberant announcement of the event, a high point of Coach Parker's career was his selection in 1963 to be the American team's wrestling coach at the Pan American Games, which were held in Brazil that year. His four-decade stint as the Davidson wrestling coach made him a legend on the campus—the wrestling room in the Baker sports complex is named in his honor.

David Grier Martin, Sr.

Dr. Grier Martin was the college treasurer after Cash Jackson retired from that post. When President John Cunningham retired in 1958, the trustees of the college chose Dr. Martin to succeed him as president.

Dr. Martin was one of the most soft-spoken and self-effacing men I have ever met. I cannot imagine that anything ever upset him. He was highly popular among town and gown. Dad was delighted that the college picked him as the new president.

Dr. Martin and his wife, Louise, had three children—Mike, David Grier ("D.G."), and Mimy. Mimy and my sister were best friends, and

I think Ginger divided her time equally between the President's Mansion and our house. I remember how Mom was green with envy when the Charlotte Country Club invited Mimy to make her debut. Davidson had no country club and no debutantes. Most people thought it was rank social snobbery and much ado about nothing. I can understand why Mimy participated—her father was president of the college, and many members of the Charlotte club had attended Davidson. This didn't seem to bother Ginger at all, and she even turned down an invitation to participate in the state debutante ball.

Kristi Scott decided that we should stage our own debutante ball, so a bunch of us marched over to her house and presented Kristi to society. For her part, Ginger had a big wedding bash, which more than made up for missing the Charlotte debutante scene. None of the girls in my peer group made a formal debut—thank goodness!

In 1967, John and I were invited to be "stags" at one of the Charlotte Country Club debutante parties. Stags are unattached males who show up at these affairs to give the debs someone else to dance with besides their fathers and escorts. Mom cajoled us into playing this silly role. I suppose it was her way of presenting her twins to society. We did it for home and hearth—we rented tux from John Mack & Son in Mooresville and headed down to Charlotte. We talked about picking up the Neil girls in Huntersville en route and making it a foursome, but we decided they probably wouldn't go on such short notice, and they might be regarded as interlopers if they did. At any rate, after thirty minutes of that awful party, we left to spend the better part of the evening at Shoney's on the Plaza, our old high school gathering spot. Mom never knew.

Young D.G. Martin was considerably older than the Puckett twins, but he always was friendly to us and even on occasion joined us in playing touch football. I will always be grateful to him for that largess of selling me his window-washing business (described in chapter 8).

D.G. was a star basketball player and scholar at Davidson. He worked so hard at basketball that Lefty Driesell established an athletic award in his honor called the D.G. Martin Hustle Award. As I mentioned earlier, D.G. became a distinguished attorney with a reputation for integrity. He worked for the University of North Carolina for a number of years, and he even made two runs for Congress, albeit losing both times. Today he is a columnist, frequent guest on North Carolina public television, and head of the North Carolina Land Trust.

D.G.'s father was president of Davidson College from 1958 to 1968. John Cunningham's successor, was a thoroughly capable administrator who presided over a period of substantial growth in the college's physical plant, including the creation of such landmark structures as the Cunningham Fine Arts Center, the Dana Science Building, E.H. Little Dormitory, Richardson Dormitory and the Patterson Fraternity Court. He also presided over the racial integration of the campus. And he shepherded such curricula innovations as the humanities and junior-year abroad programs. Also of particular note, he presided over the abolition of the college's greatly loathed custom of students' compulsory church and chapel attendance.

I remember Dr. Martin most as a people-centered college president who always listened intently to whatever you had to say. He loved to play Frisbee and could often be spotted out on the campus tossing a "Pluto Platter" with students and children. We loved him for it. It's hard to imagine any college or university president doing that on a regular basis today.

The 1960's saw more social change than perhaps any other decade in the last century. Dr. Martin's presidency stood at the boundary of a genteel conservatism and a new liberalism that was pervading college and university campuses across the land. The coming of Dr. Sam Spencer in the fall of 1968 marked a new era in the life of the college.

Samuel R. Spencer

I was in my junior year when Sam Spencer came to Davidson in the fall of 1968. Actually he was returning to the campus since he had served at Davidson as professor of history and dean of students before becoming president of Mary Baldwin College in Staunton, Virginia, in 1957. His children Reid and Ellen were among our childhood friends.

My mother had attended Mary Baldwin in the mid-1930's, and Ginger chose to follow in her footsteps, enrolling as a freshman in early September of 1963. Dr. and Mrs. Spencer invited our family to stay with them over Freshman Parents Weekend that year. I remember that it was shortly before John Kennedy's assassination—a very cold and snowy few days of my tenth-grade year. We again visited Mary Baldwin in 1967 for my sister's graduation exercises. This time we stayed in a motel in Waynesboro, Virginia, about twelve miles from Staunton. John and I spent most of the weekend with Peter Hobbie, a Davidson student and son of the minister of the same Presbyterian church that Woodrow Wilson's father had pastored one hundred years previously. Peter always spoke of Wilson as "Woody."

Dr. Spencer presided over the commencement exercises on a lovely late spring afternoon in 1967. None of us could have known that a year and several months later he would return to Davidson as the college's fifteenth president. Nor could we have guessed that Dr. Spencer would award all three Puckett children their college diplomas.

Davidson College held a big convocation for Sam Spencer's inauguration. It was the first event of that nature that I had attended—and the only one in which I would ever participate. Despite the requisite, perfunctory, and boring speakers, Davidson had a new president and a new direction.

There were a crowd of alumni and distinguished guests on campus that week. The college decorated the campus with historical markers for the occasion. For example, a sign erected in front of the Dana Science Building reminded everyone that the national physics collegiate honor society had its roots at Davidson College. A sign across Concord Road told about the old North Carolina Medical College and the first radiographs made in the United States.

Someone decided to liven up the reception. On the morning of the inaugural convocation a student rearranged all of the signs on campus. In addition, a new sign appeared on the front lawn of Chambers. It bore an arrow pointing skyward. These words appeared on the sign: "Blue Sky, Given by the God Foundation." This requires a brief explanation.

Shortly after the inauguration, the Board of Trustees approved an overhaul of the curriculum at Davidson. (The planning for this work had begun at the end of Grier Martin's presidency.) The college had adhered to a rigid semester system since its inception. Now the faculty and trustees wanted to try out a trimester schedule with three courses maximum each trimester. It was an interesting concept, but I questioned whether it would work. Dad thought it was worth a try; a lot of other faculty members felt the same way. The faculty organized the Blue Sky Committee to address the whole issue. We dubbed it the "Blue Fly Committee." During my junior year the trimester system went into effect. An enormous burden was lifted from my academic being: the system was easier. Classes were held only four days per week (Wednesday was the day off) and the hated Saturday classes were jettisoned. An A was now 90-100 percent, whereas under the old system it was 95-100 percent. From my perspective, Davidson appeared to be lowering its academic standards. The trimester concept was an experiment—one that in time outlived its usefulness and went by the boards.

Dr. Spencer led Davidson in a liberal direction. Perhaps his most notable achievement was to lead the college to introduce coeducation. I believe that the college's very survival depended on its coeducational status; to remain competitive Davidson had to open its doors to women. It was a national trend that wasn't going away, the protests of some chauvinist alumni notwithstanding.

At first there were only a few female students who attended on a trial basis in 1970-71. Then the idea caught on rapidly and succeeded beyond everyone's expectations. In the end it made the campus a much richer, more interesting, and far more diversified place. Most, but not all, of us who attended Davidson in its all-male years cheered the move. Davidson would no longer be a suitcase college with the boys heading out of town on weekends.

Dr. Spencer's administration, 1968-1983, introduced a number of other positive changes in step with the changing times, including the active recruitment of minority students, the conversion of fraternities into self-selected eating clubs, and the requirement that faculty become active researchers. And the town and college became wet—very wet.

Max Polley

Max Polley taught second semester Religion 101(*New Testament*) during my freshman year. The seminar met on a Tuesday-Thursday-Saturday schedule on the first floor of old Phi Hall. The religion department had selected as the standard textbook *Interpreting the New Testament*, written by Duke University professor James Price. It became apparent early on that whatever we learned in the course would come from Dr. Polley since the text was poorly written and virtually unfathomable. We renamed the course, "Interpreting *Interpreting the New Testament*." (Mercifully there were other more readable books on specific topics such as the apostles Paul and John.)

Dr. Polley taught well. There were only ten of us in the class that spring, so it made for intimate discussions. Dr. Polley generally rotated ends of the table from which he rendered instruction and led discussions. He knew we weren't pleased with the Price text so, he filled in the gaping holes with information I still carry with me to church each Sunday. He emphasized the role of the *Bible* as the foundation block of Western Civilization. In terms of my own development, I'm very glad Davidson made critical biblical study (incorporating history, archeology, and scholarly criticism) a required part of the curriculum.

Dr. Polley had a reputation for toughness. He expected high performance and punctuated his lessons with frequent pop quizzes. Everybody called him "Max the Axe." One unfortunate Saturday morning he lent literal meaning to his nickname. We had all arrived on time and were waiting in our seats, hoping he would be more than ten minutes late so that we could leave and salvage what remained of our weekend—in those years if a professor arrived at his classroom more than ten minutes late, the students got a free cut on the house.

Max the Axe wasn't late on this particular Saturday. He came in at the nine-minute mark, dressed casually, and carrying an axe, which he put down on the table right under my proboscis. It startled me, to say the least. I cautiously whispered to him, "Dr. Polley, are you going to live up to your nickname this morning?" Dr. Polley looked sternly at me and asked, "And what nickname might that be?" I replied, "Dr, Polley, you know, 'The Axe, Max the Axe'." I wanted out of there fast. The last train to Durango would have been just fine. Amused or miffed, I never knew which, he explained that he was going on a Scouting campout, and that's why he had brought the axe.

Twenty-three years later I was practicing in Concord when Dr. Polley came over from Davidson each Sunday for eight weeks to teach my Sunday school class a course on the *Book of Amos*. I spoke with him after the first session. He remarked, "You know, until that day in class when you mentioned my nickname, I didn't even know that the name existed." It was déjà vu. I felt the same discomfort I had felt in 1967. I replied, "You were no Axe. You gave me an A."

William Gatewood Workman

Dr. Workman was the head of the psychology department during my Davidson years. He, his wife, Mildred, and children, Bill and Eleanor ("Wookie"), lived across the street from us at the corner of Lorimer Road and College Drive. The Workmans had already completed their home in what had been Johnsie Shelton's horse pasture before we moved in across the street in October of 1956. That first night in our new home Mrs. Workman invited my family over for dinner.

We had finished moving everything into the house by mid-afternoon. John and I went about exploring our new environs. In the backyard we came across a bucket of unused tar from the waterproofing process in the basement. We decided to build a tar baby. This was a big mistake. We hadn't learned anything from Joel Chandler Harris and Uncle Remus. We were soon inseparable from the monster and thoroughly covered in the gooey substance. At that point Mom called us in to get bathed before going over to the Workman house for dinner.

We came in silently and crept up the stairs. In so doing, we left behind a trail of tar. Mom was beside herself. We had to throw out our clothes. The entire family would spend the next several days extricating the house from the clutches of that tar, some of which probably remains to this day. Anyway, the dinner was great.

Young Bill Workman was considerably older than John and I. Bill was in the seventh or eighth grade when we were in the first grade. Every year the PTA held an annual talent show for the northern end of the county. Every year Bill, who had a wonderful baritone voice, would sing "Old Man River" and "Go Down Moses" and obliterate the competition. It reached the point where people threatened not to participate.

I mean that boy could sing! John and I would sit outside the window of his bedroom on summer nights and listen to him singing in the shower. We knew he was going places. Bill, like many faculty sons, attended Davidson. He later studied at the Curtis Institute in Philadelphia and became a distinguished professional opera singer. He and his wife lived in Hamburg, Germany, where he performed regularly with the Hamburg State Opera, one of the finest opera companies in the world.

I saw Bill just before my departure for military duty in Germany. He spoke fluent German without an American accent. He was familiar with the area where I would be stationed, and he gave me some sound advice about those strange German ways. Unfortunately, for one reason or another, I didn't catch up with him at all during the Army years.

When I think of Mrs. Workman, food always comes to mind. I occasionally showed up on her doorstep to see what was cooking, and she always had something good to offer me. I remember distinctly how well she fed me on the day of my sister's wedding.

John and I were working in Montreat that summer—John as a general maintenance man, dishwasher, and waiter at the William Black Home and I as a bellhop at the Assembly Inn. We had planned on coming home the day before the wedding and returning the following day. That's about all of the festivities we wanted to partake, but Mom had other ideas. She asked that we spend the entire week at home, and she insisted that we buy new dress suits. We protested that this was a waste of time and money for a single occasion, and it might jeopardize our jobs. Mom countered that we had only one sister, and this would (hopefully) be her only wedding. We grudgingly decided to placate her. Fortunately our employers allowed us to take the time off.

Ginger was engaged to William B. Grizzard, Jr., from Roanoke Rapids. He was a recent Citadel graduate and a Vietnam veteran— and one of the finest people I have known. He and his father owned several NAPA auto parts stores in eastern North Carolina and south-eastern Virginia.

This brings me back to Mildred Workman. She hosted the prenuptial dinner on her front and side yards. I thoroughly stuffed myself on her great food. I can't explain it, but my most enduring memories of that day are not of the actual wedding but of that late afternoon meal, notwithstanding Bill Bondurant's postnuptial bash and my shenanigans with Linda Hopkins in the back seat of Shaw Smith's car, which led Shaw to remark, "You're such a tiger, Puckett."

We survived the wedding and went on about our business. In time the senior Workmans retired to The Pines, where I frequently saw them on my visits with Aunt Louise. Like Louise, Dr. Workman died there among his friends.

When my son, Jim, was roaming the countryside looking at colleges, we visited Davidson. The woman directing tours of the campus looked vaguely familiar. It was Wookie Workman. We talked about the good old days.

Scotty and Peter Nicholls

We called them "Aunt Scotty" and "Uncle Pete." Scotty was the director of the dormitories at Davidson, or the "Dorm Marm." Peter ran the college student store. They had four children—Gail, Jane, Sandy, and Hope. They lived on North Main Street not far from the college cemetery, and during the summer months of our high school years, John and I practically moved in with them.

Davidson was as dead as Marley's ghost during those summers. Desperate for something to do, John, Gail, Jane and I came up with the idea of "parading." This usually meant hanging out with the Nicholls' girls, sitting on the porch of their house on North Main Street telling jokes, playing parlor games like Michigan Rummy, and raiding Uncle Pete's refrigerator (we drank a lot of milk with instant eggnog, I recall). I can still hear the Byrds' "Mr. Tambourine Man" playing on their stereo. The nightly parades kept us busy, happy, and out of trouble.

Several of the college students became regulars at the Nicholls' house during those summers. Our favorite was Tom Youngdale. A vigorous, tall, and gangling fellow, close to seven feet in height, he was a substitute center on Lefty's basketball team. Tom wasn't Magic Johnson, and we used to ask him if he even knew that a basketball bounced.

The three older Nicholls children and we Puckett twins all attended North Mecklenburg together. Gail was in our class at North, and I remember that John took her to our senior prom. She was very bright, with a wicked sense of humor. Sandy was very athletic and a fine basketball player. Jane? Well Jane was Jane. She was pretty, bright, had a very dry wit, and was fiercely independent.

In the summer before my freshman year, Uncle Pete asked me to be the poster child for the football and basketball programs for the 1966-67 seasons. I agreed. Somewhere in the college archives is a picture on the back cover of a football or basketball program of a skinny Davidson freshman, red beanie and all, weighted down by about twenty books. I thought I looked silly and had to endure it for the year. I never saved a copy.

Gail attended N.C. State, and Sandy went to UNC-Chapel Hill. Jane married Alan White, son of physics professor Locke White. Alan is a professor at Williams College, where I spent the summer of 1958. Gail died in 1982 from cancer. Sandy still lives in the family home on Main Street. Both he and Hope work in Charlotte. Uncle Pete died in 1999. Scotty did TV commercials for a while. I last saw her at my thirtieth college reunion. She hasn't changed a bit over the years. Some people seem to have eternal youth.

James Purcell

Dr. Purcell taught in the English department at the college. Students affectionately called him "Gentleman Jim" because of his quiet demeanor and subtle humor. In the 1960's Davidson required two core courses in English for graduation. I enrolled in Dr. Purcell's American literature class in the autumn of 1967. It would be one of the most enjoyable courses I had in college.

The course dealt predominantly with nineteenth century American literature. The workload was voluminous—covering in the end approximately three thousand pages. Dr. Purcell's reviews and exams were very difficult to spot. He delighted in giving identification tests.

He would extract some small detail such as a chimney or a shoe from a work and expect us to give the name of the book or short story and its author. Nothing like "a great white whale" ever found its way onto the pages of a Purcellian examination.

Jim and Betty Purcell and their two children lived just up the street from us on the corner of Hillside and Lorimer. We got to know them well because for over eight years we shared a telephone party line.

It is hard to imagine there was a time before cell phones, inexpensive long distance, and a host of competing companies such as ATT, MCI, and Sprint, to name but a few. We grew up in the years of the Ma Bell monopoly. We had to use their lines, rent their phones, and pay their outrageous rates. Long distance calls within North Carolina were approximately $5 for a three-minute call. Out of state and out of country calls were simply out of reach.

One of the idiosyncrasies of the system was the party line arrangement. To cut the cost of phone service, families were allowed to share the cost of the line with other families. Incoming calls were no problem—they reached the appropriate house without disturbing the other party. There were some problems with outgoing calls, however—you had to get a free line.

I exploited the system. Throughout the winter and spring months of 1964, I spent seemingly endless hours on the phone with Julie Eatman and her pals from North High. Because they lived in the Derita community of north Charlotte, physical contact outside of school was limited to occasional weekends only. I resorted to the phone, much to my mother's and Betty Purcell's chagrin.

I had a two-way brain. Phone time found me carrying on a conversation almost every night with a book in hand. Mrs. Purcell was very gracious about all of this and never complained to Mom, although Mom knew perfectly well what was happening. Usually after Mrs. Purcell made two attempts to break in on the line, I relented only to resume my conversations once she was off the phone.

Mrs. Purcell didn't end my little monopoly. Mom and Shaw Smith, Sr., did that for her. One Saturday night in the summer of 1964, Mr. Smith asked me to work the desk at the college union from 7 to 11 p.m. The union phone was the only line into the college administration on weekends. A number of calls came in between 7 and 8. Then things quieted down, and I decided to take a break and call Julie Eatman. The break lasted three hours. The following week the college received several complaints, and Mr. Smith relayed them to Mom, who squelched my frequent phoner days.

William McGavock

Dr. Bill McGavock taught mathematics at Davidson and was one of the most beloved professors in the history of the college. He and his wife, Sarah, had two children, David and Martha. They lived just off Grey Road, across from Frontis and Lucy Johnston and their family.

My earliest memory of the McGavocks dates to 1952. My twin brother and I were both born with a congenital eye problem called alternating strabismus. Neither of us had binocular vision. John was using only one eye, and our ophthalmologist in Charlotte was concerned he would lose his sight in the other. He scheduled corrective eye surgery for John that summer. Mom and Dad went with him to Charlotte and left Ginger and me overnight with the McGavocks.

I was a miscreant. After running all over their house and raiding the refrigerator, I found myself across the drive in Frontis Johnston's living room. The Johnstons didn't know I was staying with the McGavocks and drove me back to our house on Main Street. I didn't say anything. When the Johnstons found that no one was at home, they called the McGavocks and straightened things out. No one was pleased.

My fondest memories of the McGavocks involve a trip to the beach in 1968. Dad (along with the rest of us) was recovering from Ginger's wedding. I had finished working in Montreat for the summer. Dad and several faculty members decided to arrange a fishing trip to the Carolina coast. It was early September, so there were cottages available on short notice. We made the trip a father-son outing. The party included Bill and David McGavock, John and Tom Hopkins, A.H. and Heath Whittle, Jr., and Dad and I. We rented a cottage in North Myrtle Beach and planned to fish for a few days.

It was my first beach excursion since the outing with my Sunday school class in 1964. There was just enough room in the house for all of us to find a bed. We brought plenty of groceries along, and Dad did most of the cooking—for which he was locally famous. The Lions Club members called Dad, "Hot Cakes Willie" (his full name was William Olin Puckett). Every morning he served us hot cakes, eggs, bacon, and sausage—not so healthy by today's standards.

Dad and the other fathers planned fishing excursions out of the Merrell's Inlet area. I thought we were going deep-sea fishing. Dad explained to me that we weren't and told me about a fishing trip gone awry years before—one he had never mentioned to me before.

One summer in the early 1950's, Dad and several faculty buddies drove down to the beach and hired a boat for the day to do some fishing about ten miles out at sea. Sometime in the middle of the afternoon, as they were preparing to return to shore, the boat's motor died. When they tried to radio for help, the radio didn't work. After they turned up missing, the Coast Guard finally tracked them down—all of which was unsettling to Dad, who couldn't swim.

For two days we fished the inner coastal waterways around Merrell's Inlet. Each night Dad and Dr. McGavock cooked up a special fish stew. This concoction included the day's catch and shellfish cooked together. It remains the best seafood I've ever eaten. Sadly, their recipe is lost to posterity.

Dave McGavock was a licensed professional pilot. Heath Whittle, Jr., and Dave wanted to spear some eel. They planned to fly in Dave's plane to scout out the area for an ideal spot. Having found a promising area, they set out late that night by car and on foot. The next morning they returned empty-handed and a little shaken. There were police at the door. They were almost arrested for trespassing. Fortunately no eel turned up in the fish stew.

Dr. McGavock and Dad both had strokes at roughly the same time in 1970. They were both disabled and spent time together at the Charlotte Rehabilitation Center. Our families were mutually supportive, and the ordeal brought us closer together.

Martha McGavock settled in Brevard with her husband who is a police officer. My last contact with her was in the early 1990's.

Martha had suffered a heart attack and was in the hospital in Asheville. I visited her and Sarah at that time.

Dad and Dr. McGavock both appear on the college's sesquicentennial poster. Dr. McGavock loved to play chess and is shown doing just that. Dad and Dr. McGavock were campus legends, and I'm pleased that the college chose to depict them side-by-side in that picture.

Frontis Johnston

Dr. Johnston taught in the history department and was the dean of faculty. He and his wife, Lucy, had three children—Tish, Currie, and Martha. Currie was in my sister's class, and Martha was one year behind us in school.

We sometimes called Currie "Arch" because his full name was Archibald Currie Johnston. Even though he was a few years older, we enjoyed playing basketball with him. He was an excellent player. He also masterminded getting us into Johnson Gymnasium, which was off limits to faculty children outside of regular college events. Currie always found a way to get us in. During the school year we could usually mingle in with the students on the gym floor, but after an hour or so of play, Mr. Howard or one of the other gym personnel inevitably smelled the rat and ran us out.

On holidays and in the summer, getting in was more problematic. Whenever he was with us, Currie had us on the hardwood within a few minutes. Usually there was an open window or one that could be forced. Currie would work his way through the window and open the doors. To thwart intruders, the gym personnel locked the basketball court doors and pushed the bleachers to the walls. This was no problem since we simply went up into the balcony at the southern end of the gym and climbed over the railing onto the top of the bleachers and slid down to the floor.

Currie went on to basketball stardom at North Mecklenburg. In his senior year *The Charlotte Observer* named him to the All-County team. After graduating from North, he attended Southwestern in Memphis, where he was a Rhodes finalist. After a stint as an Air Force pilot, he became a Ph.D. seismologist. After Currie left town, David

Lloyd and C.W. Stacks took over his role of getting us into Johnson Gym.

Currie's sister Martha was a year behind me. We were casual acquaintances over the years. We became closer friends during two summers of water balloon fights. At the end of our tenth grade year, John and I met with Martha and plotted the first annual Davidson water balloon fight. We invited all of the kids in our church group, filled hundreds of balloons with water, and placed them into cardboard boxes in the middle of the Johnston's side yard. We then divided into two sides. At the agreed upon signal we all rushed the boxes, and what followed closely resembled a riot hose down. The following summer we did it again, this time with several thousand balloons. Somebody put ink and food coloring in some of the balloons, and a few people showed up with eggs. We ended up stomping through Mrs. Johnston's rose garden. She was distraught and not a little outraged. She banned the sport forever from her premises.

Frontis and Lucy Johnston are gone now. Tish married Lawrence Kimbrough, the oldest son of math professor Dr. John Kimbrough, and they live in Davidson. A few years ago, I read an article on minor earthquake fault lines written by Currie in *Scientific American*. Tish recently told me that Martha is an attorney in Philadelphia. I last saw all of them together at the time of Dr. Johnston's death.

On the night Davidson College dedicated the Baker Sports Complex, I fantasized about rounding up the old gang and breaking into the new gym for some hoops—to give the place its proper townie dedication. It nearly took a passport to get into the game, and the place was all but under armed guard. Currie could have found a way in, but I don't suppose the powers that be would have been as lenient with us as they were in the 1960's.

Thomas Logan

Tom and Dell Logan and their daughter, Susan Van Lear, lived up the hill from us on Woodland Drive. Dr. Logan taught chemistry at the college. Ginger and Van Lear were and remain the best of friends.

My earliest memories of the Logan family are from Pawley's Island. They rented a cottage during our summers there. Van Lear frequently visited at our cottage, which was on the northern end of the island.

Every time I think of Van Lear, watermelons come to mind. I somehow came up with the notion that watermelon seeds planted at just the right depth in the sand would actually germinate and give rise to the sweet fruit. Van Lear tried to convince me otherwise. I told her that I could disprove her, and I went ahead and planted some seeds that were left over from a watermelon feast we had just finished. I watered the area every day and watched carefully for weeds and the precious fruit, both of which, to my dismay, never appeared.

Van Lear was a frequent visitor at our home in Davidson, and Ginger was up at the Logan's house almost as much. Occasionally I would drift into their living room for one reason or another, but that's about all I ever knew of the interior of the house. Theirs was one of the few faculty kitchens I didn't raid.

During my high school years Van Lear held socials in her living room and occasionally invited John and me. It gave me a sense of being grown up. She was very bright and sophisticated, and we felt very special around her. I had my first taste of alcohol in the Logan's living room. Van Lear invited some of the faculty children in the neighborhood to one of her socials and offered us all some brandy. I had only a few sips, and that was it for me.

Mrs. Logan's brother was a judge in Charlotte. Her nephew Howard Arbuckle (he of the Montreat-Mt. Mitchell saga) attended Davidson and played on the college basketball team. Howard was a favorite among the children in town. We always tagged along with him after football games. He courted his hometown sweetheart, Sarah Porter, who was an absolute dish. My mother used to say of Howard, who had a capped tooth, "The boy is so ugly, he's good looking." We didn't care about Howard's looks; we just wanted an eyeful of Sarah.

Howard married Sarah, but that didn't work out. He later married Margaret Bourdeaux, who lived next door to the Logan house and was one of the nicest girls to ever grace the town of Davidson.

After he graduated from Davidson, Howard went to work for Northwestern Mutual Life Insurance Company. He and Bob Stone sold me my first life insurance policy in 1970. The last time I saw Howard was shortly after my son was born in 1981. He cajoled me into establishing Jimmy's insurability with a small policy—a good idea. John stays in touch with Howard—he, too, carries a policy with him.

Van Lear Logan was two years ahead of me at North Mecklenburg. She was brilliant and an avid reader. Ginger told me that Van Lear had read *Gone with the Wind* in the third grade. I remember that she read Leon Uris' book *Exodus* some eight times ("I couldn't put it down") and even got a kiss from Uris when he lectured at the college in 1962. Van Lear was a senior and I was a sophomore in Miss Rigney's world history class, 1963-64. We were there together when we learned about President Kennedy's assassination.

Van Lear came to Miss Rigney's class well read. She added greatly to my enjoyment of the course. She and Miss Rigney kept up a running conversation throughout each day's lesson. I suppose that Van Lear was miffed that I made the highest grade in the class on the final exam that year. She never knew that I had unwittingly read the questions and answers before the test.

Clyde Wilson Stacks, Sr.

One of the perks granted students who attended Davidson College was the superb laundry service—for which I am certain their parents paid dearly. The laundry building was behind Belk Dormitory and was always a beehive of activity.

Clyde Stacks, Sr., directed the laundry operations for the college. Mrs. Stacks was a seamstress. They had a son my age named Clyde Wilson Stacks, Jr., who was known to everybody as "C.W." The Stacks lived in a small wood frame house in a cul-de-sac directly behind the laundry.

John and I were buddies with C.W. from cradle to grade twelve. We were at his house a lot because he shared our interest in baseball and baseball cards. I remember first collecting a few cards in 1954 and cutting all kind of deals with C.W., hoping to rip off his best cards. This was four years before we began to collect in earnest, and sadly all of those early Topps cards are now carbon somewhere.

Mr. Stacks was a big jovial fellow who always sported a huge cigar that reminded us of the tall smokestack hovering over the laundry. We sometimes called Mr. Stacks, "Mr. Smokestacks." The children at DCPC remember him as Santa Claus at Christmas—a story that appears in the next chapter.

We participated in all manner of sporting events with C.W., Jr. As I noted in an earlier chapter, we worked the college baseball games. C.W. became a talented tennis and basketball player. I hated playing basketball with him because he was such a tenacious player. I always came out black and blue.

My fondest memory of C.W. involves his college interview at Southwestern University in Memphis. He, like so many of my college children contemporaries, attended that institution, which is now Rhodes University. I remember the night C.W. asked to borrow my Sunday suit for his interview.

It was a rainy Saturday night in the autumn of 1965. We attended a North Mecklenburg High football game at Memorial Stadium in Charlotte. C.W. drove us to the game in his 1950 Plymouth. On the way back his old clunker started smoking badly—some problem with the exhaust. Having had a working muffler might have helped. We pulled to a stop in the rain to let things settle down, but it was obvious that C.W.'s car was in no condition to drive him to Memphis, some 700 miles west of Davidson, the following day.

C.W. came to that awful realization when he dropped John and me off. He said he would have to leave that night and bum rides. He asked if he could borrow my Sunday suit for the interview. I agreed and gave it to him, and he thumbed all the way to Memphis in the pouring rain wearing that suit. It wasn't anything fancy—a Botany brand Mom had purchased for me in Mooresville. A few days later he returned the suit, all neatly cleaned and pressed. C.W. had both grit and panache.

Mr. Stacks died prematurely. I last saw C.W. the night we graduated together from North Mecklenburg in 1966. He was one of my best childhood friends. I have tried to locate him since but have not been successful. How did I let people like him slip by me?

Tom Scott

Dr. Scott came to Davidson as the athletic director in the mid-1950's. He was the head basketball coach at UNC-Chapel Hill before Frank McGuire and his Tar Heels won the NCAA title in 1957 and changed the face of college basketball forever. Dr. Scott, his wife, Bess, and their children, Tom and Kristen Jo, lived on Woodland Drive. Dr. Scott laid the foundation for excellence in athletics at Davidson and brought the basketball and football programs to national prominence in the 1960's. He would serve as athletic director until his retirement in 1974.

Dr. Scott coached basketball until he brought in Lefty Driesell, who gave Davidson a ten-year carpet ride in the rarefied air of big league college hoops. Golf teams that he coached at Davidson won five Southern Conference championships. Dr. Scott presided over a fine staff that built strong minor sports and intramural athletic programs. He also made it clear, however, that academics was the college's top priority.

The Scotts' daughter, Kristi, was more our contemporary than young Tom, Jr. I remember the day I first met her—it was in the elementary school cafeteria. I was in the second grade and she was in the third grade. The lower grades always went to lunch first. I remember that I was finishing my lunch when I noticed her sitting across from me. I introduced myself and asked her where she lived. Almost immediately, Jim McEver came up behind her and planted a kiss on her cheek.

In those years lunch cost twenty cents, and milk, dispensed in eight ounce bottles, was an additional three cents. The meals usually consisted of a meat selection ("mystery meat"), two veggies, bread, milk, and usually a pudding of some sort. There usually wasn't enough to fill me up. On that particular day I wandered back over to the cafeteria line, which was empty, hoping to no avail to get a second helping. At the milk dispenser I ran into Jim McEver. He was gloating over his romantic conquest and dared me to kiss Kristi. I took him up on it and walked over to the table where she was still sitting. I sneaked up behind her and planted one on her head. Kristi turned around and smacked me with a piece of cornbread. It did not qualify as a first kiss.

In the summers the college gave the children in the community the opportunity to swim in the college pool. Everyone had to learn to swim to continue in the program. Marianne Couch, a student's wife, taught John and me to swim in the first grade.

As we approached puberty, one of our favorite pranks was to try to get a peek into the girls' dressing room. The boys rushed to get showered and dressed first, after which we would saunter down the hall to try to catch a glimpse of some skin. The idea was to stand in the front of the women's dressing room door until someone opened it to leave, thus exposing the other girls to view. I remember one day as I was walking down the hall, Kristi, for some reason, darted out in only her underwear. She ran smack into me and started screaming and scurried back into the dressing room. It startled me more than it did Kristi. Thereafter, the girls made certain that no one was in the line of view whenever the door opened, and the boys stopped pestering them. At least my voyeur days had ended with an eyeful.

I recall a party hosted by Pattie Newell and Evelyn Tyson at the college union just after Christmas 1960. Mom drove us to pick up Kristi and take her with us to the party. Mom always insisted that Kristi was my first date that night. She was wrong. That dubious honor went to Georgeanna Mayhew the following year. At all events, it was a big party, held in the union ballroom. Worried that pubescent passion might erupt in the dark corners and recesses of the large hall, the parents hired Cop Linker, the campus policeman, to keep an eye on things. I remember a stern-faced Cop spending the evening sitting with his arms folded by the door. (Martha Newell avows that Cop uncharacteristically kept a shotgun on his lap through the evening.)

Kristi hung out with Pattie Newell, Becky Caldwell, and Jane Withers, among others. She was at that backyard cookout when we played spin-the-bottle and Pattie kissed me. As I was recovering from that exhilarating moment, the bottle landed on Kristi and then spun on me. I couldn't believe my good luck. But when I stood up to receive my lottery prize from the cutest girl in town, she flatly refused to deliver the goods.

In the summer of 1962 Kristi and I enrolled in a Red Cross Junior Lifesaving course at the college pool. John Rankin, who was a student at Davidson and a member of the college swim team, organized and taught the course that summer. The old pool (long since replaced by the Olympic pool at the Baker sports complex) was seventy-five feet long, or roughly twenty-five meters. It was just eight feet deep at the diving end and supported only a one-meter springboard. We spent six weeks in that pool learning how to deal with just about any drowning scenario. Rankin was a perfectionist, and I think he actually put us through the senior program rather than the more abbreviated junior course. He literally wore us out.

Initially the girls rescued the girls, and the boys rescued the boys. The inevitable followed. The girls had to learn to rescue bigger game. I think we all handled it admirably both figuratively and literally. By course's end everybody knew every body pretty well. I enjoyed rescuing Kristi more than anyone else. She usually put up a good fight.

Rankin gave a monster final exam. After demonstrating proficiency in all manners of rescue, we each had to rescue the teacher, who was big and muscular. Initially, Rankin gave the girls a fit, but they all eventually passed after he decided to lighten up. He almost drowned me before easing off. The written exam he cooked up took three hours to finish. Fortunately, we all passed and received our badges for something most of us would never use.

The Scott family ran the concession stand at the Southern Boys Tennis Tournament on the college courts each summer. This event brought in the finest junior talent from all over the South. Much to their chagrin, the townie boys always had to take a backseat to the cadre of debonair, alarmingly good looking fourteen and fifteen year old athletes who showed up in town for the tournament and stole the hearts of the local belles. It was downright painful to watch Kristi and her friends serving concessions and fawning over these scions of the country club set from exotic places like Atlanta, Mobile and New Orleans.

During our high school years John and I became close friends with Kristi. We called her "Jo" and "Belle." We made a habit of dropping by the house on the spur of the moment to play cards, talk up a storm and pal around—Kristi did a mean lip sync of Brenda Lee. Kristi's mom, Bess—God bless her—joined right in.

One year Kristi ran for class secretary at North Mecklenburg. She plastered the restrooms with signs calling on voters to "Hit the Pot with Scott." Three years earlier my sister had run for either class or student council treasurer with signs in the halls proclaiming "Truck it with Puckett," which must have garnered a considerable amount of off-color graffiti and may have served as Kristi's inspiration. John's failed campaign for school vice-president in 1965 included Gail Nicholls' (his reprobate campaign manager) handing out lollipops with little stickers that read "Suck it for Puckett." (Subtlety was not Gail's forte.)

I saw Kristi Scott much less after she went off to Salem College in the fall of 1965. During my senior year at Davidson, Kristi was working for an airline in Charlotte, and she lined up a date for me with one of her old college friends for the Spring Frolics weekend at the college. My date turned out to be one of those classic 1960's flower children who had experimented with just about everything and burned out more than a row of brain cells. John really liked her, and by Sunday she was *his* date. By that time she probably couldn't tell the difference anyway.

Kristi's father continued as the athletic director through my college years and was at the helm when Lefty directed the basketball program to its zenith in the 1967-69 seasons. I am proud to have participated in two NCAA Division I sports during my college years under his auspices. Perhaps the greatest honor accorded Tom Scott was his election to the presidency of the NCAA basketball tournament committee. He reigned during the John Wooden/Lew Alcindor years at UCLA. Dr. Scott was instrumental in the development of the current NCAA Tournament format. I suppose, in a way, "March Madness" originated in my own little neighborhood.

I didn't see Kristi again until the spring of 1995. My son, Jim, an eighth grader at the time, was participating in the state Math Counts program finals in downtown Charlotte. During a break in the action we went over to Discovery Place, the hands-on science museum. As we were leaving, a woman shouted out my name. It was Kristi. I hadn't seen her in almost twenty-five years. She had moved back to

Davidson and was living in the Scott family home on Woodland Street. I hugged her. This time she didn't have cornbread to throw at me.

Ernest Beaty

As a young child I encountered a generation of Davidson faculty who were retired or nearing retirement, professors such as Edward Erwin, Guy Vowles, Walter Lingle, C.K. Brown, Henry E. Fulcher, Kenneth Foreman, Lewis Schenck, William Porter, James Douglas, and Ernest Beaty. My parents knew these estimable men well and would occasionally visit them and their families, with John, Ginger and me in tow.

Ernest Beaty stands out in my memory more than the others, perhaps because he was such a natural charmer and raconteur. By day he taught German and classical languages at the college; by night he was the mayor and municipal judge of the town, often holding court in the wee hours. Mayor Beaty was greatly loved by students and townspeople alike.

I remember Mayor Beaty as a gregarious, portly man who had a moustache and wore black-frame glasses and baggy suits. In the early 1950's he was a member of a *Stammtisch* that gathered at Cloyd Goodrum's drug store weekdays during the 10-11 a.m. Chapel. Students often cut Chapel just to listen to the banter that was always going whenever Mr. Goodrum, Fred Hengeveld, the college registrar, and Mayor Beaty held court at a table next to the pharmacy counter, directly under an ancient ceiling fan that always creaked along at an adagio tempo. In our pre-school years John and I would sometimes go with our father to the drug store during the Chapel hour—Dad would join the *Stammtisch*, and John and I would settle in at the magazine rack.

On Sunday mornings at DCPC Mayor Beaty sat a few rows behind our pew. He occasionally made audible comments on the quality of the sermon, which kept John and me in stitches.

Ernest's daughter, Mary, had grown up in the town about eight years ahead of John and me. The Beatys' house, built in the 1940's, was at the top of Schenck's Hill on Woodland Street, fronting a densely wooded area that was then the eastern boundary of Johnsie Shelton's horse pasture. I came to know Mary in the late 1970's, when she joined the library staff at the college. She was more reticent than her flamboyant father, but every bit as genial. She was also a scholar, holding a Ph.D. in classical studies from UNC-Chapel Hill. Mary died prematurely of cancer about a decade ago, leaving an important legacy to the town and college: her two books, *Davidson: A History and the Town from 1835 to 1937* (1979) and *A History of Davidson College* (1988). Her books were indispensable resources in my own reconstruction of town and college life.

Traditions

In this final chapter I look at several traditions that were part of my family and college life in Davidson in the 1950's and 1960's. These were the accustomed rhythms of the passing years of my childhood and youth. As these stories illustrate, my life and my family's were tightly intertwined with the life of the college.

The Cake Race

As there were no track scholarships at Davidson College, Coach A. Heath Whittle had to rummage the dorms every year in the early autumn to round up a respectable cross-country team. His recruiting difficulties led to a good idea that in time became a beloved tradition at the college. Every fall all of the freshmen were invited to participate in a cross-country race. Faculty wives baked cakes, and the first forty or fifty finishers in the race got their choice of a cake in their order of finish. Running in the Cake Race was not mandatory, but most of the freshmen showed up anyway, if not to compete seriously, then at least to have a good time. After a number of years, the Cake Race became both a welcomed athletic and social event.

I attended the races when I was a child. I remember the 1957 version in particular. While *The Charlotte Observer* sent a photographer to cover the race, no picture of the race or a cake winner ever appeared in the paper. What did show up in the next day's edition was a photograph of our dog Gizmo and our friends John and David Mason. The cut line read, "Dog and Friends." A brief description of the race followed. The photographer took some stills of John and me with Gizmo, but they never made the paper. The Mason picture is still in my photograph collection.

The Cake Race was run on a 1.8-mile course. The runners started on the lower athletic field and after approximately three hundred yards entered the woods on a trail heading east from the campus down to the gravel road below Erwin Lodge. Where the trail met the gravel road, the runners turned right and swung down to Grey Road, where they took another right, this time onto pavement, to begin a long uphill trek to Concord Road. Once they reached the top of the big hill, they ran the longest stretch of the race on level terrain along Concord and then turned right on the college campus. The Cake Race ended at Richardson Field—like marathoners, the runners entered the stadium at the north gate and ran a three-quarter lap on the track in reverse direction to the finish line.

My chance to run in the race came at the start of my freshman year at Davidson on a very warm mid-September afternoon. Approximately 220 members of the class of 1970 gathered on the lower athletic field; there were probably only six or eight of us who were really serious about running.

Coach Whittle lined us up for the start. When the gun went off, Calvin Murphy from Charlotte tore out like the proverbial bat from hell. Calvin was way out in front of the stampede. But after we reached the woods, I saw him sitting on the side of the trail laughing and saying, "Bet I scared you rabbits."

The run was more difficult than I had imagined. I had done a lot of running around Davidson over the years, but I had never run that particular course. Once in the woods, it was mostly a downhill sprint for the next half-mile or so. When we hit Grey Road, I felt like a million. The Grey Road hill was steeper that I had ever remembered. Once I got to the top, there was little reserve left in tank—I just coasted the rest of the way. My third place finish gave me a prime choice cake. Ahead of me was John, who won the race in the second fastest time ever, and without any training that summer, to boot. Mrs. Jerry Roberts was thrilled when he picked her ten-pound chocolate cake.

When all of the runners were in (including a smirking Calvin Murphy), everybody paraded over to the freshmen dorms and spread out the cakes. Everybody shared in the fruits of our labors. We pigged out. At the same time Coach Whittle was going around signing up freshmen runners.

At my twenty-fifth class reunion the college held a mini-Cake Race. Some of the old alums ran a short course around the campus, and there were a few cakes there for the early finishers. While this event bore no resemblance to the races of yesteryear, everyone seemed to enjoy it. I announced to several of my former classmates that I would run in the 2000 race on the occasion of our thirtieth college reunion wearing a shirt emblazoned with "#3 in '70." Talk is cheap— I never made that race.

Death before Dishonor

A recent publication on America's finest institutions of higher learning describes Davidson College as a school where there is no cheating. That distinction comes from Davidson's longstanding Honor Code. During my college years, students were pledged to do their own work, and they signed all submitted work with, "I pledge that I have neither given nor received aid on this [paper, exam, or project]." Most students abbreviated this statement by simply signing, "Pledged." Davidson students were expected to abide by the code, and there was considerable peer pressure to do just that. The penalty for an adjudicated violation was dismissal from the college.

When I was a Davidson student, the code was simple. A student was obligated not to lie, cheat, or steal. If he caught someone else violating the code, he was obligated to report that person to the Honor Court. Failure to do so could result in the non-reporter's own dismissal.

In the years covered by this book, the Honor Court consisted of a faculty advisor and five elected judges. An accused student was required to present his case before the judges, who always wore black robes. Refusal to appear meant automatic dismissal. My father once told me there was a hierarchy of failure at Davidson College: "First you can flunk a test. Next you can flunk a course. In either case, you can stay in school. Cheat and you're out on your ass."

A controversial issue that fell within the purview of the Honor Code was mandatory attendance at religious services. Those services, of course, had to be Presbyterian. Students were bound by the code to sign their own names on the attendance slips, in effect, pledging they were who they said they were and that they were indeed present for the service. At least up to the 1930's, students had to attend a specified number of church, Vespers, or morning Chapel services to remain in school.

The rule was strictly enforced. Recalling his own days as a Davidson student in the mid-1920's, Dad told me about an acquaintance of his who had reached his maximum number of worship service cuts. One Sunday morning he decided to drive his late model Ford down to Charlotte to visit his fiancée, figuring he could easily catch the Vespers service that night and remain in good standing with the college. Sometime around noon while he was driving in south Charlotte, his car broke down. He couldn't find a ride back since neither buses nor trains were running that day. He abandoned his car and fiancée and began the long twenty-six mile trek back to campus on foot. He arrived back in Davidson in the wee hours of the morning. His credible excuse notwithstanding, this poor lad was expelled for one semester by Professor Mark Sentelle, the designated faculty officer for disciplinary matters.

By the early 1960's the student body was clamoring for the abolition of required religious functions. On Sunday nights students packed the balcony at DCPC. They did this in protest. Some brought typewriters and typed their papers right in the middle of the service. Sterling Martin told me that anything and everything, including condoms, began showing up in the collection plates.

By the time I attended Davidson, the religious requirements were less vigorous. Attendance at Sunday morning church or Sunday evening Vespers was no longer required. The only requirement was Chapel, which met at 10:30 a.m. several days a week. Each student was allowed six unexcused cuts. The penalty for over-cutting Chapel was an automatic six-week grounding on the college campus—a fate some considered worse than expulsion.

We soon learned that Chapel had nothing to do with religion. It was simply an anachronistic carryover from the old days—a vestige of a tradition some of the trustees wouldn't allow to go gently into that good night. The dean of students office roamed the highways and byways searching for speakers to ruminate on just about anything to fill up the thirty minutes before the 11 a.m. class bell. Over time the system deteriorated terribly. The student body was slowing organizing resistance to what most felt was a colossal waste of time and an infringement of student rights. Student proctors, positioned in the balcony of Love Auditorium, took attendance by counting heads—students sat in assigned seats. Dummies began to fill the seats of the orchestra section of Love Auditorium.

My brother over-cut Chapel in the last week of his sophomore year. Because he was scheduled to spend his junior year in Marburg, Germany, he couldn't be "campused" (the *in loco parentis* term for being grounded). The assistant dean told him not to worry, that the odorous policy would probably be gone when he returned to campus his senior year—and it was. John got a good laugh out of that one.

Chapel ended the following year in the wake of a performance by a short, corpulent middle-aged woman who arrived at Love Auditorium one fateful morning. She wore a Duke-blue sweatshirt emblazoned with the words "Peace Pilgrim." She told the students that she had dedicated her life to bring peace to the entire world. She had already walked over twenty thousand miles for that purpose, living on the good will of people she met along her way. Unfortunately she would find no peace in Love Auditorium that day.

The wind was up and the surf was rising. Catcalls and hisses emanated from all corners of the auditorium. The noise reached a resounding crescendo when Peace Pilgrim cried, "Sears and Roebuck has announced that this Christmas it will remove from its shelves all toys of destruction!" The place went berserk. Poor Peace Pilgrim went down in a hail of balled-up paper.

The next day an article on Peace Pilgrim appeared in *The Charlotte Observer*. She declared that her reception at Davidson was the rudest she had ever experienced. From my perspective, she just happened to be at the wrong place at the wrong time. The students were looking for a head, any head, to roll on the Chapel issue. Shortly thereafter, the board of trustees abolished compulsory Chapel. My brother had his official reprieve.

A few years ago I caught the national evening news in my home in Asheville. At the conclusion the network did a segment on an elderly, short, corpulent woman decked out in a Duke-blue sweatshirt. Could it possibly be? I strained forward in my chair. It really was! Peace Pilgrim brought more peace to the Davidson campus than she would ever know. I owe that woman.

Open House

Davidson College prided itself on its small student-faculty ratio. Most of the classes enrolled at most ten to fifteen students. Only the required science classes had more—perhaps thirty at the most. There were no graduate students or teaching fellows to segregate students from their professors. Our professors were completely accessible—they held regular office hours every afternoon, and students were free to come to discuss problems concerning the course or simply to chat.

In my freshman year the college required an advanced math course for its premedical majors. I had done very well in high school math, so I thought advanced calculus would be a cinch. It was almost my undoing. That most of us in the class had trouble greatly distressed our professor, J.B. Stroud. Dr. Stroud believed we weren't trying hard enough. To make matters worse, Steve White, son of physics professor Locke White, was making A's on every review. Steve was a high school student who won the state high school math competition three years running—and he was still in high school when he took Dr. Stroud's course.

Dr. Stroud held court daily in his small office in the old Jackson fraternity court. I recall spending at least thirty minutes every afternoon there. He must have hated to see me come with such regularity. The course was much tougher than I had anticipated, and I was lucky to get out alive with a passing grade.

Basic physics at Davidson was also no free ride. It was so hard that many of the premedical students went to summer school at Duke to take the course there and hold up their grade point averages. I was working in the summers and didn't have the luxury of doing that.

Professor John Hopkins taught the first semester physics in my junior year. I worked hard in that class. I came out with a B+ and resolved to pull it up to an A the following semester. Then something unexpected happened that still sends shivers down my academic spine. The department changed professors for the second semester.

Dr. Allen Wolf had come to Davidson in 1965 to join the physics department. I heard that he was hard, but because the course I would be taking was for premeds and involved little higher calculus, I had no concerns—at least not until the first review, which I thoroughly flunked with a grade of forty-eight percent. The next reviews were not any easier. Dr. Wolf would beam us down to some fictitious celestial sphere and give us some parameters and expect us to come up with gravitational pull, atmospheric pressures, and the like. I was lost in space.

Every afternoon there were two lines at the Dana Science Building—one outside Dr. Wolf's office seeking mercy, and the other outside my father's office begging his intervention now that some of the premedical students would have no chance at all of getting into medical school because of their failing grades in physics. Dad, the college's premed advisor, told everyone to tough it out. In the end there was a monster curve, and I miraculously passed. It was the hardest course I ever took.

The faculty's accessibility extended into their homes. Every Sunday night after Vespers faculty members, on a rotating basis, opened their homes to any students who might wish to drop by. I remember how Mom used to fret that another faculty wife might outdo her; so she turned those nights into somewhat lavish occasions. Dad was very popular, and there was always a crowd of students when our turn came. Mom usually served punch, cookies, and small chicken salad sandwiches. I remember some nights when students filled the living room, dining room, kitchen and hallway of the first floor of our house.

By the time I was a student at Davidson, the lifting of the mandatory church rules had all but done away with Vespers, and the open houses, which always followed that service, tapered off in attendance. I don't know what became of the custom after my graduation.

When I departed Davidson in 1970, I left behind the freedom to freely and liberally associate with my professors. In medical school some of my professors had research obligations, and they purposefully made themselves inaccessible to students outside of the classroom. That rankled. I suppose Davidson had spoiled me.

I miss those Sunday nights. They were exciting for John and me. Even when we were small children decked out in pajamas, Mom and Dad allowed us to freely mingle with the students. I came to know many of them over the years. Mom told me shortly before she died that two of those students, James Holshouser and James Martin, actually babysat John and me on occasion. They were the only two Republican governors of North Carolina in the twentieth century. I don't know if she got things confused, but it was a good story all the same.

Homecoming

Davidson held its homecomings in October every year. The campus was ablaze in color, and the weather was always cool. In my twenty-two years in Davidson I don't recall that it ever rained on homecoming weekend.

As children we looked forward to that special weekend each year because all the fraternities built projects on the front lawns of their houses on the old Jackson Court. There was a heated competition, and some of the projects were quite elaborate—including a gallows for hanging the Erskine, Catawba, or Pfeifer mascot in effigy. The court was always open for display on the Friday night of homecoming weekend.

When the fraternities moved to the new, more spacious Patterson Court, there was a loss of intimacy. Jackson Court had been small and crowded. Touring the annual exhibits was like walking through a carnival. All of that vanished with the new houses. Over time the project competition simply died out altogether.

With the demise of the old system, fraternities came up with new traditions at homecoming. Among those were the stealing of frat mystic goodies and house symbols.

My sophomore year my ATO brother Ken Hill and a few others hatched a plot to steal the Sigma Chi cross. One very rainy October night a few days before Homecoming Ken and his accomplices put a ladder up to the Sigma Chi chimney and unbolted the cross. They carried it off into the night. The next day a sign appeared on the Sigma Chi lawn that read, "I will lift up mine eyes unto the hills." My frat brothers had tied the cross to the top of the water tower behind the old college cemetery.

Thanksgiving

Burnished in my childhood memories are the Thanksgiving holidays my family spent on Warren Street in Wilson, North Carolina, where our material grandmother lived in an aging white frame house. Virginia Hale House was a widow who had lost her husband, John, in 1942. "Papa John," as we called the grandfather we never knew, was a wholesale merchant in Wilson whose livelihood had been damaged by the Depression. I suppose the trials and tribulations of that period took years off of his life. Mom wanted us to call her mother "Nana", but we got it mixed up, and it came out "Now-Now." She was a short, stocky, bespectacled lady who was a devout Christian.

We were in Wilson every Thanksgiving from 1948 to 1957. On the Wednesday afternoon before the great day, we would load up the car and drive to Wilson—a six-hour trip along the winding state highways that took us from Davidson eastward to Durham and Raleigh and into eastern North Carolina.

My earliest memory of her house is of me looking inquisitively into her bedroom mirror wondering who I was and what role I had in God's scheme of things. At age four I began to delve into the meaning of human existence. It was one of my life's profound moments. That image of me in my grandmother's mirror still haunts me to this day.

Now-Now was an English professor at Atlantic Christian College in Wilson. At nights during those Thanksgiving visits she would gather John, Ginger and me on her bed and tell us Greek myths and sagas like *Beowulf* and Coleridge's "The Rhyme of the Ancient Mariner." I remember being fascinated by the great mead hall in *Beowulf* and the image of Beowulf's companions being snatched untimely from their drunken slumber by a green-scaled monster—although I didn't appreciate what mead was until forty years later on a trip to Ireland, where I had some and learned first hand why the Norsemen were such easy pickings for Grindel.

John and I spent Thanksgiving mornings in Wilson roaming the neighborhood, which was filled with children. We were particularly attracted to the Carr house across the street. Mary Gilliam Carr, an old friend of my mother, was a widow raising three children, Betsy, Joe, and Nancy. We were perpetually up to no good over there.

One Turkey Day, Joe and John came up with the brilliant idea that Joe's box kite could support and fly three-year old Nancy Carr. They tied the screaming child to the large kite and tossed her off the front porch, expecting moon shot results. Fortunately she landed in the bushes and was unhurt. Mary Gilliam ordered Joe into the house and called our mother. By the time the mothers were through with Joe and John, little Nancy wasn't the only kid crying on Warren Street.

The top of Warren Street intersected Nash Street, which at one time was considered one of the most beautiful thoroughfares in America. Even in my childhood it still retained much of the elegance and charm of its halcyon days in the 1920's. The street was lined with fine old mansions dating from the late nineteenth and early twentieth century. Most of the homes were large columned affairs. I thought they were the biggest houses on earth. The owners didn't seem to mind when we walked through the front door for a peek inside.

Wilson was the largest bright leaf tobacco market in the world. I suppose that much of the wealth of the town came from that odious leaf. Mom was a good friend of Speed Riggs, who was the most famous tobacco auctioneer of his day. I remember visiting the Center Brick warehouse, which was the largest tobacco storage and auction facility in the world. At least it was until the night it burned down in 1953.

I don't know how the fire started. Fire truck sirens awakened us as the multi-county alarm went out. The night was so lit up by the conflagration that Dad was reading a newspaper out on the front porch.

It was frightening. We could see the blaze well above the trees. The scene still reminds me of the burning of Atlanta scenes in *Gone with the Wind*. We saw the building the next day as it continued to burn. The devastation was incredible. Someone mentioned arson, but I don't believe they ever knew for sure. Mom suspected that someone had dropped a lighted cigarette, which really would have been ironic.

Also, during those Turkey Day weekends in Wilson, we visited the Hunter family, whose house was on the north end of Nash Street. Dr. Bill Hunter, a general practitioner in the town, and his wife, Martha, had three children—Betsy, William, and Ted. We were all fast friends.

Ted Hunter was mentally challenged, but as a child I didn't understand what this meant. He was just one of the gang to me. He called John and me, "the James-John boys," and we liked him a lot. When Ted developed seizures, the Hunters took him to Duke University Medical Center, but there wasn't much the doctors could do. His parents cared for him at home through the years.

We spent a lot of time at the Hunter home partly because the boys had the largest and finest toy collection we had ever seen. Mom and Martha Hunter were lifelong friends, and our parents spent a lot of time there also. A gentle, well-liked man, Dr. Hunter would tend to whatever minor medical emergencies arose on our visits—one summer in the late 50's John showed up at his house with a raging boil on his backside.

In 1958 Now-Now moved to Davidson to live with us. The two years she was in our house were some of the happiest I have known. My grandmother had a vast knowledge of English literature and history and was always enthusiastic about sharing that with us. I suppose much of my interest in those subjects comes from the time I spent with her.

Now-Now died in her sleep on March 12, 1960. We took her back to Wilson for burial. Mom requested a reading of Alfred Lord Tennyson's "Crossing the Bar" at the funeral, which was held in the Methodist Church where my mother and father had been married in 1942. Fittingly that poem would be read at my mother's funeral twenty-five years later. In my opinion, it is the most beautiful writing in the English language.

William Hunter and Joe Carr attended Davidson College. In 1967, my freshman year, William, Joe, John, and I drove to Wilson over spring break. Joe's mother had remarried—a wealthy physician named Beatty Clark. They had a huge house out on Raleigh Road. We visited them, and I remember spending the greater part of one evening discussing Josephus Daniels with Dr. Clark, who had the man's entire life memorized.

That same week someone had the bright idea of arranging dates for John and me with a pair of identical female twins for a night on the town. We dined on bad hamburgers and saw an awful Elke Sommer movie—on all counts the evening was a bomb. I also ran a red light and narrowly avoided an accident. The girls were furious.

In 1973 my wife and I passed through Wilson on our way back to Chapel Hill from a trip to the Outer Banks. I wanted to show her Warren Street. Sadly, much of the ambience had changed. The old mansions on Nash Street had fallen on hard times. On Warren Street the residential zoning regulations must have eased up considerably because a dental office stood on the site of my grandmother's former home.

Fortunately my memory has no zoning changes. I can still clearly see her house and that wonderful street. I can still run in and out of lovely old mansions that lined what was once considered one of the most beautiful streets in America. I can still follow Beowulf as he chases the dragon Grindel into his lair beneath the sea. At my grandmother's house the good guys always win.

A highlight of every Thanksgiving for me was the ROTC-sponsored Turkey Shoot at the college. The event was held on the Tuesday afternoon before Turkey Day. The ROTC department (hence taxpayers) footed the bill and provided entertainment for young and old alike.

After school on that special day, we always headed straight to the ROTC department. It was great! The military kept us thoroughly entertained with all kinds of short films—from mountain goats in the Rockies to World War II documentaries.

At 5:30 p.m. everyone would gather in the basement of Belk Dormitory for the finals of the Turkey Shoot. The ROTC staff would always have a big live turkey in a cage to remind us that the winner would take home a plump frozen counterpart. Coach A. H. Whittle won each and every year—no one was ever close.

On Thanksgiving Day, spent at home after 1958, we gathered around the table as Dad pontificated about the evolution of the turkey. We rushed through dinner, knowing that there would be plenty of food left for us after the big game.

The big game wasn't the Detroit Lions' traditional holiday game. It was our own Turkey Bowl. Many of the kids in my peer group would gather at the college baseball field or the lower athletic field for a rousing afternoon of touch football. These games were not for the fainthearted. As we grew older, there were some serious injuries— Curtis Smith, for example, ended up in the hospital with a bruised kidney. In inclement weather we would break into the college gymnasium, with Currie Johnston leading the charge, for an equally rousing afternoon of basketball.

By the mid-1960's a Charlotte tradition was competing with the Turkey Bowl. Every Thanksgiving the good people of Charlotte held a parade called the Carrousel Parade. This was hardly on a par with the Macy's Thanksgiving Parade, but it was impressive for a low-budget affair. I fondly remember the time we attended the parade with Dick and Belle Banks from Huntersville.

Dick Banks, a Davidson graduate, and his family lived in his ancestral family's plantation home, Cedar Grove, on Gilead Road in Huntersville. Built in the 1830's, Cedar Grove replaced a nearby pre-Revolutionary War structure that was a ruin by the time I came to know the Banks family. The house was (still is) a magnificent brick structure with fifteen-foot high ceilings and numerous fireplaces. It's on the National Historical Registry.

The chief attraction at Cedar Grove was young Margaret Banks, who for some unfathomable reason was nicknamed "Chuck"—unfathomable because she was gorgeously proportioned. John and I fawned over Margaret on the front steps of that storied house in the summers of our youth..

We fancied ourselves as modern day Tarleton Twins, and Margaret was our version of Scarlett. We would spend hours during those summer evening visits just talking on the front stoop. If the mosquitoes were active, we moved indoors. Standing in the hallway at twilight always gave me an eerie sensation of being back in antebellum days. There was something deeply Southern about Cedar Grove. It remains among the most beautiful and enduring images of my youth.

In 1965 Belle Banks invited John and me to sit with her family in the main grandstand at Independence Square in Charlotte for the Thanksgiving Day parade. We had a ball watching the floats, marching bands (lots of local high schools were represented), and local celebrities waving jubilantly from the backseats of late model convertibles. After the parade someone long forgotten introduced me to Colonel Harland Sanders—the KFC man. The Colonel looked just as he appears today on the KFC logo, an impeccably coiffed, white-haired man sporting a goatee, dressed resplendently in an antebellum-style white suit. At the time he was making the rounds of fairs and parades advertising his famous chicken. He had recently sold his interest in the company, some 600 franchises in 1964, and signed on as the public spokesperson and symbol of the new KFC Corporation. I tried to strike up a conversation with the Colonel, but he wasn't at all interested. I suppose his mind was in a deep fat frier somewhere.

John and I chased Margaret Banks along the primrose path until she went off to college. After that we all went our separate ways. In the late 1980's my wife and I took our son to the Fourth of July celebration in Faith, North Carolina. As we wound through the crowd, a man confronted me with, "Are you John Puckett's brother?" This had happened to me many times over the years. John is about as well connected as Dad was. I explained that I was indeed said sibling, and as we were speaking, a lovely woman walked up behind us. It was Margaret, his wife. Reacquainting ourselves after a twenty-year hiatus, we sat around for an hour or so talking about the old days at Cedar Grove.

I visited Cedar Grove again in 1989. The family had restored the original wooden pre-Revolutionary War house. Belle gave me the grand tour of the property. When Dick Banks died some years back, I wrote Belle a note of gratitude, sharing with her my memories of Cedar Grove. That Belle was a Yankee from Pennsylvania always struck me as a very curious anomaly.

Christmas

Around 1953 the town board of Davidson decided to plant a Christmas tree in the commons area that we called the Grove (a grove of oaks and pines stood there until Hurricane Hugo took them out in the late 1980's). The Christmas tree was planted fully-grown, and it thrived in its plot on the edge of Main Street in the good hands of the town garden club. That year my father proclaimed me the "Vice-President of the Christmas Tree." In my august new position, at the tender age of five, I looked out my parents' bedroom window toward the newly lit tree and swelled with pride. It was a glorious sight. A simple pleasure that evoked the joy and excitement of Christmas, the tree's variegated lights were a touchstone of my childhood and youth.

Every year on the Sunday before the college's Christmas recess, DCPC held a Vesper's service featuring the college choir, the aptly named Male Chorus. Performing with an orchestra and the church's thunderous organ, the Male Chorus generally played to a packed church.

DCPC's annual White Gift Service took place the following Sunday—a service that included a pageant followed by the laying of food gifts (always wrapped in white paper) for the poor at the foot of a cradle bearing a reasonable facsimile of the baby Jesus. We have all seen movies or read books where the Christmas pageant goes hopelessly FUBAR. Davidson's annual pageant was no exception. The church did more or less the same thing every year, and somewhere along the way one thinks somebody would have gotten it right. It never happened that way.

I remember one pageant in particular from my high school years. Every Sunday afternoon after Thanksgiving that year we walked through the agony of the entire Christmas story. On the first day of rehearsal the pageant director declared that this would be the finest pageant in our church's history. She took great pains to appoint the appropriate baby boomer for each figure of the crèche scene. I had been a reader in the previous pageant and had messed up big time. This year I was demoted to a lowly shepherd. That meant a burlap bag over my person, and I was allergic to burlap! Brother John got the male lead that year—a colorfully costumed Joseph; Sandy Wheaton was the Virgin Mary.

The pageant consisted of the costumed crèche crew and several readers. Barbie Doll played the Infant Jesus. The director told us to "feel" the parts. We were supposed to imagine that we were in fact shepherds, kings, angels, etc. That first rehearsal the director had us do a walkthrough, exhorting us, "Feel the part!" I certainly did feel the part—I was itching to death. For verisimilitude the director even had the readers dress up like the prophets they were supposed to portray. She also had them coached by a speech specialist in the town. She was after realism, and that called for an authentic presentation. She demanded a believable reproduction of the birth of the Messiah.

Like it did every year the pageant took some turns nobody expected. Shepherd Doug Cantrell approached the crib and on bended knee, crook and all, smiled up at John and said, "Bite me, Puckett." John looked down at Doug for a few seconds in stunned disbelief and started laughing convulsively. Doug's miscreant behavior happened just as the lights were going down for the grand entrance of the gentlemen from the Orient. As the sanctuary darkened, everybody at the crèche scene was laughing. A spotlight came on in the rear of the sanctuary; then the huge church organ pealed, and the building reverberated with the sound of "We Three Kings of Orient Are." The spotlight followed three elaborately costumed kings, marching in slow, deliberate cadence (it really is a plodding piece of music), up to the manger, where by the time the sanctuary lights were back on, the crèche crew was back on good behavior. The evening would have passed without further mishap had not one of the readers forgotten the director's admonition and looked directly into the spotlight—temporarily blinded he bravely carried on with the pronouncement of "uh, uh, uh" into the microphone, much to the merriment of the crèche crew. I would have enjoyed all of this a lot more had I not been in a pruritic hell, wiggling like a worm on a hook.

There was universal agreement among the DCPC congregants that the annual Christmas pageant, for all its snafus, was a good thing. What became contentious and reached a boiling point in 1964 was the Christmas tree service that took place under church auspices on Christmas Eve.

Since 1921, Mary Beatty tells us in her history of the town, children of the DCPC congregation had been gathering around the church tree on Christmas Eve in eager anticipation of an appearance by Santa Claus. In my childhood we assembled in the reception room in the church basement or, on occasion, in the basement of Chambers Building. After a brief service and some carols, Clyde Stacks, who directed the college laundry, would come in dressed as Santa Claus trailing a sled stuffed full of goodies—orange string-mesh bags filled with fruit and candy, which he would quickly dispense to the throng of outreached hands.

I believe this tradition originated in simpler times when churches gave out pokes containing candies and small presents. I've seen this custom in other churches where congregants gave Christmas gifts to the poor.

It was my junior year in high school when an obstreperous faction of the congregation led by a cadre of young faculty members and their spouses spoke out that the Christmas tree service, as a secular practice, violated the church constitution. My peer group labeled the grinches the "Anti-Santas." While there was no denying that Santa Claus had nothing to do with the theological significance of Christmas, we felt that booting out Santa (i.e. Big Clyde Stacks) was a bit extreme, considering our deep attachment to him and the service. At probably the only spirited congregational meeting of my youth, the church finally voted on the matter. After impassioned speeches from both sides, the good people of DCPC voted out Santa Claus.

During my high school years the young people of the Senior High Fellowship and college students who were home on break went caroling on Christmas Eve. Every year we assembled at the church at around 7:00 in the evening and paraded up Main Street or out Concord Road, going door to door. I think the folks we serenaded enjoyed our noisy exuberance if not the quality or piety of the off-key singing—the kids with nice voices were usually drowned out or nullified by a sizable group of B-flat crooners. Refreshments at somebody's house always followed the caroling. My tenth grade year my mother sacrificed our living room for that purpose. Jim McEver spilled a cup of hot chocolate all over Mom's new white wool carpet. She never did get the stain out—every time she looked at it, she would mumble something about "that McEver boy." For years thereafter a chocolate stain on a rug, a mud spot on an old bedroom ceiling, and a smattering of tar here and there remained as telltale signs of my passage in that house over forty years ago.

EPILOGUE

There have been many changes in Davidson over the years since I left in 1970. The town has changed physically, and like the rest of America its attitudes and values have also changed. Some of these changes, the passing of Jim Crow comes first and foremost to mind, unquestionably have been necessary and good. Yet, I also think that something valuable has been lost along the way. A lot of moneyed people have moved to the area in and around Davidson and Lake Norman, transforming it into exurban Charlotte. In response to that invasion in some ways the town has become Disneyfied—ornamented artificially to resemble something like "Main Street USA." The town center is pristine and immaculate; you won't find any aesthetically displeasing stores like Pop Copeland's Jungle or the workroom at Withers Electric—businesses that once served a very vital function in town despite their uncomely appearances. Trendy restaurants and shops are the order of the day. On Main Street First Union Bank, now suddenly Wachovia, long ago devoured tiny Piedmont Bank and Trust, not to mention other banks from Florida to Philadelphia. But corporate giants will never erase my fond memories of the neighborly face-to-face relationships in the business hub of my formative years. To me the epitome of the new upscale Davidson is the Ben and Jerry's Ice Cream shop located across the street from the old Blake house, where I lived from 1949 to 1956. That old house, by the way, was moved several years ago to make way for a Harris Teeter complex— a deal that fortunately went belly-up, but not before the house was transported.

There have been changes that would please my youth. It's hard to quibble with the splendid new elementary school that was built about a decade ago at the far end of South Street—affectionately known to us as School Street—just across from the McEver Field ballpark, which has been upgraded over the years. And a new town library stands on the fringe of the old Grove commons area. My old friend, Nancy Withers Dishman, is the librarian. Unfortunately, the town had to move Mrs. Agnes Brown's house, a lovely prefabricated structure that was ordered from Sears and Roebuck in the 1930's, to build the new library. At least the town council saved it—the house now stands on a rise overlooking Lorimer Road behind the old Blake House property.

Other positive changes from my perspective have involved the college. In the late 1970's the college built a beautiful, first-class library befitting its rise to prominence as one of the nation's leading liberal arts institutions. Embellished with a Rodin statue, a new art department building has been built on the site of a former parking lot on North Main Street. And new dormitories have arisen in the woods north of the former Patterson Court fraternity houses. I am pleased to have seen the old fraternity system pass by the way. There was a social snobbery about it that I didn't like at all. My old frat, Alpha Tau Omega, later became an eating club called "Apple Turn Over." The stadium at Richardson Field has been renovated, replete with a new track, and the facility has hosted NCAA national soccer tournaments in recent years. A beautiful athletic complex has grown up on the shabby old baseball field. Johnson Gymnasium has been converted into a spectacular student union. Perhaps best of all, women attend Davidson, as they have since the early 1970's, and now comprise approximately fifty percent of the student body.

The small Southern college town I encountered as a child now belongs to the province of history and remembrance. To retread a cliché, we will not pass that way again.

In this book I have described the strengths and foibles of the town as I remember it. In the two post-World War II decades, Davidson reflected a simpler, more innocent time than was to follow. It was a place where a traffic jam was a single car frozen on red at the only stoplight in town. A writer from *Sports Illustrated* once wrote that Davidson was the kind of place where cars would stop to let a mama beagle cross Main Street with her pups. I remember a place where a quarrel was settled promptly and usually amicably on a front porch or yard and not in a courtroom. It was a place where the only lawyer in town was the trust officer at the bank, and a shaken hand or a person's word was as good as any signature. It was a time and place when groups of neighbors regularly brought out their lawn chairs on summer evenings and chatted amicably for hours while their children chased fireflies in the gathering darkness. There was a sense of neighborliness, trust, and reciprocity there that I have not experienced in any other place.

I left Davidson to begin my adult life and work over thirty-two years ago. I became a cancer specialist, taught for several years in academic medicine, and finally settled down to clinical practice, first in Concord, later in Asheville. After pursuing what my twin, John, calls a "checkered career," which included a spate of stopgap jobs and six years of school teaching, he is an Ivy League professor, which makes two of that genre in my immediate family—Dad at Princeton and John at Penn.

And that leads me to one final thought: Whatever goodness, whatever Godliness, and whatever decency I possess; I owe in large part to Davidson. As I enter the autumn of my years, I continually draw strength from childhood experiences that shaped my character and serve as touchstones in my adult life.